The Meanings of
Mass Higher Education

SRHE and Open University Press Imprint
General Editor: Heather Eggins

The Meanings of
Mass Higher
Education

Peter Scott

The Society for Research into Higher Education
& Open University Press

Published by SRHE and
Open University Press
Celtic Court
22 Ballmoor
Buckingham
MK18 1XW

and
1900 Frost Road, Suite 101
Bristol, PA 19007, USA

First Published 1995

A catalogue record of this book is available from the British Library

ISBN   0 335 19443 5 (hb)   0 335 19442 7 (pb)

Library of Congress Cataloging-in-Publication Data
Scott, Peter, 1946–
    The meanings of mass higher education / Peter Scott.
        p.   cm.
    Includes bibliographical references and index.
    ISBN 0–335–19443–5. (hb) ISBN 0–335–19442–7 (pb)
    1. Education, Higher—Social aspects—Great Britain.
2. Educational sociology—Great Britain.   3. Education, Higher—
Great Britain—Aims and objectives.   4. Higher education and state—
Great Britain.   5. Universities and colleges—Great Britain—
Administration.   6. Education, Higher—Cross-cultural studies.
I. Title.
LC191.8.G7S36   1995
378.41—dc20   95–10593
                                                                              CIP

Typeset by Graphicraft Typesetters Ltd., Hong Kong
Printed in Great Britain by St Edmundsbury Press Ltd,
Bury St Edmunds, Suffolk

For Cherill and Anna

Contents

Preface

This book is an attempt to offer a general account of mass higher education. It takes as its starting point the development of British universities and colleges, the subject of Chapter 2. But it is impossible to write about this key shift from élite to mass higher education solely from a British viewpoint. Mass higher education is a much wider phenomenon – in two senses. First, higher education systems in all developed countries are being transformed by the same pressures and in similar ways. So comparisons with the rest of Europe, Australia and the United States are unavoidable. These comparisons not only illuminate, but also domesticate, what could otherwise appear an alarming transformation. Second, the development of mass higher education is only one of several modernizations under way in late-twentieth century society. It cannot, therefore, be regarded as an isolated and autonomous phenomenon. These larger changes in the nature of society and structure of the economy, shifts in intellectual culture and in science and technology, which are considered in Chapters 3 and 4, are integral parts of the story of mass higher education.

The first draft of this book was an inaugural lecture with the same title, given at the University of Leeds on 16 May 1994. The part of Chapter 2 which refers to the new universities (the original new universities of the 1960s) is based on an article originally published in *New Universities Quarterly*, which itself was based on a lecture given at the University of Kent. The part on unified and binary systems grew out of a paper given at a conference organized by the Academia Europaea and the Wenner Gren Foundation in Stockholm. My ideas about the links between the welfare state and the development of higher education were first developed for a conference held at the Autonomous University of Barcelona. One of my substantial debts, apparent in Chapter 4, is to my fellow members of the so-called Gleneagles group (because we first met at Gleneagles) which considered how the production of science and knowledge was changing: Michael Gibbons, Camille Limoges, Helga Nowotny, Simon Schwartzmann and Martin Trow.

Finally, I would like to acknowledge the help of many colleagues, first at the *Times Higher Education Supplement* and then at the University of Leeds.

This is inevitably a hybrid book, a mixture of journalistic opinion-mongering and (I hope) more academic reflection. I am particularly grateful to my colleagues at the Centre for Policy Studies in Education: Catherine Bargh, Alison Moore and David Smith. Last, but really first, I want to thank Jean Bocock. Most of my ideas have been launched, tested and matured in long conversations with Jean over many years.

1

Introduction

This book is an attempt to interpret the changes under way in British higher education, notably the rapid expansion of student numbers and the establishment of an open post-binary system. The interpretative framework which has been adopted is that of a transition from élite to mass higher education. Devised originally to analyse the explosive growth of American higher education a generation ago, this idea of an élite–mass paradigm shift has become the standard account of how higher education systems develop. In one sense it is an inadequate framework for interpreting the evolution of the British system, because it tends to mask the subtleties which characterize the experience of British universities and colleges in the 1990s. It imposes a linear regularity on developments which are neither linear nor regular. Indeed, non-linearity and irregularity are a recurrent theme of this book.

But, in another sense, the élite–mass transition offers an illuminating explanation, because it enables the experience of British higher education to be contextualized by using a common language to describe its development and that of analogous systems. A second theme of this book is the erosion of British exceptionalism; the distinctive qualities of British higher education, derived from and reinforcing the particularities of our national culture, have been undermined by widening access beyond traditional élite (and meritocratic) constituencies and creating an open system in which institutional boundaries and hierarchies have become more fluid. The élite–mass account also allows the British experience to be generalized, by emphasizing the affinities between the growth of a mass system and other socio-economic trends and wider shifts in intellectual and scientific culture. A third theme is this synergy between massification (ugly but convenient shorthand) and post-industrial change. Mass higher education systems are among the most distinctive, and powerful, secular institutions of modern society.

The transformation of British higher education during the past two decades has been intense, but remains curiously incomplete. The number of universities has doubled; they have become large and complex organizations; and they have taken on new roles. The number of students has quadrupled;

as a result, novel academic programmes, course structures and learning strategies have been developed. The proportion of young people going on to higher education has risen from fewer than one in ten to almost a third. A social revolution has been accomplished. A political and administrative revolution, too. A unified system has been established in place of the former binary division between universities, their 'donnish dominion' still shielded by the University Grants Committee (UGC), and the new polytechnics only recently admitted – and only as second-class members – to the higher education club.

Yet, despite these rapid and radical changes in the 'public life' of higher education, the rhythms of its 'private life' are less regular. In its broad cultural intentions there seems to be an underlying continuity. Many universities and colleges still embrace notions of education, rooted in subtle and stealthy socialization and acculturation rather than explicit intellectual formation and skills development, which are recognizably élitist. Consequently they remain committed to a personal engagement between teachers and students, and to individualized (even charismatic) styles of scholarship and, less so, research, which appear to take little account of either the values or the imperatives of a mass system.

In the inner worlds of academic disciplines the high excitement of the Robbins era has arguably receded. Already two decades ago, the philistinism and provincialism of Britain's intellectual culture had been sloughed off. A proper 'sociology', in Perry Anderson's terms, had been established.[1] The prefix 'socio' was launched on its ubiquitous ascent. The New Left's creative effects were accomplished, and perhaps exhausted, before a mass system was born. The old humanities, too, had abandoned their anti-intellectual gentility, the 'urbane trade' denounced by George Steiner, and begun powerfully to absorb the lessons of the new social sciences.[2] Science, notably the biological sciences, had discovered a dynamic inter-disciplinarity. The prefix 'bio' was becoming as promiscuous as 'socio'. Professional education, its centre of gravity shifting from engineering to caring, had acknowledged its wider socio-political contexts and responsibilities. This academic opening-up had occurred while higher education was still élitist, although liberally extended by the Robbins expansion.

The result is a disjunction, even a paradox. British higher education has become a mass system in its public structures, but remains an élite one in its private instincts. According to the linear sequence suggested by Martin Trow, it is undeniably a mass system. He defines élite systems as those which enrol up to 15 per cent of the age group; mass systems as those enrolling between 15 and 40 per cent; and universal systems as those which enrol more than 40 per cent.[3] The current age participation index in British higher education is 32 per cent, which suggests that the system is more than half-way towards becoming a universal system. As American higher education includes the two-year community colleges, it is necessary to add in post-18 students in further education colleges to secure a fair comparison. So the true participation index is already nudging 40 per cent.

The decline and fall of totalizing themes

But British higher education still feels much more like an élite than a universal system. Why? Three broad answers will be suggested that mirror the three themes mentioned at the start of this chapter. The first, which will be discussed in greater detail in Chapters 3 and 4, is that the late twentieth century world is not a uniform or linear place. Instead, ambiguity is embraced and grand schemas distrusted. The velocity and reflexivity of modern society inhibit the emergence of settled patterns. Consequently the tension between mass structures and élite manners is not surprising. Nevertheless, it is difficult to accept, as a permanent feature of mass higher education systems rather than simply the pains of transition from élite to mass forms. Universities have always been attracted to the solace of ideological regularity.

In the mid-nineteenth century Cardinal Newman could speak confidently of *The Idea of a University*.[4] His Dublin audience, and later readers, recognized the university as a distinctive, and privileged, institution, and acknowledged that it required a grand theme, an Idea. It did not matter that Newman's ideal university existed only in the imagination; most Victorian universities and colleges were much grubbier functional institutions. Even, a century later and a generation ago, during the bright dawn of the American multiversity before the Fall into leftist revolt, when the élite–mass paradigm was first being developed, Clark Kerr, then President of the University of California, could still speak confidently of *The Uses of the University*.[5] A single idea had become plural uses. Victorian idealism had been replaced by Parsonian functionalism. But the essential unity between form, or structures, and function, or purposes, continued to be taken for granted.

In contrast, the mass higher education systems of the 1990s (including the British system), the heirs of Kerr's university-as-service-station, are characterized by radical discontinuities. They no longer embody plural, but compatible, uses but starkly different representations, or meanings, which cannot be integrated satisfactorily or for long. They are anti-organic, anti-systematic, anti-totalizing. Part of the story is the highly diverse social constituencies from which they recruit students; part the dispersal of a common culture; part the volatility of post-industrial change. Mass systems are not only heterogeneous in sociological terms and heterodox in intellectual ones; they resist all but the most ephemeral classification.

But still there is a reluctance to accept that it has become impossible to construct a grand unifying theme (or that, even were it possible, it would be undesirable). The university, because of its title, cannot easily abandon an ideology, a rhetoric at any rate, which emphasizes moral integration and intellectual synthesis. Ronald Barnett has acknowledged that modern higher education systems have been doubly undermined – sociologically, because of their social (and professional) diversity and institutional pluralism; and epistemologically, because of the collapsing belief in the possibility of objective knowledge and scientific truth. Nevertheless, he argues that, even if the grander claims once made by the university can no longer be sustained, higher education in a broader sense is still a distinctive category, a coherent conceptualization, because its project is to emancipate its students through a process of critical self-reflection. Indeed, he further argues that, by institutionalizing these values of critical theory, higher education has become a key instrument in maintaining an open society.[6]

Others have attempted to derive a totalizing theme from shifts in organizational paradigm, reflecting wider socio-economic change. Christopher Duke has written of the learning university, aligned with the learning organization and learning society. He argues that the university has ceased to be a finishing school for school-leavers and instead is predominantly engaged in providing continuing education for adults.[7] There is empirical evidence to support Duke's thesis, notably the growing number of mature students and the growth of continuing professional development within universities and colleges. But there is also contrary evidence. Because of increased participation, mass higher education systems have intensified rather than abandoned their role as finishing schools. As suggestive rhetoric, and as a political agenda, Duke's thesis is persuasive; as an overall explanation it remains contested.

Other accounts are multi-dimensional. Accordingly, they find it easier to incorporate the fluidities and ambiguities characteristic of mass systems. Tony Becher and Maurice Kogan have proposed a model of higher education which can be applied more generally to social policy arenas. Their model is based on a matrix, one axis formed by distinguishing between values (norms) and activities (operations) and the other by the various levels within the system – individuals, basic units (i.e. departments), institutions and systems.[8] Although their matrix can be interpreted, in the context of system-wide equilibrium, as a totalizing explanation that excludes others, it is also compatible with the persistence of unresolved tensions, incommensurable roles and volatile purposes. Burton Clark, in his account of higher education, has written of the legitimation of disorder. 'Colleges and universities themselves do not need a great deal of consensus, since their structures and activities are only mildly interdependent.'[9]

More pragmatic explanations of this tension between mass forms and élite instincts, of course, are available. One is that recent policy changes, notably the 'elevation' of the polytechnics to university status, have reinforced the latter. Signs, redundantly, are significant. It is a paradox that, at the very moment when an irreversible momentum towards mass higher education had been established, the university title (and all its associated socio-cultural values and academic practices?) should be promiscuously extended. According to one account, the institutional diversity guaranteed by the polytechnic alternative has been sacrificed to university *revanche* – Robbins revenged on Crosland. According to a rival account, the autonomous university tradition has been subverted by this radical enlargement of the university system. In normative terms the first may be more plausible; in operational terms the latter.

In the short term, the creation of a unified system has produced a number of unintended, even contradictory, effects which seem likely to reinforce its élitism. Through research assessment, the spread of a system-wide research culture has been stimulated; while a small number of élite universities have come together to promote their particular interests, in the process redefining themselves as American-style research universities. In the long run, more radical effects, such as a more explicit division of institutional missions, may well emerge. But the confusion between the short-term and/or normative reinforcement and long-term and/or operational subversion of the élite system is a factor in the tension between mass forms and élite instincts.

Another explanation of this tension emphasizes the novelty of these mass forms. Two-thirds of Britain's universities were established after 1960. Except for Oxford, Cambridge and London, existing universities were small, closer in scale to a provincial grammar school than an American multiversity. Most had fewer than a thousand students. The poet Philip Larkin recalled his arrival at the then University College Leicester as an assistant librarian in 1946 in these words:

> The atmosphere was almost familial. The staff lunched together in what was then called the Outer Hall. The first two courses were brought in by waitresses, but the two puddings were put in front of the Principal and Vice-Principal, who sat at opposite ends of the table and served their colleagues. The conversation was genial. 'What's in that jug,' one senior member of the staff asked. 'Not what you think,' replied another.[10]

The first significant break, in scale and ethos, came only in the 1960s when, in fictional terms, the 1950s world of *Lucky Jim* was superseded by that of *The History Man*.[11] The Robbins expansion and, a little later, the establishment of the polytechnics, created a new kind of higher education, a 'campus culture', closely linked to the opening-up of post-war society and the growth of popular culture. But it remained a recognizably élite system, enrolling barely 8 per cent of the age group. The second, and more decisive, breakthrough did not take place until more than two decades later, the late 1980s and early 1990s. Leslie Wagner has pointed out that in 1981, which is as far as the Robbins committee's student number projections went, the participation rate of 13 per cent had fallen behind the Robbins prediction. Only in the mid-1980s did it reach 15 per cent, the threshold figure that marks the boundary between élite and mass higher education. Between 1987 and 1992 participation almost doubled from 14.6 to 27.8 per cent. It was only yesterday, during that turbulent half-decade, that Britain irreversibly acquired a mass system.[12]

The erosion of exceptionalism

The second broad answer arises from the erosion of British exceptionalism. This is both a specific phenomenon, because British universities, in particular

Oxford and Cambridge, are (were?) acknowledged to be exceptional institutions, love them or hate them. It is also a general phenomenon, in the sense that all élite systems tend to be exceptional while most mass systems are similar. Exceptionalism, in the first sense, has often been admired. The government of British universities was traditionally regarded as a *via media* between the bureaucratic excesses of other European higher education systems and the market excesses of the American system. Recently, admiration has been replaced by more critical scrutiny. Political scientists ceased to celebrate the UGC even before it was summarily dispatched in 1989. An American exchange student, Rosa Ehrenreich, recently recalled her experience at Oxford in excoriating terms which recall Steiner's denunciation of literature's 'urbane trade'. Her section-headings tell the story: idealization; bewilderment; disillusionment; insight.[13]

This élite academic tradition, which she experienced in its dog days, mistaking its oblique irony and complicit values for shuffling amateurism, has been defined by Claudius Gellert as one of the three dominant strands within the European university tradition. These are the 'knowledge' model, represented historically by the Humboldtian university in Germany, which placed graduate study and research at the heart of higher education; the 'professional' model, represented by France's *grandes écoles*, which concentrated on producing professional workers and, in particular, state functionaries; and the 'personality' model, centred on Oxford and Cambridge, which aspired to 'civilize our gentlemen' by initiating them into a liberal intellectual culture.[14] His categorization underestimates the pluralism of all higher education systems, including the British (which will be discussed in the next chapter), but describes their broad orientation well enough.

Of these three traditions the last has been least robust in its encounter with massification. Of course, the Humboldtian university did not provide an ideal template for a mass system. The scientific dynamics, and logistics, of modern research demand concentration. Not everyone can, or wants to, participate in the grand professor's seminar. But the Humboldtian ideal does not discourage the establishment of alternative forms of higher education, unlike the Anglo-Saxon 'personality' tradition with its all-embracing holistic ambitions. Perhaps the polytechnics could only be fully and finally accepted into higher education by becoming universities. Certainly they were subject to subtle status pressures from which *Fachhochschulen* in Germany, HBO (higher professional schools) schools in the Netherlands and *instituts universitaires de technologie* in France are exempt.

Similarly, the 'professional' model can only provide a basis for a mass system if root-and-branch stratification of prestige and resources is introduced. But the incestuous links between many of the systems which have been most heavily influenced by this tradition and the commands of the state have made such planning simpler than in the autonomous arm's-length systems that predominate within the 'personality' tradition. System-wide planning is difficult to achieve in a British system regulated by the unwritten consents of a club rather than bureaucratic rules. The proposal in the late 1980s to grade all institutions on a three-point scale – R for those with comprehensive research roles; X for those with mixed missions; and T for teaching-mainly institutions – failed, not only because of a lack of political will to implement a controversial reform, but also because, crucially, it offended the inarticulate affection for informal hierarchy rather than planned stratification endemic in the British university tradition.[15]

However, the main difficulty encountered by the attempt to reconcile the 'personality' tradition with mass access is that its intimacy – social, professional and intellectual – appears to be directly threatened by the imperatives of mass higher education. This intimacy is not a uniquely British characteristic. Sheldon Rothblatt has contrasted the rival ideals of the college and the university: the former private, even inward, familial (in Larkin's revealing phrase), all pastoral warmth and pedagogical engagement; the latter public, responsive to its external environment, a factory of scientific research and professional expertise.[16] In the United States these rivals are clearly distinguished, and separately institutionalized, in liberal arts colleges like Bryn Mawr on the one hand and the great multi-campus state universities in California, Wisconsin and Michigan on the other.

In Britain the two ideals remain awkwardly combined. The largest university must still be 'collegiate' in ethos. Even the Open University was obliged to construct mechanisms of intimacy, such as summer schools, and permit the construction of myths of intimacy, as in the film *Educating Rita*. Attempts to label the colleges of higher education, since 1992 a residual or immature university sector, as liberal arts colleges have foundered. As a result, intimacy and access coexist uneasily in the same institutional settings. In practice the latter imperative has become dominant. Intimacy is being abandoned, privacy invaded. Two-thirds of British universities have now introduced, or plan to introduce, credit accumulation and transfer and modular degree schemes.[17] Terms are being transformed into semesters. Formal quality systems are being introduced in teaching. Access in a starkly different sense, as political and market intervention, is also dominant. Research assessment, based on bureaucratized peer review, is accepted. Scientific priorities are influenced more and more by so-called 'users' of research.[18]

Yet, nostalgia, even grief, for a lost intimacy, an academic Arcadia, acts as a silent drag on progress towards wider access and advance towards mass higher education. A mass system enrolling a third of the age group, mass institutions with tens of thousands of students in which donnish collegiality is a fading memory, mass practices in teaching and research are confronted by the instincts of an élite age. Nor is this longing for intimacy, and its attributes, a peculiarly academic regret. It has its analogues in the informal solidarities, tacit values and archaic institutions which mark the British (or English) experience, such as our unwritten constitution and the common law. Massification, therefore, is caught up in a larger modernization.

This erosion of the exceptionalism of British higher education is compounded by the convergence that underlies the general transition from

particular, élite systems to similar, mass systems. The three traditions identified by Gellert have all to be represented in mass higher education. The
'research' tradition needs to be clearly delineated; élite research universities cannot be left to sink or swim among mass institutions. The 'professional' tradition must be strengthened as the supposed links between higher
education and the production of highly skilled labour are increasingly
emphasized. The 'personality' tradition, too, is likely to be reinforced as
many more students, with less focused professional ambitions, are enrolled
and as old-style liberal education is reinterpreted in terms of the development of adaptable and transferable skills. Mass systems, therefore, while
struggling to encompass this diversity of traditions, are likely to become
more alike in their policy responses.

However, time and place are important determinants of the character of
mass higher education. The first mass system developed three decades ago
in the United States. The spirit of the 1960s was different from that of the
1990s. Faith in the efficacy of ambitious social policies, themselves seen as
a realization of democratic entitlement (especially, in America, for ethnic
minorities), was still strong. Belief in the benefits of a progressive science
was unshaken. Radical protest reflected a culture of political optimism.
Thirty years later, the wider welfare state is under siege by neo-conservatives
and abandoned by faint-hearted liberals. Science has been undermined
from within by epistemological doubts and from without by growing public
consciousness of environmental and other risks. The adventurous optimism
of the 1960s has been abandoned as either naive or subversive. Mass higher
education systems are coloured by the spirit of the age of their creation.
Part of the hesitation about massification in Britain can be attributed to a
wider ambivalence about the development of society.

Differences between America and Europe are also significant, because
recognizably mass higher education emerged first in the United States. As
a result, the American system came to be regarded as a hegemonic model.
It is no accident that the interpretative framework adopted in this book,
and by most writers about universities and colleges, the transition from élite
to mass higher education, was developed in America. But too little attention perhaps has been paid to the particularities of American political culture,
with its paradoxical combination of extensive state regulation (the result of
a multi-layered federal–state–local government) and strong commitment to
the market. The American system was shaped by this culture. Planned stratification on the one hand; an open market on the other.

The political culture of most European countries, including Britain, is
different. The state, normatively, is more authoritative, but its operational
authority is expressed as much through (passive) administrative regulation
as (active) political interventions. Its effective power is restrained in arenas
such as higher education by powerful, if informal, constraints. At the same
time faith in the market is much less. As a result, most European higher
education systems are less responsive than American universities and colleges, either to politics or the market. According to one interpretation, this

inwardness is a reflection of their underdevelopment; as they become mass systems, they will become more responsive. In part, this is true. But, according to another interpretation, the distinctive orientations of European and American higher education arise from differences in political cultures – or, more broadly, 'public doctrines'. Therefore, they are likely to persist.

Mass higher education in post-industrial society

The third broad answer arises from the links between the development of mass higher education systems and wider socio-economic trends, generally labelled post-industrialism or post-Fordism, and shifts in academic and scientific culture, which include so-called post-modernism but embrace other intellectual currents. The keynotes of both, trends and shifts, are acceleration, volatility, non-linearity, simultaneity and reflexivity (which will be discussed at the end of Chapter 3). These characteristics can also be observed in mass systems, which helps to explain the difficulty of devising overall interpretative, or policy, frameworks. The same anti-totalizing imperatives apply.

As a result, élite instincts and mass forms presently coexist and are likely to persist, not only in the sense that mass higher education includes within it élite institutions or that mass systems are the culmination of, or alternative to, élite systems (although both are true), but in the more radical context of the profounder ironies and irregularities which define the future world. These form the substance of this book, because massification is not so much the product of the 'internal' dynamics of the system, of its autonomous self-development, as of 'external' influences. These influences are 'external' in two different senses. Some represent grander socio-economic change (although mass systems are themselves principal agencies of change). Others are 'external' to the 'public' world of higher education, the arena of policy-making, because they are generated within the 'private' world of disciplines, of knowledge and its applications.

They include the growth of a contractual state, through which a plurality of interests are expressed rather than a single national interest and in which the demarcation between public and private has become increasingly porous; contested claims about the classless and ungendered society, in which involuntary solidarities allegedly are being replaced by individualized identities; the shift from life chances, sober and productive, to lifestyles, playful and ephemeral, in economic life; in intellectual culture the substitution of plural narratives, or discourses, for authoritative knowledge traditions; and the erosion of expert science as invention and application become elided and progressive science as epistemological doubts gather and risks accumulate.

This book's argument, in brief, is that the transition from élite to mass higher education cannot be understood simply in terms either of the evolution of higher education systems, such as the expansion of student numbers or structural reforms; or of the substitution of one paradigm, labelled 'mass', for another, labelled 'élite'. Instead it must be interpreted in the context of the restless synergy between plural modernizations – of the academy, polity, economy, society and culture. The most important, and only permanent, characteristics of mass higher education systems are that they are endlessly open and radically reflexive. In all other respects, they are in ceaseless flux. Therefore, the apparent disjunction between mass forms and élite habits, which has been discussed in this introductory chapter, can be doubly explained: as an instinctive drawing-back from destabilizing and disorientating change, and as an expression of the ambiguities and irregularities inherent in that change.

Despite this argument that structural and institutional reforms are secondary, the next chapter is devoted to them. The growth of a unified system in Britain is analysed, as well as the contrast between different types of national system. Next, the present pattern of institutions is described, to emphasize the diversity that already prevails in British higher education. Two contrasting modernization strategies are also discussed, the liberalization of the university tradition (by creating 'new universities' in the 1960s) and the development of alternative institutions (the polytechnics). Finally, in that chapter, issues of mission and management are addressed.

Chapter 3 considers two broad topics, the reform of the welfare state and the shift from industrial to post-industrial society. The impact of the former on the government (in particular, relations between universities and the state) and funding of higher education is discussed; the influence of the latter on the system's inputs, or social demand for higher education, and outputs, or graduate careers, is also considered. The chapter ends with a more general discussion of the parameters of modernity. Chapter 4 opens with a brief review of past 'moments' of affinity between the development of higher education and radical conjunctures of social, economic and cultural change. It then also considers two broad topics, shifts in intellectual culture and in science and technology. The chapter ends by considering the implications of both for teaching and research. The final chapter attempts to draw the threads of the argument together and to offer a general account of mass higher education.

2

Structure and Institutions

Universities are thoroughly modern institutions. Two hundred years ago there were only six in Britain – Oxford, Cambridge and the four ancient Scottish universities – Edinburgh, Glasgow, St Andrew's and Aberdeen (really two, King's College and Marischall College, until the 1850s). Together they enrolled fewer than 5,000 students. In no sense did they form a 'system'. Not until the mid-nineteenth century were there any public policy interventions to shape, or reform, what today would be regarded as higher education. Even a century ago the number of universities had barely doubled, to 14, although the number of students had risen fourfold, to 20,000. There was still no national system, despite the chartering of new universities in the North and Midlands and the first tentative state subsidies for technical education.

When the Robbins report was published in 1963 there were still only 24 universities, with a further six, the first wave of 'new' universities, in the process of formation. But a national system had begun to emerge as a result of the activities of the University Grants Committee, and this system was about to be extended to embrace the non-university sector. The university student population then stood at just under 120,000 (with a similar number in teacher training colleges and on 'advanced' courses in further education). But old patterns persisted. Three out of every 20 still attended Oxford and Cambridge. In other words, almost three-quarters of Britain's universities have been established during the past three decades, less than the span of an academic working life. Even if anterior institutions are taken into account, few universities can trace their origins back beyond the mid-nineteenth century. Student numbers have increased ten times over during the same period. Almost everything about higher education – system, institutions, students – is new.

This chronology is important in two senses. First, it demonstrates that the ancient pedigree of the universities is largely a myth. The universities themselves are recent foundations. Although it can be argued that the survival of the 'university' as an institutional ideal suggests that present universities, however young, are heirs to a deeply rooted tradition, it is just as plausible to argue that the persistence of the label proves how adaptable an institution the university has been over the centuries.[1] The university has survived so long because it has changed so much. Second, this chronology suggests a close association between the growth of the universities and wider developments in society.

Pre-industrial Britain had little need of universities. At the end of the eighteenth century the number of students was actually lower than it had been two hundred years before. Moreover, universities fulfilled very different purposes from those which are familiar today. They were largely concerned with the training of clergymen and teachers, entwined professions. Their mission, in today's terminology, was to sustain intellectual hegemony, the established Anglican (or Presbyterian) order, not to encourage a progressive science or provide a liberal education. Although members of élite social groups passed through universities, they rarely completed their degrees. The subsidiary mission of the pre-industrial universities was to complete the socialization of future élites, social and political. The university provided an extended form of secondary education.

During the nineteenth century three decisive shifts took place which not only created the demand for a more elaborate university system but also shaped (and continue to shape) its development. The first was the stirrings of the democratic revolution. The progressive extension of the franchise, the spread of polite culture among the middle classes and the growth of working-class consciousness contributed to a growing emphasis on education (whether as a means of emancipation, enlightenment or social control). The second, of course, was the industrial revolution which created a demand for a much more sophisticated division of labour, based on expert skills. It was in this context that the technical colleges and mechanics' institutes, later to develop into the technological universities and the former polytechnics, were established. The third was the rise of professional society. The development of organized professions and the growth of a bureaucratic state created new training needs. The civic universities were established to meet these needs, typically on the initiative of local civic, professional and commercial élites rather than of the state.

During the twentieth century universities have continued to be moulded by the same three shifts, although radically extended. The democratic revolution has passed beyond meritocratic co-option to mass entitlement, and beyond representation to empowerment. The industrial revolution, more precipitate and more volatile, has remade the division of labour many times over. It has produced other fundamental effects, spatial in the shape of urbanization and social in the twin (but jostling) forms of commercialization and collectivism. Professional society, more pervasive in its techniques but less coherent in its values, has come almost to be coterminous with the modern state. The multiversity which first emerged in mid-century America and the mass higher education systems in which it has been generalized, and globalized, are the institutional and organizational forms which have developed in the context of these larger transformations.

The subject of this chapter is not these larger transformations, which will be discussed in Chapter 3, but the evolution of these institutional and organizational forms. As has already been argued, existing systems and institutions are recent formations. But, despite their novelty, the shift to mass higher education means that both systems and institutions have to be radically reconceptualized, and reconfigured.

The rest of the chapter is divided into two sections. First, the development of a system of higher education is described, its present structure examined and various structural models discussed. Key themes are the growth of a national system, steered by the state, and the shift from binary to post-binary structures. In the second section the focus is on institutions. The evolution of different institutional types is described. Two evolutionary strategies are considered, the elaboration of the existing pattern of universities (mainly but not exclusively by establishing new universities) and the creation of alternative institutions. The changing character of higher education institutions is also examined, in terms of their governance, management, organization and culture.

Systems and structures

The growth of national systems of higher education is a by-product of the development of the modern nation state, which has acted as sponsor of new institutions, predominant funder and planner or co-ordinator. In Britain the evolution of the system has had two main elements – first, the subordination of the autonomous universities to the commands of the state; and second, the take-over by the state of responsibility for other advanced institutions once provided by local government, the churches and other voluntary agencies. The latter has been routine, characteristic of the growth of most higher education systems; the former arguably exceptional because of the high degree of autonomy once enjoyed by British universities. This process is described in the first part of this section. It is two related stories, of the decline and fall of the UGC system and of the nationalization of the former polytechnics and other colleges.

Systems require structures. The first step is simply to conceive of higher education as a coherent system, rather than an aggregation of separate institutions. That alone, if undertaken by the state, is sufficient to establish a system-wide structure; institutions are then regarded as part of a national network, not as independent units. The next step is to articulate that embryonic structure. From there it is a short third step to reforming that structure as a deliberate act of public policy. This process is discussed in the second part of this section. Its theme is the progressive integration of the system, leading eventually to the replacement of the binary division between universities and polytechnics and other higher education colleges by a post-binary structure.

Wider, and more theoretical, issues are raised by these two processes, the development of a national system of higher education and the successive structural reforms. Does the articulation of systems produce an irreversible shift from dual, or binary, to integrated structures? Here the British experience is examined in the context of the development of other higher education systems, in the rest of Europe and beyond. In the light of that examination two interpretations are considered – exceptionalism, or the survival of the special character of Britain's universities and colleges despite the scale and scope of recent reforms; and massification, those convergent effects which are reshaping all higher education systems.

The development of a national system

As has already been pointed out, a system of higher education, and indeed higher education itself as a coherent category (whether administrative or academic), did not really exist before 1945. Until the late nineteenth century the state's involvement in the development of higher education was extremely limited. Universities and colleges were essentially private institutions. Oxford and Cambridge long pre-dated the formation of the modern state, although their structure and statutes had been reformed by the Acts of 1854, 1856 and 1877. The Scottish universities, like the law and the church, were distinctively Scottish institutions which survived the union of 1707. They, too, had been reformed between the 1820s and 1880s, in a series of external interventions inspired at first by a Whiggish enthusiasm for improvement and later by a desire to modernize (Anglicize?) their practices.[2]

But the emphasis on voluntarism remained strong well into the twentieth century. University College and King's College in London were established by voluntary initiative, as were most of the colleges which later coalesced into the Victorian-age civic universities.[3] Medical schools, dissenting academies and mechanics' institutes, which developed, or were incorporated, into universities, were also established as voluntary institutions. Only in 1889 did the government offer financial help to the struggling university colleges (£15,000). In the 1890s they received additional payments, for technical education and teacher training. The *ad hoc* University Colleges Committee, established in 1906 and chaired by R. B. Haldane, was the first attempt to create administrative machinery to regulate the relationship between universities and the state. Nevertheless, the bulk of universities' income continued to be provided by student fees and industrial, commercial and civic sponsorship.[4]

The two world wars transformed the relationship between universities and the state. They underlined the vital contribution of science and technology and of highly skilled manpower to sustaining national power. Their social reverberations, combined with the final establishment of democracy in the form of universal suffrage after the First World War and the creation of the welfare state after the Second, created the conditions for the rapid growth of demand for higher education. Universities came to be seen as national institutions.[5] A permanent body, the UGC, was established in 1919 to distribute Treasury grants to universities.[6] The original purpose of these grants was limited, to make good the deficit between university income and expenditure. But, despite the Depression, and the pressure to reduce public expenditure, one-third of the universities' income was provided by UGC grants on the eve of the Second World War. By 1946 this had risen to two-thirds. Universities had become in effect public, as well as national, institutions.

However, this creeping nationalization of the funding of universities did not at first reduce their autonomy. Indeed, the establishment of the UGC as an instrument by which state funds were channelled to universities may actually have enhanced their independence. Universities were no longer dependent on local funding which was often unreliable, always insufficient and likely to involve more direct scrutiny of its uses. The decline of lay influence, and the entrenchment of the so-called 'donnish dominion', discussed later in this chapter, have been attributed to this switch in funding. The UGC itself was seen as an ingenious institution which, uniquely, allowed British universities to be both publicly funded and insulated from political pressure. That is perhaps to overstate its importance. There is no inherent contradiction between state funding and (effective) university autonomy, as the experience of the British universities between 1919 and the mid-1960s and of many other European universities, although formally incorporated within state bureaucracies, suggests.

Nor is the standard interpretation necessarily more reliable: the greater the dependence of universities on state funding, the more open they become to political pressure. In Britain the key factors seem to have been increasing public expenditure and political resistance to it, the proportion of overall public expenditure devoted to higher education, and the broadening of the scope and mission of institutions rather than the degree of the universities' dependence on state funds. The first of these phenomena, the apparent backlash against the welfare state, is discussed in the next chapter. The other two, however, are closely linked to the development of mass higher education systems. These are more expensive, in aggregate rather than unit-cost terms, and more accessible in the sense that they have more democratic purposes. The historical record suggests that élite systems, whether or not state-funded, enjoy a high degree of autonomy, while mass systems, even if they become less dependent on the state, inevitably (and beneficially) attract political attention.

This general account fits the particular experience of British higher education well enough. It was changes in political culture and the wider transformation of the higher education system, rather than their dependence on public funds, which subordinated the universities to the state today – and the 'market' tomorrow? – and led to the nationalization of the polytechnics and colleges. Between 1945 and its abolition in 1989 the UGC was gradually transformed from being a buffer body designed to insulate the autonomous domain of the universities from direct and detailed intervention by Whitehall, into an executive agency responsible to ministers for planning university development. This responsibility was inherited by the Universities Funding Council (and now the three successor funding councils). The autonomy of the universities was eroded as more and more elaborate control systems were imposed by the state.

Similar changes took place in the non-university sector, although here nationalization enhanced, rather than diminished the status of the training and technical colleges. The Percy report in 1945 and the 1956 White Paper on technical education provided the first evidence of Whitehall's interest in the colleges which became the polytechnics in the 1960s.[7] After a series of false starts, the National Advisory Body for Public Sector Higher Education (NAB), an anomalous agency representing a local–central government condominium, was established in 1982 to plan what had become an alternative national system of higher education. This task was inherited by the Polytechnics and Colleges Funding Council (PCFC) when the polytechnics and colleges were removed from the control of local education authorities by the 1988 Education Reform Act.

Both stories, the subordination of the universities and the nationalization of the polytechnics, can be telescoped into five distinct phases. The first, which covered the years between the end of the Second World War and the beginning of the 1960s, was the UGC's golden age. Still a non-departmental committee responsible directly to the Treasury and without statutory backing, the UGC's terms of reference were modified in 1946 to require the committee to take into account 'the needs of the nation'. The committee also took on a more active planning role rather than simply providing deficit funding.[8] But generally ministers were content to leave detailed university policy to the committee, including the development of the red-brick university colleges into fully fledged universities, the expansion of the existing civic universities and the designation of new universities.[9]

However, the UGC's success in promoting university development encouraged the articulation of a national system in place of an assembly of autonomous institutions. Also the post-war development of further education meant that the contribution of non-university institutions towards what was coming to be called higher education could no longer be ignored. Towards the end of this first phase, there were already signs that the government saw the need to supplement, or even bypass, the UGC regime. Sir Winston Churchill's last Cabinet tentatively discussed the feasibility of establishing élite technological institutions, a project which became more urgent with the launching of *Sputnik*. The decision in the 1956 White Paper to establish colleges of advanced technology, outside the university sector and directly funded by the Ministry of Education, suggested an unwillingness in Whitehall to leave the development of higher education entirely in the hands of the UGC.

In the second phase, the decade of the 1960s or the Robbins–Crosland years, the influence of the UGC was reduced by a series of developments. First, the Prime Minister, Harold Macmillan, established the Robbins committee to inquire into the future pattern of higher education.[10] It has been argued that the establishment of the committee was a crucial episode in the decline and fall of an autonomous university tradition, because the UGC was bypassed. It was no longer seen as representative of the burgeoning higher education system; nor, perhaps, as capable of long-range strategic planning. Much controversy has also surrounded the correct interpretation of the significance of the Robbins report. According to the standard account its university-friendly recommendations were rejected in favour of a binary policy motivated by anti-university prejudice.

That is too simple. Robbins did recommend that the university sector should be enlarged by promoting, first, the colleges of advanced technology and, subsequently, selected regional colleges of technology (which became the core institutions of the future polytechnics instead). It is true that this prescription, expansion built round autonomous universities, was rejected in favour of expansion based on accountable polytechnics. This appeared to be a decisive break with the past. No more universities. The polytechnics were established as an alternative to the universities (although the colleges of advanced technology (CATs) were transferred to the UGC list). But in the *longue durée* of the development of higher education the influence of Robbins was immense. By supporting expansion, which could only be funded by the state, the report endorsed the creation of not only a system, but a public system, of higher education.[11] And, through its work, Robbins enlarged the notion of higher education to embrace the leading technical colleges and teacher training colleges as well as the universities.

In any case changes within the machinery of government were perhaps as decisive as the 'rejection' of Robbins and the establishment of the binary system in eroding the autonomy of the universities. A second development was the creation of a new Department of Education and Science (DES) to which the UGC was made responsible, ending its privileged access to the Treasury and the universities' structural detachment from the rest of the education system. For the first time a single department was responsible, albeit indirectly, for the whole of higher education. Third, the accounts of individual universities were opened to Parliamentary scrutiny. The practical effects of this change were slight, despite the apparent intrusion into the autonomous domain of the universities. Fourth, the public expenditure survey system was introduced to plan social expenditure as a whole. It was this fourth change, the first shot in a continuing Whitehall revolution, which proved to be the most decisive.

In the third phase the UGC was increasingly absorbed into the wider Whitehall system.[12] The tension between the old quinquennial system, which guaranteed university grants in five-year tranches, and the developing Public Expenditure Survey (PES) system was resolved in the mid-1970s by the collapse of the former under inflationary pressures. After the IMF-induced recovery universities were offered a three-year rolling triennium instead. But, in practice, rapidly increasing expenditure on universities made it inevitable that the old arm's-length relationship could never be restored. Just as the UGC's success in stimulating university development during the

1950s and early 1960s led to the emergence of a university system, which demanded a degree of national co-ordination the UGC was unable to provide, so another UGC success, the successful development of this system in the 1970s, undermined its traditional role as buffer between universities and the state. Paradoxically this role was most revered, and the UGC celebrated as a uniquely successful device for reconciling the public funding of universities with their autonomy, when it had already become an anachronism.

During the 1970s the growing weight of the polytechnics, although still under inchoate local authority control, obliged ministers to take a more active role in determining higher education policy, if only to secure better co-ordination between the two sectors.[13] Initially this was resisted – or, rather, ignored – by the UGC, and by university leaders, in the hope that the government would permit two separate economies to coexist in higher education, a high-cost 'university' economy built round a defence of the unit of resource and a low-cost 'polytechnic' economy based on productivity gains. For a while the government was too absorbed by the difficulty of redefining, or unravelling, the complex relationship between polytechnics and local education authorities to insist on the illogicality of the UGC's position.

Seen in this light the 1981 cuts, experienced as a grand caesura in the post-Robbins development of the British universities, were a pyrrhic victory for the UGC. Its waning influence as an advocate for the universities was cruelly exposed by the severity of the cuts. Yet the detailed distribution of the reduced university grants remained the UGC's exclusive responsibility. Universities were asked to cut their intakes by 5 per cent to provide (partial) protection of the unit of resource in the face of a 15 per cent cut. In effect, the UGC was still attempting to pursue a policy at odds with the wider drift of the government's higher education policy. Even in the early 1980s, ministers had begun falteringly to develop a strategy based on rapid growth in student numbers *and* ruthless productivity gains. This expansionary strategy was whole-heartedly pursued in the second half of the decade and sustained until a pause for 'consolidation' was introduced in the mid-1990s.

The fourth phase began with the after-shocks of the 1981 cuts. The UGC was doubly undermined. First, its claim to provide the universities privileged protection within (or rather, without) Whitehall was exploded. The interests of the UGC and those of the universities diverged. Public opinion within the universities turned against the UGC which was regarded, however unfairly, as the enemy within.[14] Also, university leaders no longer saw the UGC as their champion. Increasingly, if hesitantly, they made their own arrangements to influence political and public opinion. Second, the UGC's attempt to run its own, apolitical, policy for universities had to be abruptly abandoned. Never again would ministers be informed about key decisions affecting the university system hours before they appeared in the newspapers. Never again would DES assessors be asked politely to leave when sensitive issues were discussed by the UGC.

Paradoxically, the collapse of its claim to stand outside politics gave the committee a new, and final, lease of life. The UGC took on an increasingly executive role in its dealings with universities – determining (and policing) student number targets, carrying out subject reviews, embarking on research assessment, even dealing with delinquent institutions such as University College Cardiff.[15] But the UGC's subordination to the DES increased. Although detailed decisions, and tactical issues, were still left to the committee, university development now had to conform to the strategic direction set by the government. Two years after the 1981 cuts the NAB began work. This transformed the higher education policy environment. The two evolutionary strands, the subordination of the universities and the nationalization of the polytechnics and colleges, came together.

The UGC now had to work with, or against, the new NAB with the DES as arbiter, accelerating the politicization of higher education policy. Moreover, although the creation of the NAB did not turn out to be a full and final settlement of the 'polytechnic question', it provided a context in which, for the first time, a higher education system could be managed, as opposed to discrete university and polytechnic sectors. It had only been possible previously to conceive of, and seek to shape, a system of higher education in terms of high policy-making; the creation of the NAB alongside the UGC provided a managerial structure through which the system could be articulated. The UGC, and the 'old' universities, were only part of that system – and, as the 1980s went by, a dwindling part. The system's centre of gravity subtly shifted from universities to polytechnics.

Finally, the fact that the creation of NAB did not resolve the tensions between the DES and local education authorities over the management of the polytechnics and colleges of higher education set off a chain reaction which led to the creation of a unified system and – sad necessity – the abolition of the UGC. The UGC was a casualty of the war between local and central government during the 1980s, collateral damage. When the decision was taken to remove polytechnics from local authority control, NAB's convoluted constitution became unsustainable. In the interests of administrative symmetry the replacement of NAB by the PCFC had to be balanced by the substitution of a Universities Funding Council (UFC) for the UGC, although the Croham committee established to inquire into the latter had proposed no more than constitutional tinkering and there is little evidence that ministers were dissatisfied with the UGC's performance under Sir Peter Swinnerton Dyer.[16]

But the UGC system was also a casualty of deeply rooted secular shifts in the constitution of British higher education. It was undermined by external factors – the emergence of a higher education system which embraced much more than the 'old' universities; the inexorable politicization of university policy-making; the desire to plan (i.e. curb) the growth of public expenditure; the raising of the age participation index from fewer than one in ten to, currently, 32 per cent of school leavers; the democratization of institutional missions. It was also undermined by internal factors. The

UGC in its classic form was designed to channel state grants to a limited number of élite, homogeneous, self-referential and autonomous institutions. When universities ceased to be like that, which began to happen not in the 1980s but in the 1960s, the UGC constitution became an anachronism. A death long foretold, in other words, rather than a murder committed by Thatcherism.

The evolution of the non-university sector was shaped by similar forces. As early as the 1956 White Paper, if not the Percy report a decade before, it was clear that its development could no longer be regarded as a purely local, or voluntary, matter. The articulation of the binary policy a decade later was an ambiguous phenomenon, in part a reassertion of local government's stake in higher education but, more powerfully, a recognition that to maintain a credible stake quasi-university institutions had to be established in the form of the polytechnics. During the 1970s efforts were made to create a national planning framework for the polytechnics and colleges, notably the Oakes initiative. Well before Margaret Thatcher came to power in 1979, the slow but sure differentiation of the non-university sector from the mass of local authority further education was under way. The creation of the NAB in the early 1980s and the PCFC in the late 1980s, far from being policy disjunctures, were the culmination of 40 years of creeping nationalization.

The fifth, and most recent, phase of the relationship began with the simultaneous abolition of the UGC and the NAB.[17] In the eyes of the universities the new UFC embodied subordination, a loss of autonomy; for the polytechnics and colleges the PCFC represented nationalization (combined with greater operational freedom), a status gain. The constitutional anomalies of the UGC, a non-departmental committee with an independent chairman ranked as the DES's second permanent secretary, were swept away. The new councils were established as statutory agencies with almost identical terms of reference. In retrospect they were too alike to remain apart.

Much was made of their statutory independence during the debates surrounding the passage of the Education Reform Act. But the universities were not deceived. From the start the UFC was viewed unsentimentally as an arm of the state. The attempt by its chairman, Lord Chilver, to encourage institutions to bid against each other in order to drive down unit costs, and his unguarded remarks about making students contribute to the cost of their tuition, increased the universities' sense of alienation. The well-signalled squabbling between Lord Chilver and his chief executive, Sir Peter Swinnerton Dyer, the last chairman of the UGC, added to the UFC's instability. As a result the UFC was labelled a failure, unable to overcome its UGC inheritance. The PCFC, unencumbered by the tensions between local education authorities and Whitehall which the NAB had struggled to accommodate, was able to make a fresh start.

The wider political environment also favoured the PCFC. The expansionary climate which developed in the wake of Kenneth Baker's Lancaster speech suited the polytechnics far better than the universities.[18] Polytechnic numbers had been boosted by students displaced by the 1981 cuts and the NAB regime between 1982 and 1989 had produced impressive productivity gains. The PCFC was able to work with the grain. In contrast, student numbers in universities had grown only slowly during the 1980s. Moreover, the UFC inherited the UGC's reticence about rapid expansion which, unless carefully managed and adequately resourced, could undermine the genius of the universities. The instinct to defend the unit of resource remained buried deep in the council's collective folk memory. Both universities and UFC found it more difficult to come to terms with the expansionary climate of the late 1980s and early 1990s.

When the binary system was finally abandoned in 1992 the UFC and PCFC were replaced by unified funding councils, the Higher Education Funding Council for England (HEFCE), the Scottish Higher Education Funding Council (SHEFC) and the Funding Council for Wales (FCW, which was also made responsible for further education).[19] The significance of this reform is considered in greater detail in the next part of this section, because it relates more closely to the structure of higher education than to the development of a national system. The concern here is with broader changes in the system's contours. The most obvious, of course, was the enlargement of the university sector (Robbins vindicated?) and the creation of higher education-wide control systems in the form of the HEFCE, SHEFC and FCW. But two other changes were made which are likely to have far-reaching implications for the system's future shape.

First, three national (or sub-national) systems were created, largely by political accident. But already they have begun to diverge. The Scottish system is heir to distinctive intellectual traditions and different administrative practices. Its smaller scale also allows it to be managed in ways impossible in the much larger English system.[20] The Welsh system, too, is more intimate. It also embraces further as well as higher education, and so opens up the possibility of vertical integration of post-secondary education. In the larger transition from élite to mass higher education there is likely to be a shift from nation-wide horizontal integration to vertical integration, often in a regional context. This is an aspect of the larger shift from closed to open systems and institutions. The separation between HEFCE, SHEFC and FCW may have created, unwittingly, the conditions for such a reconfiguration.

Second, in the same political manoeuvre which created a unified system(s) of higher education, further education colleges were removed from the control of local education authorities and made responsible to a new Further Education Funding Council (FEFC). In one sense a new binary frontier has been established, between higher and further education. But, in a deeper sense, further education has been removed from purely local environments and is now funded, and planned, in a quasi-national context. Its horizons have been extended. The final result may be a radical enlargement of the higher education system to embrace further education colleges, for which ample precedents exist in the United States. Just as in the mid-twentieth century the notion of higher education was expanded to include the proto-polytechnics and training colleges as well as the universities, so in the late-twentieth century it may be extended again to include all post-secondary institutions. The potential synergy between the regionalization of higher education and the emergence of a wider post-secondary education identity is powerful. Both contribute to the meanings of mass higher education.

A *post-binary framework*

The determining characteristic of post-binary higher education is its size. Britain, in a fit of absent-mindedness, has acquired a mass system of universities and colleges. It is no longer exceptional compared to other European or North American systems. Before Robbins and Crosland, British higher education was highly selective, enrolling fewer than 8 per cent of the age group, and consequently élitist and/or meritocratic in its ethos. The binary era was a period of transition, from élite to mass forms. Between the mid-1960s and 1990 the age participation index increased more than fourfold, from 8 to 28 per cent. In 1994 the index stood at 31 per cent.

The post-binary system, therefore, is grounded in mass access. In 1990 there were 1.2 million students in universities and colleges, an increase of 41 per cent since 1980.[21] There were a further 800,000 students aged 18 and over, in further education colleges. In the United States these students would be enrolled in community colleges and count towards the higher education total. If they are included, the participation rate is pushed up to almost 40 per cent, similar to the rates which prevail in all but the most advanced American states. Comparisons with the rest of Europe also need to be adjusted. The number of students who continue after the first-year cull, common in many mass systems in Europe, is broadly similar to the British total. (The growth of student numbers in British higher and further education since 1962 is given in Table 1.)

However, mass access remains a novel experience, in four senses. First, growth rates have been uneven, with the bulk of expansion concentrated in the past decade. The 1970s were a decade of steady rather than spectacular growth. Yet this was a decisive period in terms of moulding the values and practices of British higher education, a time when the post-Robbins university system was taking shape as the older civic universities grew away from their provincial roots and the new and technological universities were

Table 1 The growth of students in higher and further education since 1962 (thousands)

	1962	1972	1982	1992
Higher education	324	602	832	1,444
Further education	446	914	1,505	2,574

established, and when the polytechnics were differentiating themselves from further education. Only in the 1980s was there a resumption of the impressive growth rates of the 1960s. But this acceleration took place against a troubled background as universities battled an unsympathetic government and polytechnics began to kick over the traces of local authority control. Not only has growth been recent, it has taken place in what many regard as unfavourable circumstances.

Second, perhaps because of its novelty, expansion has yet to produce the culture change normally associated with the shift to a mass system. Many of the detailed practices in British universities remain rooted in an élite past. The emphasis on the privileged (even private) character of student–teacher exchanges, a strong belief in pastoral intimacy, an enduring (even strengthening) commitment to a research culture are examples. It has already been pointed out, in the last chapter, that despite the quantitative indicators, which suggest that British higher education is now a mass system, in qualitative terms it still feels like an élite system. Many higher education teachers continue to see the system in terms of a core characterized by selective entry, specialized academic disciplines, low wastage and high standards, even if they acknowledge this core is now surrounded by a growing periphery where these traditional characteristics are less marked or absent altogether.

Third, growth has not been equally distributed across the system. Although growth rates in the universities and polytechnics had been similar during the 1970s, they diverged during the 1980s. Student numbers increased by 72 per cent in the latter and only by 22 per cent in the former. Expansion has been concentrated in only certain types of institution – the former polytechnics, especially those in larger cities; colleges of higher education anxious to acquire first polytechnic and later university status; and, more recently, the older civic universities. Oxford, Cambridge and the colleges of London University, which form the 'golden triangle' of British higher education, have grown only slowly. Rates of expansion in the new universities established in the 1960s, constrained by campus and location, have also been modest. As a result, only some institutions have embraced mass higher education. Others have remained élitist, in scale and arguably scope. In a more differentiated system the coexistence of élite and mass sectors, and differential growth rates, would have presented little difficulty. But the British system, even in the binary era, was remarkably homogeneous, the less noble institutions deferring to the more noble.

Fourth, universities and colleges have expanded, not so much by reaching out to new student constituencies, as by exploiting existing constituencies more fully. Some argue recent growth can be explained largely in terms of well-understood phenomena, such as the expansion of middle-class jobs, the onward and upward march of credentialism and the growing number of graduate parents, rather than in terms of a fundamental shift in social attitudes towards higher education across the whole community. It is not yet clear whether Britain is developing a generic 'college culture' on the American pattern.

Table 2 Increases in expenditure on higher education, 1962–92 (£ millions)

	1962	1972	1982	1992
Universities	129	414	1,879	
Polytechnics and colleges of higher education	90	323	924	
Total	219	737	2,803	5,200

The available evidence argues for caution. Demand has come from school leavers with standard entry qualifications, not mature students. Increased female participation has been particularly significant.[22] Higher education seems to have been shaped more decisively by a gender than a social revolution. (These issues will be explored in more detail in the next chapter.) Instead of already having made the transition to a mass system, British higher education may be about to run up against the limits which constrain growth in élite systems. The decisive breakthrough to mass participation has barely been achieved. So recent it may be reversible.

However, the influence of these four factors – recent, and as yet undigested, growth; the persistence of élite practices; differential growth rates between institutions; and doubts about whether a social breakthrough has been achieved – may only be temporary. Growth is being routinized, and even internalized, across the system. The mass periphery may soon unbalance the élite core. The hegemony of slow-growing élite universities may be eroded as the system becomes more heterogeneous. And institutions are coming to rely more and more on non-standard entrants to fill their places. The British system, once characterized by rigorous pre-entry selection, uniform standards and low drop-out, is already moving closer to the post-entry selection, variable-standard, higher-wastage model common in most other mass systems. Much will depend on the future pattern of expansion. According to government plans a three-year period of consolidation, or steady state, will be followed by three more years of slow growth. If this policy is maintained, regression is possible.[23]

After size, the most important determining characteristic of post-binary higher education is its cost structure. The total income of English universities and colleges of higher education in 1992–3 was almost £7 billion. Two-thirds, or £4.5 billion, was provided by the state (£2.4 billion from the HEFCE, £1.8 billion in fees paid by local education authorities and £334 million from the research councils).[24] Three decades ago, when the Robbins report, was published, public expenditure on higher education amounted to only £219 million, including Scotland and Wales.[25] (Trends in higher education funding are described in Table 2.) This 20-fold increase far outstrips inflation. It also outstrips the tenfold growth in student numbers. This headline comparison highlights two key facts.

First, British universities and colleges are now big business. The cost of mass higher education systems, unlike élite systems, is a substantial item in state budgets. Although the proportion of non-state income has risen from 10 per cent to almost a third, the state has provided the bulk of the resources required to create mass systems. Also public expenditure on higher education has risen much faster than public expenditure overall. Second, the constant pressure from government for 'efficiency gains' has been less successful than is commonly supposed. Politicians have had to fight a rear-guard battle against rising unit costs. Moreover, the widespread perception within institutions that budgets have been cut is inaccurate, at any rate over the long haul. Successive 'cuts' have generally been temporary blips on a sharply rising curve.

The common-sense expectation that mass higher education systems will be cheaper, that their economies will inevitably be lower-cost, is not borne out by the British experience. The opposite seems to have happened. Mass institutions, such as the former polytechnics, are funded more favourably today than élite universities were a generation ago. Of course, the increase in national wealth, and rising expectations produced by higher living stand-ards, and the so-called sophistication factor and the relative price effect in the public sector make such inter-generational comparisons problematical. Nevertheless, they suggest that the relationship between lower unit costs and massification is not straightforward.

One interpretation is that there is no particular relationship. Mass sys-tems are not inherently cheaper than élite systems, although their cost structures are different. Lower unit costs are balanced by higher drop-out and longer courses. A comparison of teaching costs per student has sug-gested that, if annual costs are multiplied by average course lengths and completion rates taken into account, the price of a British graduate is almost the same as that of a German graduate, and significantly cheaper than that of a Dutch graduate.[26] Indeed, institutional diversity and mission spread may even lead to higher costs. The American experience offers some support for this interpretation. There, tuition fees in both private and state institutions have risen much faster than inflation, provoking a cus-tomer and taxpayer revolt.

Another interpretation is that, although it may be true that the early stages of massification unit costs remain high (and even increase), as mass systems accelerate towards wider access costs tend to fall again. The British experience supports this second interpretation. Since the mid-1980s, when expansion got properly under way, unit costs have been driven down. Pub-lic expenditure on higher education has continued to grow, faster than inflation but not fast enough to keep pace with growing student numbers. As a result unit costs in universities, which remained steady in the first half of the 1980s, were cut by 5 per cent in the second half. In the former polytechnics and colleges of higher education, where the bulk of student growth was initially concentrated, unit costs were cut by almost 40 per cent during the 1980s. In the first half of the 1990s unit costs in both sets of institutions have continued to decline.[27]

It is not impossible that both interpretations are right. A third of the income of English universities and colleges, £2.5 billion, comes from non-state sources. A significant proportion of this money is likely to be used to support teaching. Also funds allocated by the HEFCE to support research, which may represent half the total grant to some institutions, cannot easily be segregated from funds for teaching. So calculations of unit costs based on dividing HEFCE teaching funds, plus fee payments by local authorities, by the number of students may not give an accurate picture of the resources available for teaching. However, if this is accepted, it calls into question the two key assumptions which underlie the debate about funding mass higher education – that unit costs will be remorselessly squeezed as 'efficiency gains' are demanded; and that, consequently, institutions have no choice but to seek more non-state funds.

Superficially the structure of British higher education has been unified since the abandonment of the binary system in 1992. All 31 polytechnics, five Scottish central institutions and two colleges of higher education have become universities, making a total of 93, and common higher education funding councils have been established. All higher education institutions, including the 50 remaining colleges, are funded, and planned, in the same way. However, there are four important qualifications. The first, which has already been discussed in the first part of this section, is that separate Scottish and Welsh sub-systems have been created. The second is that a distinction remains between the old universities, which are chartered bodies, and the new universities, which are Parliamentary institutions established by Secretaries of State. This distinction is reflected in contrasting patterns of governance and, less tangibly but more eloquently, in different institutional cultures, collegial or managerial.[28]

Third, responsibility for research funding is now shared between the three higher education funding councils and six research councils, and between their sponsoring departments, the Department of Education, Scottish Office Education Department (SOED) and Welsh Office on the one hand, and the newly created Office of Science and Technology (OST) on the other. This awkward split between baseline and programme budgets raises the possibility that, at some future date, responsibility for all research funding might be passed to the OST which would become, in effect, a ministry of higher education and science (as Robbins recommended). Even if this does not happen, the administrative unification achieved by the establishment of the Department of Education and Science in 1963 has been abandoned. Powerful centrifugal forces have been loosed.

Fourth, the wider post secondary system remains fragmented. In England the FEFC has been established to fund the 600 further education and sixth-form colleges. But in Scotland further education colleges are funded directly by the SOED, and in Wales they are responsible to a funding council which also covers higher education. Training and Enterprise Councils (TECs), in England and Wales, and Local Enterprise Councils (LECs), in Scotland, which are dominated by business interests, allocate funds for work-related further education. The TECs are responsible to the

Department of Employment and the LECs to the Scottish Office. The Department of Trade and Industry is also involved in in-company training. Altogether, five separate government departments, six research councils and four funding councils have a primary stake in further and higher education. Subsidiary stakes are held by one more department, the TECs, LECs and local education authorities. The impression of a unified structure is misleading. (The structure of higher and further education is illustrated in Figure 1.)

However, despite these important qualifications, the three funding councils are the key agencies within the new structure of higher education. The Scottish and Welsh councils were created *de novo*, although their core staff members came from the SOED and Welsh Office. Established in an era of emerging mass higher education, they have no élitist pasts to live down. In contrast, the HEFCE, the dominant funding council, is heir to two traditions – an élite tradition, inherited from the UGC and UFC, which places a high value on institutional autonomy and is instinctively uneasy about over-rapid growth; and a mass tradition, inherited from local education authorities, the NAB and PCFC, which values responsiveness and instinctively supports a policy of expansion. The HEFCE, like the other councils, has also inherited a regulatory tradition, derived from the role once played by Her Majesty's Inspectorate (HMI) in the non-university sector.

The difficulty of integrating these traditions, in particular the first two, has made it difficult for the HEFCE to develop coherent policies across a range of issues, or to establish a clear strategic orientation with regard to the development of mass higher education. Its methodologies for allocating teaching funds (based on PCFC practice) pull in one direction, broadly egalitarian, while research assessment (initiated by the UGC in the mid-1980s) pulls in another, towards greater selectivity. Of course, these different approaches could be integrated if the HEFCE were able to develop a strong strategic overview – for example, on institutional differentiation, code for encouraging the emergence of a super-league of research universities. However, the HEFCE is inhibited from thinking strategically for two reasons.

First, it lacks the room for policy manoeuvre enjoyed by the UGC, when the autonomy of the university sector was respected, and the NAB, because central and local governments interests could be played off against each other. The new funding councils are agents of government, not buffer bodies. Any advice they give to government is confidential. As a result the lobbying rights powerfully exercised by both UGC and NAB have been lost. More significantly, the influence of the funding councils over key policy decisions is limited. Good examples are consolidation, the (temporary?) shift to steady state, and frequent tuition fee changes, upwards to encourage market responsiveness and downwards to dampen expansionary pressures. The job of the HEFCE, and other councils, is to implement the government's predetermined objectives through second-order policies. The proliferation of so-called 'next steps' agencies in government, designed to separate

Figure 1 Post-secondary education in Britain

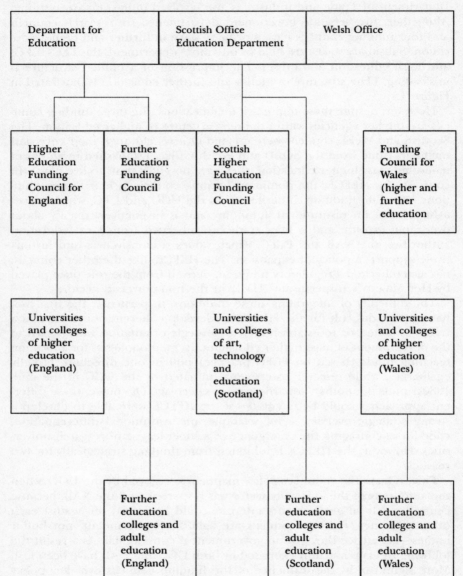

the implementation and management of policies from policy-making, has influenced the environment in which the funding councils, although not themselves 'next steps' agencies, operate.

Second, the funding councils are not designed to be planning bodies. Strategic development is supposedly the responsibility of institutions. The role of the HEFCE and the others is to fund institutions against their own strategic plans rather than to impose any system-wide pattern of development. Special initiatives to steer the system are frowned upon. Rationalization exercises are no longer undertaken. Also the funding councils lack the elaborate infrastructure of sub-committees through which the UGC in particular generated its intelligence about institutions (or, rather, about departments and subjects which, for the UGC, were the basic building-blocks of the system rather than institutions). Instead the focus is on control and information systems and audit, both academic and financial. This shift is reflected in the membership of the councils – lay chairmen supervising academic chief executives, substantial business representation and internal members drawn from senior management teams, not the professoriat.

This emphasis on funding rather than planning should have led to an increase in institutional autonomy, its ostensible political purpose. But this has turned out to be only partly true, for four main reasons. First, autonomy is more likely to be interpreted in terms of institutional leaders' right to manage than in the traditional context of the academic freedom enjoyed by teachers and researchers. This change is discussed in greater detail in the next section of this chapter. The second reason is the tension between the three administrative cultures referred to earlier – of élite planning derived from the UGC, mass markets inherited from the NAB/PCFC and external regulation taken from HMI (and, less obviously, the former Council for National Academic Awards (CNAA)).

The tension between research assessment, deliberately selective, and methodologies for allocating teaching funds on an equitable (equal?) basis has already been mentioned. Research assessment is a continuation, with minimal modification, of the policies developed by the UGC from 1985 onwards which, it can be argued, were designed to formalize, and so legitimize, the discriminatory funding patterns which the UGC had always applied. Its classic practice of 'informed prejudice', reviled as amateur and unaccountable, is alive and well, relabelled as research assessment. Although the process is ostensibly more open, the focus on subjects, rather than institutions, remains. The Matthew principle, to him that hath shall be given, continues to determine allocations. In contrast, the characteristics of the funding councils' funding methodologies can be traced back to the NAB policy of guaranteeing institutions core funding while requiring them to bid for a flexible margin, a policy which was reluctantly adopted by the UGC in its final days. The focus is on institutions, with mode not subject of study being the more significant variable, and on equitable outcomes.

A less blatant, but still suggestive, tension exists between the research assessment and the assessment of the quality of teaching, by which the research reputations of university and college departments are graded and teaching standards assessed. Superficially both rely on external scrutiny, although in the benign form of peer review. Yet they are entirely dissimilar processes. The former, derived from the UGC regime, is a planning intervention with the power radically to reshape the system – although policy-makers have no clear ideas about the desirable outcomes of such reshaping, which adds to the confusion. Its efficacy as a planning instrument has been increased by recent changes, increasing the number of grades from five to six and widening the funding differentials.[29] Quality assessment, in contrast, is a regulatory function, derived from the practice of HMI and the CNAA. Its purpose is not to reorder the system, but to guarantee threshold standards and identify excellence. Revealingly, no attempt has been made to link quality assessment to funding. Recent changes introduced by the HEFCE have reduced its already limited applicability to planning.[30]

The third reason why the switch from funding to planning has not increased institutional freedom, in a strategic rather than operational sense, is that control systems have not been relaxed; they have simply been repositioned. Institutional development plans must still be approved by the funding councils. But the emphasis has shifted from planning inputs to auditing outcomes. This shift is a general phenomenon not confined to higher education, and is discussed in more detail in the next chapter. However, the fourth and most significant reason is that it is government, not the institutions, which has filled the strategy 'gap' created by the funding councils' retreat from planning. This was an inevitable outcome. The state is unlikely ever to abandon its steering role in higher education, for reasons which were rehearsed in a historical context in the first part of this section and will be discussed in more theoretical terms in the concluding part.

The effect has been to replace the kind of strategic overview generated by the UGC that, at its best, was sophisticated, long-haul and reflected the inner values of higher education, with a strategic overview generated within government which is likely to be crude, short-term and more heavily influenced by external considerations, leaving the funding councils responsible for attenuated 'business plans'. This shift can be observed in the context of 'consolidation'. After five years in which universities and colleges were encouraged to recruit large numbers of above-quota students, to meet ambitious growth targets while cutting unit costs, student numbers are again to be planned with penalties for over- or under-recruitment. The HEFCE and the other councils have had to resume a planning role, but on less advantageous terms. They have to plan, first, according to the government's and not their own agendas, and second, without the intelligence needed to plan properly.

As a result the strategic horizons of British higher education have shrunk. The sense of system, and structure, has become weaker. Arguably this is characteristic of the shift from an élite to a mass system. Planned hierarchies are undermined as institutional roles become more volatile. However, many mass systems, as will be demonstrated in the final part of this section, do not share these characteristics. A more explicit stratification of institutions has emerged, partly prompted by the market but also planned by the state. In the case of Britain this loss of strategic vision does not appear to be a consequence of the move towards a mass system. Instead it is a complicating, and possibly retarding, factor.

The absence of strategic direction is not new in British higher education. From the start the binary system only approximately demarcated the missions of universities and polytechnics. Despite attempts to construct an alternative 'polytechnic' philosophy of higher education, the real binary demarcation was administrative rather than educational.[31] The allocation of institutions to one or other sector was largely a matter of historical accident. The key distinction between universities and polytechnics was summed up in the phrase used to describe the latter, the 'public sector', which located binary differences in Trow's 'public' rather than 'private' worlds of higher education. Only in the loosest sense could the polytechnics and colleges ever be regarded as even approximating to the mass component of British higher education and the universities to the élite component.

No attempt was made to limit mass institutions to undergraduate and taught postgraduate courses and only to allow élite universities to provide doctoral and post-doctoral programmes and to engage in substantial research. The polytechnics were always able to offer PhD programmes and many had vigorous research cultures. Nor were they restricted to providing narrowly defined professional and vocational education, although efforts were made in Scotland to distinguish more clearly between the roles of universities and central institutions. Most subjects were offered on both sides on the binary line. Indeed, in the 1970s and 1980s growth in the polytechnic and colleges was most rapid in business, management, applied social studies and humanities rather than in science, engineering and technology, the bedrock subjects of advanced further education in the 1960s. The binary system was always fuzzy.

The abandonment of the binary system, explicable in terms of long-term convergence between two inadequately demarcated sectors, has produced greater fuzziness. As an act of policy it is difficult to interpret. Was it a vote of confidence in the polytechnics (and a vote of no confidence in the universities), or final confirmation that, despite the polytechnics' efforts over two decades to establish an alternative brand image, the university has remained the only valid institutional currency in higher education? And its consequences, intended and unintended, are equally difficult to predict. Will the new unified structure open up new democratic possibilities, or undermine yesterday's élite system by levelling down academic standards and destroying what remains of the old donnish culture? Will the former polytechnics receive increased resources and more equitable funding, or will the new post-binary framework facilitate divergence, leading eventually to a stratification between research universities and institutions devoted mainly to teaching?

Convergence or divergence? Institutional differentiation is the key. But it can take two contrasting forms. Either institutions will develop market niches, within broadly uniform missions: here the danger is continuing academic drift. Or a more organized division of institutional missions will be prescribed: but suitable policy instruments seem to be lacking. As has already been argued, a strategic forward look is unlikely to come from the funding councils, although it is perhaps only through root-and-branch institutional differentiation that the contradictions between top-down planning and bottom-up enterprise, between selectivity and equity, in their detailed policies can be resolved. Government is also unlikely to develop, and sustain, system-wide strategies. Administrative time horizons are too short, while political ideology favours market solutions. Informal (and ineffective?) clubs of the 'top' universities are preferred to planned stratification as proposed by the former Advisory Board for the Research Councils.[32]

It is possible that, even (or especially?) within the new unified structure, the growth of mass higher education will be seriously inhibited by the absence of a strategic forward look. Élite universities may suffer because of the failure to concentrate, and target, resources, while the cost, and value structures, of other institutions may delay the development of a truly open system. If that happens, two outcomes are possible. Either, which seems more likely in the short run, the necessary strategic integration will take place within the narrower framework of research policy, the instruments of integration being the OST and its advisory apparatus, and the research councils. In a significant sense that would represent a regression to older élitist forms.

Or, a more likely long-term outcome, that integration will be achieved within the wider arena of post-secondary education. The diversity of actors – government departments, research and funding councils, TECs/LECs and other agencies – is likely to increase the pressure for integration in any case. And beyond mass higher education and an integrated post-secondary education lies the learning society, an even more radical enlargement to embrace education and training in non-educational settings – in the so-called 'corporate classroom' in industry and business, within the community and in voluntary organizations, through the mass media, along the information technology super-highways, in the context of Total Quality Management or Investors in People.

It may appear that such disparate activities can never be integrated within a common structure, or even a loosely defined system. But systems, and structures, exist first as reconceptualizations. Only later, if ever, are they operationalized. The language of the learning society, therefore, is significant because it suggests a growing affinity between hitherto incommensurable worlds, just as today further and higher education are increasingly seen as closely aligned and a generation ago higher education ceased to be largely synonymous with the universities.

Making sense of systems

The sub-text of both the previous parts of this section, the development of a national system and the emergence of a post-binary framework, is that

British higher education is becoming less exceptional. In scale, if not yet in 'feel', scope and organization, the differences between the British systems and analogous systems in the rest of Europe and North America seem to be less marked than they were a generation ago. One interpretation emphasizes catching up; the development of the once immature British system has made it more like the others. Another stresses all-round convergence; all higher education systems are becoming more alike. In other words bilateral, or multi-lateral, movement by all systems, not unilateral movement by British univer-sities and colleges. The transition from élite to mass higher education is a global phenomenon comprising not only the inner dynamics of higher education systems (which in their British manifestation are the subject of this chapter) but also deeply rooted secular trends in the character of the state, society, the economy, science and culture (which is discussed in the next chapter).

To choose between these interpretations – underdevelopment or massi-fication? – the British experience needs to be considered in the wider con-text of the development of higher education systems in the rest of Europe and other advanced countries. The theme of the final part of this first section is the contrast between divided, or binary, and unified, or inte-grated, systems. Embedded in that contrast are the grand strategic choices which most countries, not just Britain, have had to make as mass systems have developed. To the extent that there has been a general drift from divided to unified systems, which, if true, tends to confirm the thesis of massification, Britain has been a leader rather than a laggard, which tends to undermine the thesis of underdevelopment. If, on the other hand, no general drift can be identified, massification becomes a less useful analytical category and Britain's exceptionalism, once immature and now in the post-binary era precocious, remains.

In the 1960s and 1970s most developed countries reshaped their higher education systems. The extended systems created during this period re-placed the much more narrowly based university systems typical of the pre-war era. They were developed in response to, first, the rapidly rising social demand for university-level education, and second, the increasing demand for a more highly skilled labour force. This reshaping took various forms. But it was a general phenomenon across Europe (and the rest of the devel-oped world).[33] The fundamental imperatives were the same everywhere and arose from the modernization of society and the economy.

To reshape higher education to meet these new demands one or both of two strategies were pursued. First, existing universities were expanded and new ones created. The 1960s and the 1970s will be remembered as one of the great ages of university building. Second, greater emphasis was also placed on less traditional forms of higher education. Even after the expan-sion of the universities, there would still be a demand for alternative models of higher education. The British experience of the new universities estab-lished on green-field sites during the 1960s and the evolution of the former polytechnics are discussed in the second section of this chapter, as textbook examples of these two strategies.

However, it is misleading to draw too sharp a distinction between these two strategies. Rarely was a principled strategic choice made between them. More often they were pursued in opportunistic combination. In France the reorganization of the universities in the aftermath of the events of 1968 represented an overdue modernization of structures which had changed little since the nineteenth century. Five years earlier, following the Robbins report, access to Europe's most selective university system had been widened; new universities were established and polytechnics created.[34] In Germany a twin-track policy was pursued. The universities were expanded and made more comprehensive, but the role of the *Fachhochschulen* was enhanced. In Sweden a decade later a unified system of universities and colleges was established. Outside Europe similar reforms were undertaken; the earliest and most notable being California's Master Plan for higher education which created a three-tier system.[35] In Australia new universities were founded and colleges of advanced education formed.[36]

Nor has there been a consistent approach to the development of new, arguably alternative, forms of higher education. In some countries 'non-university' institutions were subsumed within the expanded and reformed universities. For example, in France the *instituts universitaires de technologie*, designed to offer more vocationally oriented courses, were linked to the traditional university faculties. In Sweden a more radical variant of this policy was pursued. After 1977 previously separate, and subordinate, institutions such as nursing and teacher training colleges were incorporated into the universities.[37] In other countries an explicitly binary policy was developed. Britain and Australia were good examples. In still other countries policies were adopted which incorporated features of both these approaches, the unified and the binary. The superior position of the universities was confirmed, indeed enhanced by the expansion of student numbers, but efforts were also made to upgrade technical high schools and similar institutions. This, broadly, was the approach in Germany and the Netherlands.[38]

Even within formally unified systems binary characteristics persisted. In Sweden, for example, the fault-lines within the expanded universities between the traditional faculties and recently merged colleges persisted, as did the distinction between universities and smaller university colleges. Equally, no binary system was entirely consistent. In Britain, as has already been explained, the former colleges of advanced technology, established in the mid-1950s outside the university sector, became technological universities in 1965 just when another tranche of alternative institutions, the polytechnics, was being established. Also key institutions, such as the Open University, in effect lay outside the binary structure.

In Germany and the Netherlands informal binary systems emerged initially, not as a result of deliberate policies to establish alternative institutions to rival the universities, but as the result of a gradual development of identifiably post-secondary education institutions, first within the narrow framework of technical education and subsequently on the larger canvas of professional education. The key change was not the reordering of institutions within higher education, still largely regarded as synonymous with universities, but the rearrangement of upper secondary education. In Europe there was nothing to compare with the California Master Plan, which aimed to create a coherent higher education system out of the uncoordinated fragments of university, professional and technical high-school education.

Only later was this radical challenge addressed outside the United States. The Swedish reform of 1977 came at the end of one phase and the beginning of another. In the first phase higher education reforms were generally the product of *ad hoc* modifications of the inherited pattern of institutions. Even the most radical example, an apparent exception to this rule, the establishment of the polytechnics in England, had a much stronger political than educational rationale. In the second phase, starting with the Swedish reform, the radical consequences of constructing wider post-secondary education systems began to be more systematically confronted. The effect seems to have been to produce a shift from binary to more integrated systems.

In the Netherlands it was recognized that the HBO sector (higher professional schools) could no longer sensibly be regarded as an extension of upper secondary education. So the relationship between the HBO and university sectors had to be properly articulated. Although a dual system has been maintained (for the present), the two sectors are now embraced within a common legal framework. Because of close links between the English and Dutch higher education systems, the promotion of the polytechnics strengthened the resolve of the HBO sector to secure similar recognition. In Germany the relationship between universities and *Fachhochschulen* appears, for the moment, to be more stable.[39] In Britain and Australia this second phase has led to binary systems being replaced by integrated structures.

Within this organizational complexity four broad types of higher education system can be identified. The first is a dual system, in which universities and other post-secondary education institutions are regarded as entirely separate and treated differently, the latter typically less favourably than the former (although the non-university *grandes écoles* in France are an important exception). The second model is a binary system where alternative institutions are deliberately established to complement (and rival?) the universities. It is the degree of deliberation which distinguishes binary from dual systems. Binary systems are designed as dynamic systems; dual systems represent the continuation of existing institutional patterns. The third model is a unified system in which all institutions belong to a common system and are not formally differentiated. The best example is Sweden. Since 1992 England has also had a unified system of higher education. The fourth model is a stratified system where higher education is conceived of as a total system and institutions are allocated specific roles within it. The classic case remains California's Master Plan.

However, as with the modernization strategies, too sharp a distinction should not be drawn between these four models. In practice the distinction between the first and second models, dual and binary systems, is often blurred. There is a tendency for stable dual systems within which different types of institution have inherited distinct and generally complementary roles to develop into more volatile binary systems which encourage competition and permit rivalry. This is certainly true of the Dutch and, to a lesser extent, the German systems. But it has not happened in France where non-university sector institutions enjoy equal, or superior, prestige. The highly selective *grandes écoles* designed to train the future leadership class have no reason to envy universities obliged to admit all *baccalauréat* holders. The ability of even the less grand professional schools, particularly in business and management, and of the IUTs to select their students also places them in a stronger position than the traditional university faculties.

Neither the Swedish (since 1977), Australian (since 1988) nor British (since 1992) systems is truly unified. In Sweden the 13 universities remain a distinct group of privileged institutions. They receive the bulk of the available research income.[40] In Australia and Britain similar differences can be observed. There are no examples in Europe of stratified systems on the Californian pattern, although elements of stratification can be observed. The differences between full universities and university colleges in Sweden have already been mentioned. Often universities retain a monopoly of doctoral programmes; sometimes this extends to all higher degrees. But this is not necessarily evidence of deliberate California-style stratification. An important distinction must also be drawn between anachronistic monopolies typical of dual systems which are generally eroded in the transition to binary and/or unified systems, and the division of institutional labour and differentiation of missions typical of stratified systems.

This typology is perhaps too simple to capture the complexity of existing higher education systems. The relationship, if any, between the four types is also unclear. Are they independent models, genuine alternatives, or do they describe a dynamic sequence? In other words, are dual or unified systems stable, or do they have a tendency to develop into, respectively, binary and stratified systems? The Dutch experience tends to support the latter interpretation. Not only have the HBOs been heavily influenced by the success of the English polytechnics, but also the inner dynamics of higher education in the Netherlands seem to be encouraging the development of a more coherent, and therefore more self-confident, non-university sector – for example, the aggregation of smaller and more specialist HBOs into larger and more comprehensive 'polytechnics' (the English category has been widely adopted).

An analytical framework within which to the general development of higher education systems can be described is suggested in Figure 2. Using that framework, Figure 3 tries to indicate the shifts which have taken place in the main higher education systems. However, this framework cannot capture all the subtleties of policy change. First, it does not give insufficient weight to the circularities, or regressions, which characterize recent developments in some European higher education systems, notably in Germany.

Figure 2 The evolution of higher education systems

University-dominated systems:
in which any other institutions are seen as part of the secondary or, at the most, technical education sectors, and in which the universities and these embryonic post-secondary institutions are regarded as separate sectors.

Dual-systems:
in which these other institutions are now acknowledged to be properly post-secondary and the need for coordination with the university sector is recognized, although the latter are still seen as structurally superior.

'Binary' systems:
in which two parallel higher education systems, one consisting of the traditional universities and the other based on 'alternative' institutions, develop (There is a tendency for the relationship between these two systems to drift away from complementarity and towards competition).

Unified systems:
in which a comprehensive higher education system is created embracing both the traditional universities and other institutions, although important differences of status and reputation remain (particularly in respect of research).

Stratified systems:
in which a common system is maintained by the missions of individual institutions, externally and internally, become differentiated (This differentiation may come about as a result of political action or through the operation of the market).

Second, the tendency for binary systems to reproduce themselves at lower levels when unified systems of higher education are being established is not covered. A good example is Britain, where the distinction between universities and polytechnics has been replaced by a new demarcation between higher education institutions and further education colleges. However, in time – and in turn – this new demarcation is likely to be eroded as unified post-secondary education systems develop.

Figure 3 The development of selected national higher education systems

	Dual	Binary	Unified	Stratified
Sweden			1977	
	>>>>>>>>>>>>>>>>>>>>>>>>>>>>>>>>>			
Holland	1992			
	>>>>>>>>			
Germany	>>>>>			
Britain		1965	1992	
	>>>>>>>>>>>>>>>>>>>>>>>>>>>>>>>>>			
France	1969			1969
	>>>>>>?			?<<<<<<<
Australia			1988	
	>>>>>>>>>>>>>>>>			
California			1960	
	>>>			

The detailed differences between national systems, and also the general convergence among them, reflect the changing balance between their exceptional and common characteristics. The former arise from the contingencies of national systems. Their structure grows out of national cultures – administrative as well as educational. The British binary system of 1965–92, therefore, should not be compared too closely to the Dutch dual system. Common characteristics arise from the overarching trends which affect all higher education institutions and systems. These trends are political – the drive for wider access and, correspondingly, increased accountability; socio-economic – the role played by higher education in shaping identities in a modern society which have transcended older demarcations of class, gender or ethnicity, as well as its role in producing a highly skilled and adaptable labour force; and cultural and scientific – intellectual fashions sweep the world, while new configurations of science and technology are truly global phenomena.

Among the exceptional, or particular, characteristics which have shaped higher education systems, four are especially significant. One is the pattern of school education, in particular the persistence, or otherwise, of divided secondary school systems.[41] Those countries with divided secondary school systems are more likely to have dual, or binary, higher education systems. For example, in the Netherlands the HBOs, on the whole, recruit their students from the five-year vocational secondary school system, while the universities take most of their students from the six-year academic stream. On the other hand those countries which have abandoned, or modified, the traditional demarcation between grammar schools / *lycées* / gymnasia and other, less noble, types of secondary education are more likely to have unified – or, at any rate, binary – higher education systems.

However, the links between comprehensive secondary education systems and unified higher education systems are unclear. The United States and Sweden have both. But the comprehensive reorganization of secondary education and the establishment of the binary system in higher education in Britain took place at the same time, during the 1960s. Superficially, therefore, they were complementary, not contradictory, policies, although it can be argued that the former was bound to lead to the abandonment of the latter. On the other hand, there are no examples of divided secondary schools and unified higher education systems coexisting.

A second exceptional characteristic is the differences between higher education systems in 'Atlantic' and 'Mediterranean' Europe. These two generic types have been diffused world-wide: Australia has an Atlantic system and Brazil a Mediterranean system. Broadly, in Atlantic Europe there are more examples of dual, or binary, systems, while in Mediterranean Europe the university has remained dominant. Italy, Portugal, Greece and, less categorically, Spain all have higher education systems in which alternative institutions are only weakly developed. There are, however, important exceptions. Sweden, and now Finland, have unified systems (although they are post-binary rather than pre-binary). There are also countries which are both Atlantic and Mediterranean: France is the best example; its mixed orientation is reflected in the exceptional structure of its higher education system. Another perhaps is Austria which, unlike Germany, has only recently begun to develop a *Fachhochschulen* sector.

An explanation of this Atlantic–Mediterranean contrast is different paces of industrialization. On the whole the industrial revolution came earlier to, and was more intense in, Atlantic Europe. The growth of an industrial economy was the most powerful factor in both reshaping the university sector and stimulating the development of non-university higher education. In Mediterranean Europe there was until recently less pressure to reform the universities. There was also less need to develop elaborate systems of technical education out of which alternative higher education institutions could grow. These differences in industrial structure, although still visible, have been sharply reduced during the past 25 years. To the extent that the development of higher education systems is influenced by these industrial structures, the broad division between Atlantic Europe, with its binary systems, and Mediterranean Europe, with its university-dominated systems, is likely to be eroded.

There is some evidence to support this, notably in Spain where short-cycle academic programmes have been developed in the universities. This points to an important generic distinction between Atlantic and Mediterranean higher education systems. In the latter a binary distinction is more likely to be created by establishing short-cycle programmes within universities, while in the former formal binary systems based on institutional differentiation are more common. But it may also reflect a more general phenomenon associated with massification, the growing fuzziness of binary and unified structures.

A third exceptional factor is the influence of research organization on the structure of higher education systems. In much of central and eastern Europe, and in the former Soviet Union, research was the responsibility of academies of sciences, and their associated institutes and units. The stake of universities, at any rate in cutting-edge scientific research and in techno-logical development, remains limited; since the fall of communism there have been moves in Poland and the Czech Republic to (re)integrate acad-emy institutes into universities, although these moves have been resisted.[42] In central and eastern Europe a strongly instrumental tradition, based in monotechnic institutions, which pre-dated but was reinforced during the communist era, also undermined the influence of the universities.

But this separation between research and higher education is not con-fined to the former Soviet bloc. In France the main agency for research is the *Centre Nationale des Recherches Scientifiques* (CNRS), and its linked laboratories (many of which, however, are sited on university campuses). Also CNRS and university researchers actively collaborate.[43] In Germany high-level research is undertaken in the Max Planck institutes outside formal university structures. Even in Britain, where higher education and research have always been intimately associated, there has been a proliferation of semi-detached research institutes which do not receive core funding from their universities and of research and graduate schools.[44]

The organization of research exercises an important influence over the structure of higher education systems. If most research is undertaken out-side the university, or in loosely linked research institutes, there is less incentive to establish binary systems. However, if it is undertaken within higher education, the case for a unified system (or, at any rate, a system in which it is difficult to discriminate between institutions) is much weaker. But, as the British experience suggests, it may be more difficult to limit the ambitions of non-university institutions with regard to research within a rivalrous binary system than in a formally unified, but informally stratified, system.

The fourth arena of exceptionalism arises from the contrast between the three distinct strands, or models, within the European university tradition described in the previous chapter – the knowledge, professional and per-sonality models characterized respectively by Germany, France and Eng-land. These models have been exported to the rest of the world, although in the United States the first two, and arguably all three, have been sub-sumed within the multiversity. The influence of these models on the struc-ture of higher education systems is significant. In countries where universities have become associated with the transmission of either a scientific or liberal culture the incentive to develop a dual system has been strong. Motives have been mixed – to protect the university from non-cognitive, or philistine, values or to bypass them by creating more socially and economically relevant alternatives – but the effect has been the same. In other countries, where universities have retained a more pronounced professional orientation, the pressure to establish a powerful non-university sector has been much less.

Although these exceptional, or particular, features of higher education systems remain significant, the balance is tilting towards their common characteristics. The socio-economic environments in which higher education systems find themselves are becoming increasingly alike. The shift towards a knowledge-based and services-oriented economy, the rethinking of the welfare state in a post-scarcity age, the globalization of culture, the acceleration of science and technology, the radical extension of the higher education 'franchise' – these are phenomena which affect every European country. As a result the differences between particular university traditions have been reduced.

As has already been indicated in the previous two parts of this section, British higher education, once sharply distinguished from other European systems in terms of access (more limited) and autonomy (more extensive), apparently offers a good example of convergence. In the past decade Britain has achieved participation levels broadly similar to those of other developed countries and British universities have largely lost their privileged status. Wider convergences can also be observed. In western Europe, for example, the European Union, although only obliquely involved in higher education, has the potential to become a powerful centralizing and homogenizing force. As common labour-market, industrial, financial and social policies develop, the challenges which EU higher education systems face will become increasingly similar.[45] Other regional groupings, and the globalization of higher education more generally, have similar effects.

However, this convergence of socio-economic environments will not necessarily produce more homogeneous higher education systems. Distinctive structural arrangements may be compatible with common missions. The result may be not so much convergence as fuzziness. Also it has been argued that there is likely to be less emphasis on grand structural reform at times of slower growth, partly because there may be less need to diversify into new kinds of higher education, and so to differentiate institutional missions, and partly because root-and-branch reform of the structure of higher education demands increased resources which are not available.[46] The former seems unlikely – the slow-down in growth during the 1980s was a temporary phenomenon which has already been overtaken by wider conceptions of post-secondary education and the learning society. The latter, retreat from grand reforms, seems more plausible.

There is certainly little evidence of a reduction in the complexity of the demands made of higher education systems, despite the slow-down in the growth of student numbers and restrictions on university budgets. And increasing complexity is the key to institutional and sectoral differentiation.[47] Also, the retreat from grand structural reforms is compatible with the analytical framework described earlier. The shift from tightly structured binary systems to more open, or fuzzy, systems, formally unified but actually stratified, is part of that framework. Finally, the erosion of binary systems does not mean that the process of differentiation in European higher education systems has slowed; rather it has become too rapid and volatile to be expressed through sectorization. Instead differentiation has begun to operate at the institutional, or sub-institutional, level.

Dual systems developed and binary systems were established in many countries to handle the heterogeneity which accompanied the rapid expansion of higher education in the 1960s; but, as the inflexibility of these divided systems has become apparent and the prospect of mass higher education has appeared less forbidding, a drift to more adaptable forms of differentiation may be under way. In the 1960s and 1970s there were many reasons why governments preferred to articulate dual systems and/or create binary structures to cope with the strains of rapid growth. First, the traditional ethos of the universities was respected. With the move to much higher levels of participation there was a fear that universities would be contaminated by less 'scientific' values. Second, it was believed that undifferentiated systems inevitably produced 'academic drift' which undermined attempts to produce more vocational forms of higher education. There was a need therefore to create alternative institutional models protected from the universities by *cordons sanitaires*.

Third, most institutions, universities and others, were small and homogeneous. Their managerial structures were underdeveloped. Large institutions with multiple missions were regarded as both undesirable and unworkable. The problem of complexity had to be addressed by establishing new (kinds of) institutions. Fourth, the 1960s and 1970s were an age of enthusiasm for social and economic planning. This enthusiasm encouraged large-scale systems building rather than reliance on the initiative of individual institutions. Fifth, divided systems were the norm. In nearly every country other higher (or advanced-level) institutions – colleges of technology, art and business, teachers' colleges – already existed alongside the universities. Dual, or binary, systems were simply rationalizations of the status quo.

These reasons are less persuasive today. First, binary systems are difficult to reconcile with either democratic or 'market' values. This is especially true when, as is usually the case, there is a clear association between top-tier institutions, universities, and student recruitment from privileged socio-economic groups. These policies are also seen as incompatible with 'market' values, because they inhibit institutional initiative and discourage entrepreneurial behaviour. Second, divided systems appear to have encouraged 'academic drift' rather than prevented it. Normally the university has remained the ideal model to which less 'noble' institutions continue to aspire. But, at the same time, the university may have become a less dynamic, even a closed, institution because new challenges have been met by non-university institutions.

Third, significant changes have taken place in the relationship between universities and the state.[48] These changes have not been consistent across Europe. In some countries, notably Britain, the autonomy of the (traditional) universities has been sharply eroded; in others, such as Sweden, universities have been granted increased administrative autonomy. Yet there is perhaps a common theme, the desire to recast higher education as an open rather than closed system. The links between the transition from élite to mass higher education and the development of the welfare state are considered in more detail in the next chapter.

Fourth, overload is no longer seen as a problem. Universities have become large and complex organizations well able to handle multiple missions. The collegial university governed by the academic guild assisted by low-profile administrators has been succeeded by the managerial university dominated by an expert cadre of senior managers. Finally, large-scale system-wide planning has gone out of fashion. The taste now is for 'market' solutions, even within state systems of higher education. This 'market' approach is difficult to reconcile with structured binary systems which assign missions to classes of institution. Instead it encourages much finer-grain and more flexible differentiation between and within institutions regardless of their formal nomenclature.

In higher education systems, as in many other kinds of system, the growth of complexity has produced two very different responses. The first is the imposition of more elaborate control mechanisms – in areas such as budgetary accountability, research selectivity and quality assessment. The second is an increase in volatility as institutions, and individuals, adapt to new environments; evidence of this is provided by the growing fuzziness of higher education systems. If, as seems probable, this dialectic between control and volatility can be more easily reconciled, or expressed, within formally unified but highly differentiated systems than in binary systems, most higher education systems are likely to evolve in that direction.

Institutions

The binary shape of British higher education, until 1992, suggested a simple, and misleading, dichotomy of institutions. The fault-line between universities (now 'old' universities) on the one hand and polytechnics ('new' universities) on the other was emphasized at the expense of other fault-lines, within the binary sectors and cross-cutting binary demarcations. Within their respective classes universities and polytechnics were imagined to be essentially homogeneous. Their actual diversity was disguised. The pattern of institutions was made to appear much simpler than in fact it was. The abandonment of the binary system, whether or not it encourages future convergence, highlights the pluralism which already exists in British higher education.

At least 12 sub-sectors of the university system can be identified, more if higher education and more still if post-secondary education as a whole is considered. First come Oxford and Cambridge, recognized as exceptional but far from being marginal. They no longer dominate the university system numerically. At the time of the Robbins report they made up 15 per cent of the 'old' university sector. Now their share has halved, to 7 per cent. But Oxford and Cambridge are still among the top ten universities in size. Together they have 27,000 students. Furthermore, their academic hegemony has not been seriously eroded. They are both colonizers, because their graduates dominate the upper reaches of the academic profession, and leaders, because their contribution to research and scholarship is unparalleled.

However, in terms of governance and organization Oxford and Cambridge have remained exceptional. No other university is governed solely by the academic guild. None has followed the collegiate pattern. It is in the United States, not Britain, that the ideal of the 'college' has thrived. A few British universities have residential colleges, but only Oxford and Cambridge have made the college and its fellows, rather than the department and its professors, the primary academic unit. The reasons for not following the Oxbridge model are straightforward. Colleges are expensive; Oxford and Cambridge receive additional funding because the state pays college as well as university fees. Colleges are also ill suited to an academic environment characterized by disciplinary specialization, and as research institutions. Significantly, in Cambridge, with its stronger science base, colleges are weaker than in Oxford. In both universities there are tensions between colleges, which want to employ wide-ranging teachers, and departments, which favour more focused (and, therefore, more productive) researchers.

The second sub-sector is formed by the University of London. Despite devolution of academic controls and funding decisions to its larger multi-faculty schools, London is Britain's largest, and only federal, university (leaving aside the Open University, discussed below). Again, federal universities have flourished in the United States but not in Britain. The university has 50,000 students, or 15 per cent of the 'old' university total. Like Oxford and Cambridge, London receives more than its nominal share of resources, largely because of a heavy concentration of (high-cost) medical education in the capital. Like them, London is also exceptional in its organization, comprising large schools like Imperial College, University College and the London School of Economics, and small specialized institutes. Unlike Oxbridge, London is the archetype of the English university, because it was here that the pattern of departments and chairs was first established. Together these three universities form the 'golden triangle' of British higher education.

The Victorian civic universities – Manchester, Leeds, Liverpool, Sheffield, Bristol and the rest – form the third sub-sector. They make up a quarter of the 'old' university total, and have a fair claim to be regarded as the university heartland. They were founded a century or more ago by provincial lawyers or doctors, utilitarian industrialists and Unitarian politicians. Today the civics are the most comprehensive of Britain's universities, ranging across all the arts and sciences and embracing education, medicine, law, engineering and other professional fields. Their historical commitment to extramural studies is now reflected in a growing number of 'access' partnerships with local colleges and school compacts. Research is also strong in the civics. Between the expansion of the 1960s and 1970s and the cuts of the 1980s they seemed to lose ground to the 'golden triangle'. But the most recent research assessment exercises suggest they are closing the gap again.

The fourth sub-sector comprises the so-called redbrick universities. D. H. Lawrence was their memorialist, in the case of Nottingham, and Kingsley Amis, more controversially and half a century later, in the case of Swansea (although, as a college of the University of Wales, the latter is not, strictly speaking, redbrick). The redbrick universities are, or were, smaller-scale civics, more homely in scale. Their early role was to train grammar school teachers, rather than lawyers and doctors. As university colleges they were also academically dependent on the University of London. Today they are indistinguishable from the older civics in all but three respects. First, on average they are smaller. Second, their subject range is not so wide (several lack medical schools). Third, they are concentrated in the Midlands and the South of England, a shift which reflects the comparative decline of the nineteenth-century heavy-industry heartland in the North and the rise of consumer-goods manufacturing between the wars further south. The redbrick universities make up 12 per cent of the system.

The fifth sub-sector comprises two universities that are *sui generis* and were founded more than a century apart, Durham and Keele. Durham, after a false start in the seventeenth century during the Commonwealth, was established at the same time as the early London colleges, although for a long time the infant university remained in the long shadow thrown by the cathedral. Today Durham has bits of civic, bits of redbrick, even bits of new university in its make-up. Its local hinterland has been restricted by the break with Newcastle in 1963 and the promotion of the polytechnics in Sunderland and Teesside thirty years later. But it is essentially a national institution. Its location among the closed pits and abandoned shipyards of the North-East is incidental. Keele is also one of a kind, bravely designed in the 1940s to provide a broad undergraduate education, adapted from Oxford but with an extra-mural twist to reflect its Potteries location. Sadly, such liberal-paternalistic ambitions are out of fashion. Keele lacks heavyweight professional subjects to act as ballast. Until recently, its research structure was also weak.

The technological universities – the former colleges of advanced technology – are the sixth sub-sector. They make up 15 per cent of the 'old' university sector. Their individual fortunes have been mixed: Bath and Loughborough have boomed, while Aston and Salford have struggled. Although they have diversified into other fields, notably business and management, their engineering bias has sometimes made it difficult to recruit enough students to fill their places and their unit costs have remained uncomfortably high. The technological universities have failed to match implied models such as the Massachusetts Institute of Technology (with the possible exception of the University of Manchester Institute of Science and Technology (UMIST), which is not a former college of advanced technology). Nor have they developed into élite institutions modelled on the Robbins report's SISTERs (special institutions of scientific and technological education and research). However, the balance of political advantage may be swinging in the technological universities' favour. Pure scientific excellence and academic collegiality, the standards by which they were judged and found wanting in the 1970s and 1980s, are less persuasive politically in the 1990s. Their lack of inhibitions about collaborating with industry and business, and their tauter management structures inherited from further education, have been transformed from liabilities into assets.

The seventh sub-sector comprises the Scottish universities, which themselves can be sub-divided into the 'ancient' (Aberdeen, Edinburgh, Glasgow and St Andrews); civic (Dundee); technological (Strathclyde and Heriot-Watt); old 'new' (Stirling); and new 'new' (Napier, Glasgow Caledonian, Abertay, Robert Gordon and Paisley). The first four, of course, have played an inestimable role in forming Scotland's national culture. Along with the Church and the law, they make up the troika of institutions which have embodied Scotland's distinctive identity. George Davie's 'democratic intellect' remains a poignant myth. The general ordinary degree has survived, just, the onslaught of specialized honours degrees. The Scottish secondary school system is different than that of England and Wales, culminating in Highers rather than A levels. The central institutions, from which the new 'new' universities were drawn, were more professional and less 'alternative' than the polytechnics, which meant that the Scottish binary system was less rivalrous. Although some of these differences have become less marked, they are still formidable. The establishment of a separate funding council, described in the first section of this chapter, is likely to produce renewed divergence.

The eighth sub-sector is made up of the University of Wales and the University of Glamorgan, the former Polytechnic of Wales. They are less distinct from the mainstream of English higher education than the Scottish universities, because a common system of secondary education (and examinations) has encouraged large-scale flows of Welsh students into England and vice versa. Nevertheless, the University of Wales has two distinctive characteristics. First, its foundation was an important element in the re-awakening of Welsh national consciousness in the nineteenth and early twentieth centuries. Along with the pits of the Rhondda and the disestablishment of the Church in Wales, it formed a more modest troika of national pride. Second, it is a federal university, although its constituent colleges enjoy effective autonomy. Its federal structure has enabled a greater diversity of institutional types to survive, from large institutions like the University of Wales College of Cardiff to St David's University College in Lampeter, Britain's smallest university institution. As with Scotland, the establishment of a separate funding council is likely to encourage divergence, although on a more modest scale.

The two Northern Irish universities, Queen's and Ulster, form a ninth sub-sector. The former shares many of the characteristics of the English civic universities, while the latter is the product of a merger between an old 'new' university, the New University of Ulster, blighted by its sectarian siting in Coleraine, and the Polytechnic of Ulster. Ulster is the only example of a university–polytechnic amalgamation. Once considered likely to be the first of a series, it remains in a class of its own. Both universities are funded by the Department of Education Northern Ireland. In the past their allocations, in practice, had been determined by the UGC. The creation of four sub-systems within Britain is likely to encourage the DENI to take a more independent line.

The tenth sub-system is formed by a single institution, the Open University (OU). Arguably, the OU has done more than any other to reshape popular attitudes to higher education in Britain. Yet cross-fertilization with other universities has been limited. In terms of research and scholarship the OU, and its staff, have been fully accepted. But, as a teaching institution, the OU has been kept at arm's length, and seen as one of a (very special) kind. As a result other universities have dabbled in distance learning, though without recourse to the OU's quarter-century of experience. The OU is also exceptional in another respect. Once funded directly by the government, it is now funded by the HEFCE, although it operates throughout the United Kingdom and in many other countries.

The final two sub-sectors of universities comprise the old 'new' universities established on green-field campuses during the 1960s and the new 'new' universities, the former polytechnics promoted to university status in 1992. Both will be considered in more detail in the next part of this section, as examples of the two main reform strategies adopted by higher education systems, the creation of new (and new kinds of?) universities and the development of the non-university sector. The new universities and the polytechnics, it can be argued, were the key formative institutions in post-war British higher education. The former embodied an extension, or modernization, of the university tradition; the latter an alternative to it.

Although the bulk of the growth in student numbers took place in existing universities, hopes for the Robbins expansion came to rest symbolically with the new universities (despite the fact that the decision to establish them pre-dated Robbins). The Robbins project, and their success, were bound up together. The decision to establish the polytechnics brought into sharp focus the fragments of an alternative tradition rooted in technical and vocational education. Arguably, the élite component of that tradition had been absorbed into the university mainstream through institutions like Imperial College and UMIST. But the bulk had remained outside. The polytechnic project produced a radical reordering of institutions and of these traditions, culminating in the creation of a unified system of higher education.

These 12 sub-sectors comprise the expanded universities sector. The complete higher education system goes still wider. One way to categorize non-university institutions is by country – there are 50 colleges in England, eight in Scotland and six in Wales. Another possible demarcation is between general and specialized colleges. A more elaborate typology consists of four sub-groups. The first is the small number of larger multi-faculty colleges which aspire to be universities. These include the Cheltenham and Gloucester College of Higher Education, Nene College, Roehampton Institute, Bolton Institute of Higher Education and Southampton Institute of Higher Education. They are much larger than the average university of a generation ago. Two colleges formerly in this sub-group, Derby and Luton, were designated as polytechnics in the nick of time to become universities.

The second sub-group is made up of liberal arts colleges, which were once rooted in the training of teachers but now have colonized the adjacent arts and sciences and applied social studies. On average they are smaller than the would-be universities, although some are more mature in academic terms. For example, Bath College of Higher Education has the power to grant its own degrees, while three of the larger colleges are still required to have their awards validated by universities. Several institutions in this second group are Church colleges. Their religious affiliation, reinforced by their more intimate scale, has contributed to the development of a distinctive ethos which emphasizes pastoral commitment and the collegiate community. This ethos is reminiscent of the American ideal of the liberal college, as opposed to the gigantism of the multiversity. However, its institutional foundations are far from secure in the British system. Small size is increasingly seen as a liability, to be overcome by seeking mergers with neighbouring institutions.

The third sub-group is those colleges which operate a mixed economy of further and higher education courses. They are often to be found in urban settings. As a result, they emphasize their community responsibility to provide progression opportunities to local, often mature, students, and have a strong commitment to adult and continuing education.

The fourth sub-group comprises specialized colleges. Some, like the Royal College of Music or the Glasgow College of Art, have national, even international, reputations. In no sense are they inferior to the universities. For historical and administrative reasons agricultural colleges have also remained free-standing institutions (a pattern which is common throughout Europe). Only in Scotland, with its monotechnic tradition, have separate colleges of education survived.

Higher education courses are also provided outside the higher education system. Seventy-six further education colleges in England receive funding directly from the HEFCE.[49] In 1992–3 £26 million was provided to fund 32,000 students. One-third of all Higher National Diploma (HND) students are enrolled by FE colleges not higher education institutions. Even more colleges have some involvement in higher education. The number of access courses (special programmes designed to facilitate entry to higher education by students without standard entry qualifications) increased from 130 in 1984 to 1,500 in 1993. Foundation courses, which form the first year of integrated four-year degrees, enrolled 14,975 students in 1992. In total, it is estimated, there were 139,000 students on higher education courses in further education colleges in 1992–3, the majority on part-time sub-degree and professional courses. This so-called FE-in-HE makes up the last, but not the least, element of the higher education system.

British higher education, therefore, comprises at least seventeen sub-sectors and sub-groups. Its keynote is not homogeneity, as is commonly alleged, but institutional diversity. This impression of diversity is height-ened if the whole of post-compulsory education is considered. In 1992 further education colleges ceased to be part of the local authority educa-tion service and became free-standing corporations. Their direct stake in higher education has already been discussed. But an increasing number of FE students, although not on higher education courses, are aged over 18. The Further Education Funding Council divides colleges into three broad types: general FE and tertiary colleges; sixth-form colleges; and specialist colleges. Sixth-form colleges cater almost entirely for students aged be-tween 16 and 18 and, consequently, do not form part of the post-secondary education system. However, the other two types of college enrol significant numbers of adult students. They fulfil many of the roles undertaken by community colleges in the United States.

The proportion of older students in further education colleges has been increased by the reorganization of adult education. Previously separate adult education institutes or colleges were provided by local education authorities. Since 1992 a new demarcation has begun to emerge, between recreational or other non-vocational classes (which may still be organized by local au-thorities but often on a full-cost basis and no longer as a responsibility of education departments) on the one hand and more vocational or community-education classes on the other (which are likely to be offered by FE colleges or through TECs). In addition, earmarked funding is no longer provided for extra-mural courses in universities, the heartland of liberal adult educa-tion. Publicly provided adult education is fast ceasing to be an independent sector. It has been either leisurized or mainstreamed.

The final part of the post-compulsory education and training system is the so-called corporate classroom. In the United States it is estimated that as much education and training takes place outside as inside educational institutions. In Britain its scale is thought to be less. But the corporate classroom still represents perhaps a third of the total 'system', whether in terms of student/trainee hours or of resources. This provision is heterogen-eous and volatile. Much is low-level training in routine skills or socialization into corporate cultures. However, a significant proportion is more advanced, especially in areas such as technology updating and management training.

An important characteristic of the corporate classroom is its increasingly incestuous links with universities and colleges. British Telecom's training department was an 'associated institution' of the former Council for National

Academic Awards, which meant that in-house training could count towards a degree. There are now many examples of co-operation between the corporate classroom and the higher education system. Typical is the MBA programme for Peugeot managers run by Coventry University.

To the seventeen distinct components of higher education, therefore, must be added a further three to complete the post-compulsory education and training system – further education, adult education and the 'corporate classroom' (all three can be sub-divided many times). This simple enumeration of the various elements of this wider system, which is rapidly subsuming higher education, illustrates its current diversity. But the system is not only diverse; it is also dynamic, in a double sense. First, its diversity is the product of its history. Second, it is projected forward into future policy-making.

The demarcation between 'old' and 'new' universities, derived from the old binary system and still widely regarded as the key operational divide in British higher education, is bad history. Its bogus dichotomy obscures the system's true pluralism. The labelling of institutions was largely a matter of timing. The colleges of advanced technology ended up on the 'university' side of the binary line; regional colleges, colleges of art and, later, colleges of education ended up on the 'polytechnic' side. Nor, as this demarcation misleadingly insinuates, were 'old' universities mature institutions, rooted in traditional values and ruled by diurnal donnish routine, and 'new' universities innovatory institutions able to strike out in radical new directions without inhibition. Arguably, it was the other way round. The new universities of the 1960s started from scratch, designing and building their campuses in open fields and drawing new 'maps of learning' which sought to encompass the entire territory of the arts and the sciences. The polytechnics, usually on cramped city-centre sites in a jumble of college buildings, were further constrained within a tradition of vocational education and, for many of their courses, by over-rigid professional requirements. And they were unable to award their own degrees. The Council for National Academic Awards, anxious to ensure compatibility of academic standards with those in the 'old' universities, was cautious, even conservative, in its approach to academic innovation in the early years.

Finally, the 'old' university sector did not come first, followed later by the 'new' universities in their polytechnic guise. As has already been pointed out, the former is substantially a post-Robbins growth, despite the weight of older traditions represented by Oxford, Cambridge, London and the Victorian–Edwardian civics. The old 'new' universities and the technological universities have no pre-Robbins history, the former at all and the latter as universities. Much of the development of older universities also took place after 1960. This novelty is also reflected in teaching and research. 'Old' universities, even the genuinely old, teach subjects which did not exist a generation ago and even those which bear traditional labels have been greatly changed. Their research agenda, too, has been transformed.

The trajectory of the 'new' universities has been equally, or even more, exhilarating. They are totally unlike the gaggle of colleges which were amalgamated into polytechnics following the 1966 White Paper. They have been transformed from narrowly focused vocational institutions, with the ethos of a technical high school, into comprehensive universities likely to bear the brunt of mass higher education. They have moved from municipal dependence to corporate independence. Despite the occasional caution of the CNAA, they have been at the forefront of curricular innovation, elevating the academic level of subjects once constrained within a narrowly based training tradition and pioneering new patterns of course delivery such as modular degree schemes and credit accumulation and transfer systems (CATS).

But these two development processes, equally radical in their different ways, took place almost at the same time. At the most, the 'old' universities had five years' start. Their lift-off was in the early 1960s; that of the former polytechnics in the late 1960s. Both 'old' and 'new' universities, despite their labels, have been moulded by similar forces – political, socio-cultural, scientific and technological. It is largely because of this parallelism, their near-simultaneous development and exposure to the same or similar forces during the 1970s and 1980s, inevitably with convergent effect, that in the 1990s they have come together in a unified system of higher education. The pluralism of British higher education, therefore, is reflected not in a clear-cut post-binary divide but is expressed through the much finer-grain differentiation of institutional types.

This pluralism is prospective as well as retrospective. The wider system, and its component institutions, are not static. Dynamic change is under way, most intensely at the 'top' and 'bottom' of the system. An élite university segment is struggling to emerge; and the further education sector is being transformed. The first process remains inchoate. The recommendation by the Advisory Board for the Research Councils in 1987 that all higher education institutions should be graded R (research universities on the American model), X (institutions with selective research missions) or T (teaching-mainly institutions) was allowed to lapse, although the language of RXT entered the vocabulary of British universities. One reason was that the political obstacles were thought to be too formidable, even if a market-oriented government had been convinced of the need for state-sponsored *dirigisme*. Another was that research universities are peculiarly, even exceptionally, American institutions which relate to a distinctive pattern of undergraduate education and professional and research schools. They cannot easily be replicated in Britain.

Existing policy instruments, therefore, are not favourable to the emergence of an élite sector. So soon after the abandonment of the binary system, the government is unlikely to embark on system-wide stratification. The funding councils, for reasons outlined earlier in this chapter, have little room for strategic manoeuvre. Their methodologies for allocating teaching funds are formula-driven. Quality assessment is not designed to drive selective funding. Three rounds of research assessment have led not to a concentration, but to a broadening (arguably, an attenuation) of the research base. Yet the pressure to create an élite sector, able to compete globally, is growing stronger. It is reflected in the emergence of an informal grouping of the vice-chancellors of Oxford, Cambridge, the main London colleges and the big civics, the so-called 'Russell Group' (named after the Russell Hotel where they meet). Typically British, a 'club' strategy is unlikely to be robust enough to institutionalize a university élite. A more decisive intervention, inevitably by the state, will eventually be required.

The second process, the transformation of the further education sector, is more immediate. For almost a quarter of a century FE colleges have been engaged in a long revolution, sloughing off their technical school past and evolving towards a broader community-wide comprehensive college future (their trajectory is uncannily reminiscent of that followed by the former polytechnics). As long as they were local authority institutions, the depth of this transformation was partly obscured by the persistence of political localisms. The FEFC now has to forge a national sector out of more than a hundred mini-sectors. Consequently, it cannot, like the higher education funding councils, eschew planning.

Yet, although the means are clear, the ends are obscure (in the first process, the emergence of an élite university grouping, it is the other way round: the goal is plain, the road problematical). There are three rival visions of further education which emphasize the colleges' relationship with schools, training and higher education, respectively. The first, and least plausible, locates FE colleges in the marketplace of upper-secondary education, for 16–18-year-olds. Competing with, or complementing, various types of school (local authority, grant maintained or city technology colleges), FE is another option, enhancing choice for students and their parents. Quality is the keynote. The second places further education in the context of the skills revolution, either as subordinate partners of the TECs or competing with other, often private-sector, training providers. Competence is the keynote. The third vision is of FE colleges as community colleges, entry-level institutions within an enlarged higher education system or, more ambitiously, catalysts of curriculum reform. Progression is the keynote.

The pattern of institutions within the total post-compulsory education and training system is increasingly volatile. There are powerful convergent forces, the most prominent being the creation of a unified, post-binary, higher education system and the nationalization of the further education sector. But, although convergent, both have produced great turbulence. Some institutions run for the cover of market niches; others seek their salvation in larger associations (and amalgamations). Whole classes of institution, notably colleges of higher education and sixth-form colleges, appear to be threatened. However, there are equally powerful divergent forces at work. Market pressure is producing institutional differentiation. Internal differentiation is accelerating, as a result of the internal dynamics of disciplinary disaggregation and of external interventions such as research assessment. The links between institutional forms and academic cultures are becoming weaker, as more learning takes place off-off-campus. The virtual university, or college, beckons.

Two paths to reform

The two main strategies adopted in the development of modern higher education systems have been the modernization and renewal of the university tradition, largely by founding new universities, and the articulation of alternative non-university institutions. In Britain these strategies were represented by the decisions in the late 1950s and early 1960s to build new universities on green-field sites and less than a decade later to establish the polytechnics. The fate of these two experiments is the focus of this second part of the section.

The idea of founding new universities was first raised in the mid-1940s. It lapsed because the existing universities agreed to increase their student numbers.[50] No new universities, with the doubtful exception of Keele (really a pre-war foundation), were established until the late 1950s and early 1960s, in the Macmillan 'never had it so good' era. But the genesis of the idea a decade earlier during the period of post-war reconstruction is suggestive. The creation of new universities was originally seen as part of a larger project, the so-called post-war settlement built round the welfare state with its promise to open up British society. They were to contribute to a wider conception of social emancipation. But, because of their long gestation, the new universities did not take their first students until the 1960s, when the tone of society had changed. The new keywords were lifestyle and liberation.

As a result, the founding values of the new universities were ambiguous: high seriousness mixed with playful iconoclasm. However, they added an important new strand to the British university tradition and made a powerful contribution to its renewal. The new universities were distinctive in three ways – physical, organisational and academic. As it has turned out, their spatial, and visual, distinctiveness has been generalized across the university system, while their bold organizational and academic innovations have been contained and compromised.

Their physical distinctiveness has two dimensions. First, the new universities were not established in the metropolitan industrial heartlands but in county towns. The only exception was Warwick, which is really in Coventry. (It may not be an accident that by the 1990s the University of Warwick, sited in the West Midlands conurbation, was the most successful, the only new university with a guaranteed place in the research university (proto-)élite.) They became known as the Baedeker, or Shakespearian, universities. York, Lancaster, Warwick, Sussex, Essex, Kent – they read like a cast list. But it is wrong to suggest that the new universities were founded in a deliberately anti-industrial spirit. The 1960s, after all, were the age of 'the white heat of the technological revolution'.

Pragmatic considerations such as the availability, adequacy and cost of sites were the most immediate and, arguably, most important. But titles are suggestive, and locations decisive. The new universities were conceived of as national institutions from the start. Although local politicians and industrialists lobbied the government to secure new universities, no attempt was made to re-create the localisms of the civics or redbrick universities. No students were going to commute to the new universities by tram or trolley-bus through cobbly, smoggy streets. Provincial England was being elbowed aside by modern Britain.

Second, the new universities were campus universities built on green-field sites. The campus was a novel idea in 1960. The idea of the college – quadrangles and courts, halls and chapels – was familiar. But it was essentially small-scale, a nineteenth-century ideal based on impressions of Oxford and Cambridge and grammar schools. By the 1950s the original 'college' had shrunk to a small core at most civics. The university was embedded in the city; its buildings scattered and unrecognizable as part of a larger whole. The new universities, therefore, represented a radical departure. The American campus, arguably the conception of the university's physical environment which underpins a mass system, was born in Britain.

Their students lived in on-campus residences, dorms not digs. Buildings were planned as a harmonious whole. The aspirations of their founders were reflected in their architecture.[51] The new universities were academic villages, visual representations of the city of learning set on the hill or by the lake. They were self-contained, providing their own social and cultural facilities. A passionate combination of Arcadia with Utopia. Now, of course, it is difficult to imagine higher education without campus universities. After Oxford and Cambridge, or even before them, it has become the most potent image of the university. And it is an influential model that other universities, 'old' and 'new', have followed. Most have tried to reorganize their estate as, if not campuses because their urban situations made this impossible, at any rate academic precincts. They, too, built residences, dug lakes, planted trees. The influence of the new universities over the spatial organization and visual representation of the university was decisive.

Their second arena of distinctiveness was their organization, both social and academic. Several of the new universities adopted a crypto-collegiate structure – crypto, because they did not follow the Oxbridge model where the college, not the department, was the primary academic unit; but collegiate, because an organizational attempt was made to create a more intimate focus for the social life of what were expected to grow into large multiversities (if their expansion had not been slowed by the subsequent growth of student numbers in the polytechnics). Colleges at Kent, York and Lancaster were designed to reconcile the inherited intimacy of British universities, most intensely sustained at Oxford and Cambridge, with the imperatives of an expanding system. Even in those new universities which eschewed colleges, the same goals were pursued by different means. Three decades later, because of shifting student attitudes and resource constraints, the reconciliation of expansion and intimacy, so urgent in the 1960s, has become largely redundant. As a social experiment, therefore, the new universities appear to have failed.

The patterns of academic organization they pioneered have been more influential. Nearly all the new universities, with the suggestive exception of Warwick, moved away from the tight disciplinary/departmental structures typical of the older universities. Instead their academic organization emphasized broader subject groupings, and gave much greater scope for inter-disciplinary studies. Typically a single-tier structure was adopted, either of broadly based schools of studies or of large comprehensive departments, in place of the two-tier structure of faculties and departments which prevailed in the civics. The effect was to cut out faculties, often the most conservative layer of academic organizations, and/or to increase the influence of front-line departments.

Because they were new foundations, and because they did not teach the most highly structured disciplines such as medicine, the new universities were able to adopt this more flexible pattern of academic organization. But they did not start with a blank sheet. Their founders came from established universities with embedded organizational cultures by which they were powerfully influenced, if only in opposition. Also, more recently the new universities have retreated from their early inter-disciplinary ambitions. Departments, and faculties, have re-emerged, partly to map on to the academic subject categories and units of assessment used by the funding councils. A process of convergence appears to have been at work. The older universities, and the former polytechnics, have tended to adopt the more flexible academic structures pioneered by the new universities. Also cost-centring, the devolution of budgetary responsibilities to primary academic units, has produced *de facto* single-tier structures.

The third arena of new universities' distinction, academic culture, was the most evocative but also the most opaque. Did they represent a radically new approach to higher education as well as a new organizational paradigm? Certainly their founders made grand claims about redrawing the map of knowledge. High hopes of their wider influence were expressed.[52] Their ethos seemed to be part-WEA (Workers' Educational Association), part-USA, liberal education plus electives. The new universities were designed to open up, and so reinvigorate, the British university tradition. They were a peculiarly British response to the same social and economic forces that had already produced in the United States a mass system, described by Clark Kerr in *The Uses of the University*, written in the same year as the Robbins report.[53]

These claims and hopes appear to have been exposed as naive. In the early 1960s it was widely assumed that large-scale expansion of student numbers would be accompanied by a growth of more general forms of higher education. Lord Robbins based his expansionary project on this assumption. The founders of the new universities made similar assumptions. The opposite happened. Disciplinary and professional specialization intensified as the university system grew. The new maps of learning were rolled up. But perhaps the development of general higher education was merely delayed. With true massification of the system has come a renewed commitment to generalism, although more often in the form of CATS and competences than of the Leavisite culture which lurked within the public doctrines of the new universities.

Were the new universities successful in their primary aim, to renew the British university tradition? They can too easily be disparaged as just another misconceived product of the much maligned 1960s. The case against their wider influence seems strong. First, it is clear that the ideals of their founding fathers were not shared by the majority of staff and students who had more pragmatic, and less radical, ambitions. The new maps of learning were always for show. Second, the new universities did not become the cutting edge of an expanding university system, quantitatively or qualitatively. After the mid-1970s growth rates were faster in the old civics; city-centre clubbing proved more attractive to new generations of students than late-night conversations in halls of residence. In research the new universities, with the exception of Warwick, have struggled to maintain their early promise. Third, it was the polytechnics, not the new universities, which opened up British higher education to increased participation.

But, in each case, counter-arguments are available. First, a new teaching culture developed in the new universities, perhaps not guided by grandiose maps of knowledge but rooted in imaginative subject combinations and more relaxed relationships between staff and students. The democratization of British higher education began here, not in the hierarchical world of the older universities or the instrumental world of the polytechnics. Second, it was the creation of the new universities which enabled the university sector to maintain its numerical superiority over the rival polytechnics well into the 1980s. Today there is broad parity between the 'old' and the 'new' universities. Without the new universities there would be an imbalance, with two painful effects – a more elitist and inward 'old' university sector; and a more functional and philistine 'new' university sector.

Third, it can be argued that, during the 1970s and 1980s, the polytechnics stole many of the new universities' clothes, building plate-glass campuses and devising their own modular maps of learning. Their great expansion was not in the types of student and course they had inherited from further education, part-time certificates and sub-degree diplomas in vocational subjects, but in *ersatz* new-university provision, full-time degrees in academic and professional fields. Moreover, it is the intellectual culture developed in the universities, especially the new universities, during the 1960s and 1970s which continues to dominate British higher education. A culture that is sociological rather than scholarly (as it was in the older universities) or functionalist (the value inheritance of the polytechnics), and critical rather than either donnish or instrumental. Finally, British higher education remains a middle-class enterprise, inevitably so perhaps given the role that even mass systems play in social stratification. To the extent that the new universities were (and are) middle-class, but modern, institutions, they may be closer to the centre-ground of the system than the older universities or the former polytechnics.

The second strategy for modernizing higher education, the articulation of institutional alternatives to the mainstream university tradition, was represented by the polytechnics, and to a lesser extent the multi-faculty Scottish central institutions. In one sense the success of this strategy is beyond question. Today the 'new' universities make up perhaps the most powerful block within the post-binary system. Without a doubt they have reshaped the popular imagination of the possibilities of higher education. Once peripheral, they are now mainstream institutions. In another sense the success of this strategy is less certain. The attempt to maintain a distinction between universities and other higher education institutions, which was the object of the binary policy, has been abandoned. The 'alternatives' strategy, therefore, served a transitional purpose, to provide a protected arena in which practices and values unfamiliar (or even uncongenial) to traditional universities could develop until they were sufficiently robust to be able to survive on their own. Consequently its ultimate success remains to be determined.

The most striking difference between the new universities and the polytechnics was spatial. They represented different maps of English higher education. (In Scotland, for complex historical and administrative reasons, neither modernization strategy was properly implemented. Only one new university, Stirling, was founded, and the central institutions never became Scottish polytechnics despite the ambitions of some principals). Of the original English polytechnics two-thirds were established in the old industrial England of the North and West Midlands or in inner London. (The only Welsh polytechnic was established in Pontypridd, in the industrial heartland of South Wales.) Their distribution reflected the geography of that England. Even the exceptions had suggestive associations with the industrial base – the navy at Portsmouth and Plymouth, automobile and aeronautical engineering at Oxford and Hatfield. The polytechnics were also unambiguously urban institutions. Only two new universities, as has already been pointed out, were established in the North and none in London. All were established in small towns or at a discreet distance from large ones.

This spatial distribution underlines two key characteristics of the polytechnics. First, they were vocational institutions with deep roots in technical education. Their primary role was economic, to supply skilled labour. So they grew up alongside industry. The new universities, in contrast, had an educational focus, which most interpreted, at any rate initially, in liberal terms. As a result they sought Arcadian locations. Second, the polytechnics were municipal institutions, not simply in terms of governance and administration but, more significantly, in their values and orientation. They were rooted in particular communities. This rootedness could not easily be reconciled with notions of autonomy. The new universities, of course, were *de novo* national institutions, accountable only to their more ancient peers.

A third key characteristic may also be partly a product of spatial geography. The polytechnics were open rather than closed institutions, inheriting the wider access traditions of further education. They were, physically, more accessible than the new universities. Most were in conurbations, at the centre of extensive travel-to-work regions. Nearly all were on city-centre sites. As a result they were convenient for part-time students. The out-of-(small)-town campuses of the new universities, in contrast, were inaccessible to all but full-time students. But the polytechnics were also more accessible ideologically. Their mission was not to reproduce élites, even the comparatively meritocratic élites addressed by the new universities, but to maximize the local and regional skills base. Consequently their instinct was not to be exclusionary or selective, which the new universities were bound to be, but to provide a wide range of training opportunities and to respond to student demand for progression to higher professional skills.

Two points are worth emphasizing. First, the emphases on student responsiveness and vocational outcomes, which are now seen as characteristic of the 'new' universities, are not recent innovations, products of the post-incorporation era, but reflect their *longue durée*. Although the 'new' universities of the 1990s are immeasurably more powerful institutions than the polytechnics of the 1970s, their underlying value structures are little changed. Second, the three key characteristics of the polytechnic alternative – heterogeneity rather than the academic orthodoxy to which the 'old' universities ostensibly aspire; a commitment to vocationalism; and a greater emphasis on accountability than on autonomy – are easier to understand in an evolutionary than in an ideological context. Several attempts, none especially convincing, have been made to describe the differences between polytechnics and universities in terms of first principles by constructing rival ideologies of higher education.[54] Fewer attempts have been made to describe these differences in terms of historical evolution, except as a prologue to such ideological interpretations.

The first characteristic, heterogeneity rather than orthodoxy, is essentially social. It is derived from the institutional histories of the polytechnics and 'new' universities, and the class origins, academic ambitions and job destinations of their students. The former influence, institutional histories, waned as the polytechnics left their further education past far behind. They sought to impose a coherent pattern on the wide range of courses, in plural modes, which they offered – directly by establishing modular and credit accumulation and transfer schemes and/or indirectly by emphasizing the quality of the total student experience across the whole institution. Arguably, this led to a tilt back towards older, and more organic, notions of academic orthodoxy. External influences, notably from the CNAA, may have had a similar effect.

However, the latter influence, student diversity, increased as the system expanded. The bulk of that expansion took place in the former polytechnics during the 1980s. As a result they had to make more radical adjustments than the 'old' universities to increasing heterogeneity – in terms of inputs, because they recruited a higher proportion of non-traditional students; outputs, because expansion eroded the old links between higher education and élitist occupations; and process, because new students and new graduate jobs demanded new approaches to the content and arrangement of courses and to teaching and learning strategies. On balance the latter influence has been much more powerful than the former, with the result that the 'new' universities are more heterogeneous than the polytechnics were a generation ago.

The second characteristic, a commitment to vocationalism, is educational in orientation. It, too, reflects the values and practices the polytechnics inherited from their antecedent institutions, the regional colleges of technology, colleges of commerce, colleges of art and design and colleges of education. This commitment, it is sometimes argued, has been eroded as a result of 'academic drift', an impression apparently reinforced by the abandonment of the binary system and adoption of university titles. But what has changed is not so much the polytechnics' (now the 'new' universities') commitment to vocationalism but the market for high-level skills and even the nature of vocationalism itself. In particular, two key shifts have taken place since the polytechnics were established.

First, new occupations, especially those for which the applied social sciences and business and management studies are seen as appropriate preparation, have increased in significance while traditional industrial occupations have declined. This reflects deep-rooted secular changes in the occupational structure which have influenced subject choices in the 'old' universities almost as much; in other words the 'pull' of the economy has been more powerful than any 'push' from within the academic culture. The jibe that the polytechnics, instead of becoming technological institutions, wantonly expanded into the social sciences is based on a failure to appreciate the scale of these changes in occupational structure. Second, vocationalism itself has undergone a sea change. No longer expressed through detailed and disparate technical qualifications, it is now mediated through more broadly conceived competences. Again this reflects deep changes in the demand for professional skills in a labour market characterized by post-industrialism and privatization. These trends are discussed in greater detail in the next chapter.

To the extent that the distinctiveness of the 'new' universities has been eroded, it has not been produced by a dwindling belief in the need for heterogeneity or vocationalism. In both cases their commitment has increased, although because of changes in student intake to a mass system and the rise of the new vocationalism rather than because of an explicit ideological commitment to developing alternative forms of higher education. Instead their distinctiveness has been eroded because the same external forces have shaped the development of the 'old' universities, weakly in the 1970s and 1980s but with gathering force in the 1990s. As a result, the gap between 'old' and 'new' universities has been reduced.

The third key characteristic, an emphasis on accountability rather than autonomy, is essentially political. At the birth of the polytechnics Anthony Crosland called it 'social control'. According to one view, it was largely abandoned when the polytechnics became, first, quasi-national institutions during the late 1970s and 1980s, then independent corporations no longer accountable to local education authorities in 1988 and finally universities in 1992. Although they have not been granted royal charters, the 'new' universities enjoy the same practical degree of institutional autonomy as the 'old' universities. Nor is this shift from (local) accountability to (national) autonomy a recent or remarkable phenomenon. The decision in the mid-1960s to create a new category of institution, the polytechnic, was itself a form of proto-nationalization. The establishment of the NAB in 1982 represented a further erosion of local accountability, while the creation of the PCFC seven years later confirmed the status of the polytechnics as self-governing institutions with a predominantly national role.

Nevertheless, the 'new' universities have retained a strong culture of accountability. But it is now interpreted, and operationalized, in different ways. Previously accountability took two main forms – local political control and academic subordination to external validating bodies. The first was ineffective long before the polytechnics ceased to be local authority institutions. Strategic control had succumbed to bureaucratic regulation. The second, with the honourable exception of the former CNAA, inhibited the progressive development of polytechnic education. Professional bodies, in particular, imposed reductionist (and reactionary?) requirements. Today accountability is expressed through two different mechanisms – governing bodies dominated by 'independent' members with a strong business orientation, and market responsiveness in the academic arena. Although the 'old' universities have become more responsive to customer demands, their governance is still shaped by a culture of academic autonomy.

Three points emerge from this brief examination of the two most notable initiatives to modernize higher education – the new universities of the 1960s representing renewal from within the university tradition, and the polytechnics as an organized alternative to the traditional universities. The first is that both initiatives were successful, although at different levels. The new universities helped to reshape the inner life of the existing universities. Visually, spatially, academically and socially they established a new paradigm, very different from the pre-war dichotomy between donnish Oxbridge and provincial civics. Their foundation was a powerful unifying force within a splintered university tradition. The polytechnics' most significant contribution was to re-engineer the system. They challenged the hegemony of the universities, not through ideological confrontation but by institutionalizing the different values and practices developed within further education. Their successful development replaced a static model of a circumscribed university system by a dynamic model of a higher education system with open frontiers.

The second is that these initiatives were complementary, despite the rivalrous rhetoric. It is tempting to regard the foundation of the new universities as the first (and failed?) wave of modernization and the establishment of the polytechnics as the second, and more successful, wave. In fact they were near-synchronous projects. And from the start there was greater synergy between them than is commonly supposed. The new universities were designed to enlarge, and indirectly to reform, the university sector, while the polytechnics were designed to gather together the fragments of advanced further education and professional training, so complementing that sector. The key characteristics of both, which have been briefly described, were derived from these distinct agendas, not in a spirit of deliberate rivalry. The new universities' liberality was not an indictment of the polytechnics' vocationalism; nor the latter's culture of accountability an indictment of the former's 'donnish dominion'.

The third is that, in a unified system, broad typologies of institutions are likely to become less persuasive as more emphasis is placed on the specific missions of individual universities and colleges. One reason for this is that, for reasons which have already been discussed, grand planning of the kind which produced both the new universities and the polytechnics has fallen out of political fashion. Another, more powerful, reason is that in a mass system institutional missions are necessarily highly differentiated. Consequently the polytechnic / 'new' university model, with its emphasis on heterogeneity, may be more relevant than the new university model with its organic and holistic ambitions, at any rate for mass institutions.

Mission and management

Mission and management are the twin themes of the final part of this section and chapter. The first of these terms has radically changed its meaning. Until recently the 'mission' of the university denoted a grand statement of its ultimate aims, in rhetorical descent from Cardinal Newman. Today, umbilically linked to the word 'statement', it has become an 'executive summary' of the goals of institutional management. This second term, management, is a novelty in higher education, despite its current ubiquity. It first surfaced in the late 1960s and 1970s, usually linked to planning.[55] It became pervasive in the 1980s as the 'old' universities struggled to cope with the consequences of the 1981 cuts and the NAB attempted to devise a coherent planning and funding system out of the chaos of local authority particularisms, and to encourage good management practice in the former polytechnics and colleges.[56]

Mission and management reflect changing patterns of authority in higher education institutions. Few systematic attempts have been made, in a British context, to describe these various types of authority. The dominant belief, at any rate in the 'old' universities has been that legitimate authority is exercised at the level of the basic unit, or department, and by practitioners, active teachers and researchers; other forms of authority, notably that exercised (imposed?) by managers, are illegitimate. To the extent that non-academic forms of authority have advanced, an adversarial dichotomy has developed between academics and managers. But in the United States, the best example of a mass system, a plurality of authority is accepted. Burton Clark identified no fewer than nine forms of academic authority – four based on disciplines (personal rulership [professorial]; collegial rulership [professorial]; guild authority; and professional authority); two characteristic of institutions (trustee authority and bureaucratic authority); and three operating at the level of the system (bureaucratic authority, political authority and what he called 'system-wide academic oligarchy').[57]

It is important to recognize this plurality of forms of authority – and the stake-holders they represent – in considering who should determine the mission of universities and colleges and manage them. In a mass system it is likely to increase, along with the size and complexity of institutions. The development of British universities as organizations demonstrates this growth of complexity which is reflected in multiple missions and proliferating stake-holders. The experience of the 'old' universities is considered first, followed by that of the 'new' universities. Finally, broader issues arising from the changing character of institutions in a mass system, which re-echo Clark's account, are discussed.

Four main phases can be identified in the internal government and management of the 'old' universities. The first was the 'civic' phase, the late nineteenth- and early twentieth-century university in which lay people still wielded considerable power. This was succeeded by the 'donnish' phase which emerged between the 1920s and 1950s and reached its climax in the early 1960s. In this second phase the government of universities was dominated by vice-chancellors acting in concert with senior professors, a model of élite collegiality. The third phase was that of the 'democratic' university, stimulated by student revolt in the later 1960s but which also reflected the widening of access to universities and their increasing heterogeneity during the 1970s. The fourth, and current, phase is that of 'managerial' university, a response to a harsher external environment of (fewer) resources and (more) accountability and to a radical intensification of complexity, in terms of both intellectual values and organizational structures, within the university.

Except for Oxford and Cambridge there was from the beginning significant lay involvement in the government of 'old' universities. Although autonomous, in the sense they were not state institutions, most universities were not, in their early years, controlled by academics. This point must be emphasized because, more recently, institutional autonomy and, in A. H. Halsey's phrase, 'donnish dominion' have come to be regarded as virtually synonymous.[58] Of the ancient Scottish universities both Edinburgh and Glasgow were subject to the control of their respective town councils until well into the nineteenth century. The campaign to establish the colleges which later coalesced into the University of London was led by public men, whether Parliamentary, civic, commercial or church leaders, and voluntary organizations. Their names, individual and collective, are still celebrated in college titles – Birkbeck (the man), Goldsmiths (the company) and so on. Similarly, most of the civic universities established in Victorian Britain were the result of initiatives by local political or commercial élites – Chamberlain in Birmingham, Wills in Bristol, Palmers in Reading.

The governing councils of these early universities were dominated by tightly knit networks of their provincial founders, and families and friends, and later their heirs. Only gradually did power pass from lay councils to academic senates. In this first phase management was not an issue. University administrations barely existed. Clerks sufficed. Until the twentieth century institutions were small, and departments were tiny. The council appointed the professors who then appointed their assistants, if any were required or could be afforded. Funding was generally inadequate and always precarious. Recurrent funding depended on tuition fees, capital funding on donations.

The dominant reason for the shift to the 'donnish' university was the state's growing stake in higher education, institutionalized in 1919 by the establishment of the UGC. As universities came to receive the bulk of their income in the form of state grants and, consequently, relied less on civic and industrial subsidy and student fees, the influence of lay patrons waned. Academic self-government filled the vacuum. The administration of the 'donnish' university was subordinated to the ideologies of the artisan scholar, heroic scientist and autonomous teacher. Management was minimal – civil servantish, consensual, the lightest of light touches. It was the elaboration of scientific research beginning in the 1930s and then the post-war extension of the higher education franchise which obliged universities to develop more elaborate administrations. Finance, estates and personnel became significant activities alongside the routine of student admissions and examinations.

However, the prestige of universities was such in the two decades after 1945 – they had helped to win the war; now they were building a more modern and more open Britain – that the 'donnish dominion' flourished as never before. In retrospect its final flourish may have owed as much to a congruence of interests between political and academic élites as to a principled respect for university autonomy. But that was not apparent, or suspected, at the time. When the new universities were established in the 1960s, they were conceived of as self-governing communities of scholars with lay council members reduced to a supervisory role (after they had completed their essential job as political fixers and fundraisers). This view was strengthened by a migration from Oxford and Cambridge, the only two universities which had always been truly self-governing.

During the 1960s and for much of the 1970s the focus was not on restoring the balance between academic self-government and a reinvigorated lay involvement, despite the fact that universities were moving into new fields outside the traditional arts and sciences and the liberal professions and also into applied research, arenas in which the legitimacy of lay voices was difficult to deny. Instead the focus was on making academic democracy more complete, by reducing the hierarchical power of professors and other senior staff and giving a voice to rank-and-file lecturers and students. Élite collegiality was both compromised and reinforced by this elaboration of the democratic structures within university government. This was the substance of the second shift, from 'donnish' to 'democratic' university.

Among the (temporary?) casualties of this democratization was the authority of vice-chancellors, often supported behind the scenes by powerful registrars. Charismatic leadership had been the dominant pattern during the 1950s when the ethos of the entire university system seemed to be set by a small group of influential vice-chancellors such as the Morris brothers at Leeds and Bristol. In a slightly different sense the founding vice-chancellors of the new universities – Butterworth at Warwick, Carter at Lancaster, Sloman at Essex, Fulton then Briggs at Sussex and so on – had also been dominant, even domineering, figures. However, in the 'democratic university' vice-chancellors were obliged to manage by consensus, however laboriously constructed.

The 'democratic' university proved to be ephemeral. Already in the late 1970s there were signs it was failing. The growing size and complexity of universities as organizations demanded an upgrading of managerial capacity which, by increasing the power of the centre, balanced the centrifugal forces of democratization. This upgrading could be observed right across the universities' functions – academic planning, financial systems, estates management, personnel policies, marketing and external relations. It was reflected, too, in the growing professionalization of university administration through the medium of the Conference of University Administrators (CUA) and more specialist organizations, one of the most significant but underrated phenomena of the past two decades. Much of the impetus for, as well as expertise on, corporate planning originally came from administrators rather than academics.[59] A managerial cadre began to emerge, ready to support a more executive leadership, in place of the docile clerks who had instinctively acknowledged the innate authority of academics.

From the mid-1970s onwards universities also had to confront an increasingly complex external environment in the form of a more *dirigiste* UGC and a more sophisticated research council system. These relationships could not be handled on the basis of leisurely senate discussion but required crisp managerial responses. In addition, progress towards democratization slowed. Although permanent lecturers had gained a stronger voice in university government, part-time lecturers and research staff, who now made up a growing proportion of the academic profession, were effectively disfranchised. A new generation of students, too, began to abandon the bridgehead in university bureaucracy battled for by the radical students of the 1960s. Before the shock of the 1981 cuts the outlines of the 'managerial' university of the 1980s and 1990s could already be glimpsed – the waxing of executive leadership and professionalized administration and the waning of academic self-government.

The key period in the transition to the fourth phase, the 'managerial' university, was the four years between the 1981 cuts and the Jarratt report on university efficiency in 1985.[60] But the emergence of the 'managerial' university was not a dramatic break with the past, a brusque repudiation of collegiality and academic self-government. As has already been pointed out, many of its characteristics could already be observed in embryo during the 1970s. The project-management capacity built up during the post-Robbins expansion created the skills needed for the crisis management thrust on universities during the 1980s and for the strategic planning tasks of the 1990s. The movement towards more managerial forms of institutional government was a positive response to the success of university development during the 1960s and 1970s as much as it was an emergency strategy to cope with the depredations of Thatcherism.

Cuts or no cuts, efficiency review or no efficiency review, the larger and more heterogeneous universities which had developed as a result of the Robbins expansion had to be actively managed. The diversity of roles they had acquired, their multiplying missions, led inexorably to a weakening of common purpose. Increasing incommensurability between disciplines, themselves ceaselessly reconfiguring, meant that universities could no longer be glued together by a shared academic culture. Two managerial models emerged. The first, already apparent in the 1960s, was to treat the university as a mere federation of departments which were privileged as the 'basic units'.[61] The second, which developed during the 1980s, was to reassert institutional integrity organized now around managerial routines rather than rooted in academic culture. The rights of departments as 'basic units' were qualified by their responsibilities as 'cost centres'.

The growth of managerialism in the 'old' universities owed as much to the internal dynamics of institutional development as to external pressures applied by the government or the market. Also, Jarratt was a limited exercise in two senses. First, it was merely an aggregation of detailed inquiries into different aspects of university management, plus the results of a national data study. The Jarratt report, as such, was merely the report of the steering committee which oversaw these particular projects. Like Robbins, Jarratt has come to stand for far more than its actual text. The former powerfully embodied the government's, and the universities', endorsement of expansion; two decades later, the latter came to symbolize the advance of managerialism. Second, the Committee of Vice Chancellors, prompted by the UGC, established the Jarratt inquiry largely as a defensive strategy, to avoid the imposition by the government of a Rayner-style efficiency exercise of the kind that rolled through Whitehall in the mid-1980s – and which would have been seen as an intolerable interference with university autonomy.

The continuities of university government are as significant as the invasion of managerialism. Many detailed administrative reforms were made. Registrar's and bursar's departments were combined into unified administrations; the number of committees pruned; heads of department nudged into a line-management role. But, in themselves, these changes did not amount to a managerial revolution. In the 1980s, the age of Jarratt, there was little evidence of university councils, with their lay majorities, regaining the power and influence they once possessed, despite the pressure on universities to act entrepreneurially as state grants dwindled. One reason for this was the unwieldiness of many councils. In the 1990s, the post-binary age, several 'old' universities carried out reviews of the structure and size of their councils.[62] The outcome in most cases was to recommend the creation of smaller and more executive bodies modelled on the governing bodies of the 'new' universities, although retaining more dignified and collegial features.

The main feature of the 'managerial' university, therefore, has not so far been a revival of lay power. Rather it has been a reordering of authority within the university, with the organs of academic self-government losing effective (as opposed to formal) power and senior managers gaining influence.[63] The idea of a senior management team, consisting of vice-chancellors and pro vice-chancellors, perhaps deans, and registrars and other key administrators, is still comparatively novel in the 'old' universities. The number of pro vice-chancellors has increased, and they have been allocated specific portfolios, although they still tend to be temporary appointments and many are less than full-time. However, the emergence of planning units and strategy groups, often composed of mixed teams of senior administrators and academics, is a significant phenomenon.

The government and management of the 'new' universities have followed a different evolutionary pattern. Three phases of development can be identified – municipal, transitional and corporate. Until 1989 the polytechnics (apart from the five inner London polytechnics) and most colleges of higher education were local authority institutions. Their staff were employed and buildings owned by local education authorities. As a result their government was characterized by regulation, rather than either managerialism or collegiality. Instead of managerialism the dominant mode was bureaucratic hierarchy. The considerable authority of directors or principals, deans and heads of department was derived from their position in that hierarchy. Bureaucratic status counted for more than managerial functionality. Similarly, syndicalism took the place of collegiality. Academic and other staff exercised influence, which was also considerable, through their trade unions rather than through forms of institutional democracy which barely existed in this first phase.

Governing bodies, large and inchoate, were often 'political' arenas which the majority party on the local authority sought to dominate or, more frequently, were used by interest groups to second-guess management decisions. But they lacked executive responsibility. Even when governing bodies overcame their inherent weaknesses, their effectiveness was undermined by the persistence of rival authority networks, in particular the accountability of (subordinate) polytechnic or college managers to (superior) council officers and the rights and duties of all staff as employees of the local authority. Institutional management was weakly developed, because many key functions such as estates, finance and personnel remained the responsibility of local authorities. The institutions themselves were only responsible for academic administration.

The second, transitional phase, which began in the 1970s and lasted until

1989, was distinguished by three new developments. First, following the Weaver reform of college government, academic boards had been established. Although never able to rival 'old' university senates, they became increasingly significant in the polytechnics as student numbers grew rapidly and more and more new courses were introduced. Second, the *de facto* devolution of local authority responsibilities to institutions gathered pace. On the eve of incorporation in 1989 most polytechnics had become, in practice, free-standing institutions. Third, the establishment of the NAB, after earlier fumbled attempts to establish co-ordinating machinery, created a national policy environment. Not only did the NAB itself seek directly to reform institutional management, through its *Report of the Working Group on Good Management Practice* (1987) and other initiatives; its student-number and funding policies forced the polytechnics and colleges to devise appropriate management structures. Institutional 'systems', of all kinds, had to be developed to engage the new national 'system'.

The third, corporate, phase began in 1989 when the polytechnics were removed from the control of local authorities and established as free-standing corporations, and has continued without serious modification despite the relabelling of the polytechnics as universities and the creation of a unified funding regime. New and much smaller governing bodies were established, with a majority of 'independent' members, to form the new corporations. (Significantly, in most 'old' universities the corporate body is made up of all faculty members.) New managerial capacity had to be developed as the polytechnics and colleges took over the residual responsibilities of local authorities. The two most active, and controversial, arenas were industrial relations and estates management. Finally, strategic planning took off, partly because institutional leaders, freed from the constraints of municipal bureaucracy, found a new confidence and partly because the fuzzy planning regime of the NAB was replaced by more coherent PCFC policies.

The twilight of the binary system, from 1989 to 1993, was a time of rapid change in the polytechnics and colleges. The dynamism they displayed during that period justified the subsequent decision to establish a unified university system. However, the relationship between the post-incorporation reforms of governance and management and the polytechnics' dynamic performance should not be overstated. Industrial relations, estates management and strategic planning would still have been active arenas even without these reforms. The drive to replace corporatist bargaining with personal contracts and performance pay was a general phenomenon throughout the public sector during this period. The property boom of the late 1980s encouraged all institutions to develop ambitious estates strategies. Finally, the replacement of the NAB by the PCFC coincided with a 'dash for growth', which stimulated strategic planning.

The climate of the mid-1990s is different. Rigid national pay bargaining is unlikely to be revived. So the need for active personnel policies will not be reduced, although their focus may change from labour control to staff development. But the property boom shows little sign of reviving, which has frustrated the more ambitious estates strategies. And, the new policy of 'consolidation' of student growth has led to a return to planned targets, which makes strategic planning more difficult. To argue that the development of the polytechnics, now the 'new' universities, since 1989 owed nothing to incorporation is wrong, but it may be more of a coincidence than is commonly supposed. Internal reforms of governance and management were important, but external circumstances were probably decisive.

Two characteristics of the new corporate regime have provoked controversy. The first is the suggestion that the balance of power within the 'new' universities has been distorted by removing the old checks and balances. Senior management teams, whose members are not constrained, as they are in the 'old' universities, by a culture of collegiality, have become increasingly powerful, while the influence of academic boards has been downgraded. Second, governing bodies are not seen as sufficiently accountable, because 'independent' members effectively appoint their own successors. The charge is that 'new' universities, although public institutions, are governed by closed corporations. Also the balance between supervisory and managerial responsibilities remains unclear, leading to potential conflict between governors and chief executives. In combination these concerns can seriously destabilize institutions, as happened at the University of Huddersfield in 1994.

In both 'old' and 'new' university sectors institutions have become much larger and more complex. In the first wave of mass expansion, between the late 1950s and early 1970s, new institutions, whether the green-field universities or the polytechnics, were established. It was believed, first, that intimacy had to be preserved and that intimacy and size were correlated, and second, that existing institutions could not manage complexity. In the second wave, which began in the mid-1980s, no new institutions have been established. Instead, existing institutions have been expanded. The earlier beliefs have been tacitly abandoned. Intimacy is no longer regarded as important (or perhaps feasible) in a mass system. Or, if it is important and/ or feasible, the correlation with size is no longer accepted. And, as was argued in the first section of this chapter, institutions are now seen as capable of managing multiple missions without succumbing to 'academic drift'.

The average size of universities is rising rapidly, a significant shift because British universities until recently have been small by international standards. The University of London, the largest British university if the Open University is discounted, is still less than half the size of the University of California, which is typical of large American state universities despite its global eminence. But British universities are no longer dwarfed by other European universities. Seventeen English universities had more than 16,000 students in 1993–4 and 49, or well over a third of all HEFCE-funded institutions, more than 10,000. A revolution of scale has taken place. At the time of Robbins no non-federal or non-collegiate university had more than 8,000 students. Larger institutions, it was felt, threatened British higher education's fundamental qualities, its pastoral intimacy and its donnish collegiality. Arguably, it is mass institutions, not a mass system, which are the most powerful agents of culture change.

Size is not the only dynamic. As has already been pointed out, universities and (to a lesser extent) colleges of higher education have taken on multiple missions. Even if they have only grown slowly, they still have to cope with increasing heterogeneity, which takes three main forms. The first is the inexorable growth of specialisms and sub-specialisms. Although some of the most creative thinkers operate in the more open borderlands between disciplines, most routine science and scholarship still takes place within clearly defined frontiers. Specialization remains the dominant mode (although important shifts are under way, discussed in Chapter 4).

The second is the ceaseless adding of new roles. Universities in 1994 regard as core functions activities which they would barely have recognized as fringe responsibilities in 1964. Technology transfer and continuing professional development are good examples. The third is that institutional boundaries have become highly permeable, as partnerships are established with further education and the so-called 'corporate classroom' which was discussed earlier in this chapter. In its most radical form, under the impact of new information technologies, the university comes close to being redefined as a 'virtual' institution.

These much larger and/or more heterogeneous universities have to be managed in new ways. Institutions with fewer than 10,000 students, if their missions are uncomplicated and if their students are mainly full-time, can be managed along collegial lines; academic self-government assisted by a professional (but largely reactive) administration. However, collegial management, in its familiar and regretted form, may only be appropriate for institutions with a high degree of autonomy in an élite higher education system. In the emerging mass system it may have become a historic form rather than a current option. Universities with between 10,000 and 20,000 students need to be managed on different terms. A cadre of senior managers drawn from both academic and administrative staffs, assisted by professional managers in areas such as finance and personnel, develops. In this new corporate culture strategic and executive management replaces administration as the dominant mode.

However, the development of a mass higher education system may lead to a further shift, from 'managerial' to 'strategic' institutional cultures. Universities with approaching 20,000 students, a threshold already crossed by five and likely to be breached by several more before the end of the century, are new kinds of organization. The bureaucratic and hierarchical culture which grew up in the post-Jarratt, post-incorporation era, to cope with the internal shift from homogeneity to heterogeneity and with a more exacting external policy environment, may not be sufficiently flexible to manage these much larger universities. Outwardly stratified, by both market shifts and political action, and inwardly differentiated by radical reconfigurations of the cognitive structures and social practices of disciplines, these new universities may become 'unmanageable' – but with creative rather than destructive consequences.

Flexibility, synergy and volatility will be the dominant modes of these new organizations. Flat hierarchies and loosely coupled networks will abound. The senior management team will be more like a head office, and the cost-centred departments its 'production' units. Or, rather, the other way round. Senior management may become the departments' champion, its functions reduced to strategic planning, co-ordinating and audit functions. In the post-Fordist university even looser arrangements can be envisaged, in which departments are no longer required to buy 'services' (legal, personnel, estates) from their parent institutions, but are free to shop around. It becomes instead:

> more akin to a federation or constellation of business units that are typically interdependent, relying on each other for critical expertise and know-how. They have a peer relationship with the centre. The centre's role is to orchestrate the broad strategic vision, develop the shared administrative and organizational culture, and create the cultural glue which can create synergies.[64]

The mass university has two organizational characteristics – managerialism and reflexivity. The first is most marked during the early stages of the transition from élite to mass higher education, which broadly corresponds to the shift from 'collegial' to 'managerial' modes of institutional management. Universities are forced to become more robust organizations, partly to compensate for the decay of common academic and professional cultures, and partly to counteract the erosion of public trust, which has undermined most established institutions. (The latter phenomenon, the rise of risk society and decline of professional society, is discussed in the next chapter; and the former, the transformation of intellectual tradition, in Chapter 4.) In these early stages of mass higher education internal cohesion, in the absence of shared intellectual values, is provided by management structures, which are legitimated by managerialist ideology.

The second characteristic, reflexivity, is more marked in the later stages of the growth of a mass system, broadly corresponding to the shift from 'managerial' to 'strategic' institutional cultures. Management structures are eroded by volatile post-Fordist webs or mosaics. Consequently managerialist ideology is undermined. But, at the same time, intellectual and professional heterogeneities intensify. As a result, neither managerial nor intellectual principles, by themselves, can provide the mass university's 'cultural glue'. Reflexivity, by problematizing both traditional academic culture and managerialist ideology, may offer a strategy whereby these competing ethics can be combined. Through reflexivity it may be possible to elaborate a new language, or discourse, which enables the two concepts of 'mission', as grand rhetoric and as executive summary, to be reconciled by operationalizing the former and moralizing the latter.

3

State and Society

The extended élite higher education systems which grew up in Britain and many other advanced countries after 1945 were embedded in a political culture characterized by the growth of the welfare state; economic structures designed on the Keynesian principles of full employment and planned growth; a society in which the divisions of class and gender were diminishing but within an apparently stable social order; and a feel-good culture in which materialism and utopianism were powerfully combined. The mass system which developed in the United States at the same time was embedded in a similar socio-economic environment.

That environment has been transformed over the past two decades. The welfare state has been succeeded by the neo-liberal state; many public services, including health and education, have been moved into a privatized domain, if not the private sector. The Keynesian order has been overthrown and replaced by renewed enthusiasm for the free market; at the same time profound changes have taken place in the structure of the economy and the organization of enterprizes. Society has become increasingly fissiparous; classlessness and ungendering appear to have been accompanied by greater inequality and weakened the social cement of community. The motifs of contemporary culture are deconstruction, discordance and risk, qualities which slide readily from playfulness to pessimism.

It is this transformed environment which British higher education now confronts as it evolves from an extended élite system to a truly mass one. Other European systems, more advanced in this transition, confront the same environment. Yet, as was argued in Chapter 1, the only working model of a mass system, in the United States, grew up under different conditions. The exceptionalism of place, the American experience, has been compounded by the exceptionalism of time. The value structures and operating principles of American higher education, therefore, are unlikely to be reproduced in Europe, and especially in Britain. The British mass university will need to be constructed according to different values and on different principles.

This chapter is an attempt to explore these values and principles. It is divided into five main sections. The first explores the changing nature of the state; the second its implications for universities and colleges, in particular their relationship with government and how they should be funded, issues which have already been raised in a historical and empirical context in the preceding chapter. The third discusses the changing nature of the economy and society, phenomena generally labelled post-industrial or post-Fordist; the fourth their implications for higher education, in terms of inputs (or social demand) and outputs (or graduate 'careers'). The final section examines the various attempts which have been made to theorize modernity, or post-modernity.

The post-welfare state

Most universities are state or quasi-state institutions. Although many were established before the development of the modern bureaucratic state and a few even pre-date the emergence of industrial-urban society, their present scale and scope have been largely determined by political action. It is not unreasonable, therefore, to regard the modern university as intimately bound up in the welfare state. They are near-simultaneous formations. So any retreat from, or reach beyond, the welfare state is likely to have important consequences for higher education. These consequences, for example changes in funding and governance, would be significant even if higher education itself were in a stable condition. The fact that it is passing through a period of profound transformation means that their reverberations will be redoubled.

Talk of the crisis of the welfare state has become commonplace in recent years. *The Welfare State in Crisis* was the title adopted by the Organization for Economic Co-operation and Development in 1981 to describe the proceedings of a conference on social policies held in October of that year.[1] Even earlier in the United States doubts had been raised about the efficacy of the American version of the welfare state, the Great Society. In the mid-1970s Jeffrey Pressman and Aaron Wildavsky wrote a book called *Implementation*, the sub-title of which summed up this emerging critique: 'How Great Expectations in Washington are dashed in Oakland; or why it's amazing that Federal programs work at all, this being a saga of the Economic Development Administration as told by two sympathetic observers who seek to build morals on a foundation of ruined hopes'.[2] At the time these American doubts were dismissed as exceptional, another symptom of the United States' reluctance wholeheartedly to embrace the welfare state. Later in the 1980s such doubts, in the virulent form of moralizing neo-conservatism, were injected into the mainstream of European social thought, largely through the medium of Thatcherism in Britain.

Yet, during the very period in which this apparent backlash against the welfare state has gathered force, European higher education systems have been expanded and elaborated. This apparent contradiction has been most marked in Britain. The Thatcher and Major governments, far more committed to rolling back the frontiers of the welfare state than any other European government (as has been demonstrated by their opposition to the social chapter of the Maastricht Treaty), nevertheless presided over an expansion of higher education as remarkable as that undertaken in the high noon of the welfare state following the Robbins report in 1963. This suggests that the relationship between the growth of the welfare state and the development of modern higher education systems, although close, is also complicated.

Three issues are considered in the first section of this chapter. The first is the definition and underlying dynamics of the welfare state. The second, already raised in the preceding paragraph, is the relationship between higher education and other public services associated with the welfare state. The third is the evolution of the welfare state into new forms variously labelled the post-welfare state or the enterprise state.

The welfare state, broadly defined as a state in which social expenditure has become its predominant responsibility, is a pervasive form which transcends political cultures. Although there are leaders, typically the Scandinavian countries, and laggards, significantly the United States and suggestively the newly industrializing countries (NICs) of east Asia, similar patterns of public expenditure can be observed in almost all developed nations. Health, education and social security have absorbed an increasing proportion of both state budgets and gross national products, although there has been considerable variation in the detailed delivery of such services. The balance between this broad structural convergence and these continuing differences, which are ideological as well as operational, has been described by Harold Wilensky in the following terms: 'The welfare state is at once one of the great structural uniformities of modern society and, paradoxically, one of its most striking diversities.'[3]

According to his analysis, economic level is the root cause of the development of welfare state. But this broad correlation between wealth and welfare is qualified in three significant respects. First, although economic level determines a nation's logistical capacity to develop a welfare state, its political will to do so is probably influenced more by subjective perceptions of wealth. In short, a poorer 'feel-good' country is likely to be more welfare-state minded than a richer 'feel-bad' country. This may help to explain why there is greater ambivalence towards welfare states in the anxious 1990s than in the optimistic 1960s, despite a doubling of real living standards in many advanced countries. On the other hand, to the extent that the purpose of the welfare state is seen as alleviating absolute poverty and providing a safety net, its original rationale may have been undermined by rising material standards – or, at a minimum, may need to be reassessed in the light of radically changed circumstances. However, it is doubtful whether the mature welfare state can be seen in such reductionist terms. This argument is pursued later.

Second, the propensity to develop a welfare state is mediated through other structural features. The two most significant are demographic patterns

('If there is one source of welfare spending that is most powerful – a single proximate cause – it is the proportion of old people in population'[4]) and the maturity of social programmes. The first feature helps to explain why welfare states are more developed in western Europe, with its low birth rate and elderly population, than in the NICs with their very different demographic profiles. The second feature explains the contrast between leaders such as Sweden and laggards such as the United States. In the former the welfare state has flourished since the 1930s and been nourished by much older collectivist traditions. In the latter the welfare state is a comparatively recent and still sharply contested development, supposedly inimical to a long-established ethic of individualism.

Third, other factors come into subsequent play, hastening or slowing the development of welfare states. These include the perceptions of political élites; the influence of the intellectual climate based on both empirical research and partisan inquiry into the costs and benefits of the welfare state; popular pressures, whether to cut taxes or to increase expenditure (or, typically, both at the same time); and the inertia and/or momentum of welfare-state bureaucracies. All three factors are related. Perceptions of economic well-being, 'feel-good' factors, academic fashions and the maturity of welfare states reflect important differences in political culture and, at a deeper level, social ethic.

This volatile mixture of determining factors – some, such as economic level and demographic pattern, part of the deep structure of modern society and so relatively impervious to shifts in political fashion, and others, such as political and academic perceptions, more open to ideological reversal – has made it difficult to construct a stable and satisfactory model of the welfare state. In the 1960s the argument was between theories of convergence and divergence; in the 1990s it is between those who emphasize the essential continuity of the welfare state, with only minor modifications, and those who predict, whether gloomily or triumphantly, its decline and fall. The continuity thesis is supported by statistical evidence collected by the OECD. In 1993 in only one of the 14 leading industrial countries (which happened to be Britain) was the public sector debt proportionately lower than it had been a decade ago. Although part of the increase reflected higher state borrowing in a period of recession and, in particular, the cost of unemployment, these OECD statistics indicate that the public sector, dominated by social expenditure, has barely contracted at all, despite the palpable sense that the welfare state is in crisis.

However, it is possible to exaggerate the contradiction between continuity and decline-and-fall theses, certainly if these are seen as representing alternative social policy options. Part of the political backlash against the welfare state can be attributed to ideological factors. It is this aspect which has received most public attention. For that reason perhaps too much emphasis has been placed on the decline-and-fall thesis. But part of the 'backlash' is not really a backlash at all. Changes in the structure of the welfare state, for example the shift from universal to selective benefits and greater use of user payments, can be explained in terms of its foundational imperatives – economic level, demographic profiles and the inner dynamics of bureaucracies which manage social expenditure. The welfare state, accordingly, is being not so much repudiated as restructured.

Of course, there can be no doubt about the shift in the ideological climate. Twenty years ago Wilensky's verdict on the impact of the welfare state was an uncontroversial summary of mainstream political and academic opinion:

> The welfare state is in the process of humanizing industrial society. Over a century it has meant great gains in economic and psychological security for the least privileged; in the short run of each generation it produces some income redistribution. It is a prime source of consensus and social order in modern society, pluralist or totalitarian.[5]

Such a benign account is no longer acceptable – to the left or the right. The neo-conservative critique of the welfare state has been raucously promoted, especially in the United States where welfare-state values have never been properly incorporated into public doctrine as they have been in Europe. According to this critique, the welfare state is responsible for producing an under-class and, more generally, a dependency culture, which has sapped the spirit of enterprise on which wealth creation depends and undermined the ethic of personal responsibility.

More significant perhaps, although less obtrusive, have been left-wing critiques of the welfare state. Particularly influential among these left-wing critiques have been those from, broadly, a social-democratic perspective, because historically the welfare state was a social-democratic project. Marxist and neo-Marxist analysts have always emphasized how precarious, indeed illusionary, have been the gains attributable to the welfare state. For example, Immanuel Wallerstein argued that the welfare state reflected the interests primarily of the 'middle strata' of well-paid skilled workers (including, or especially, professional workers). Social-democratic reformers never had the power to 'destroy or even seriously cripple the economic viability of the network of world private economic and financial enterprises which they claimed to regard as their antagonist'.[6] The concessions they had been able to wrest from the upper strata were due to the latter's fear of communism, an interpretation reinforced by the parallel growth of the welfare state and the national security state. The National Health Service and the Red Army, allegedly, were once the two largest employers in Europe!

What was new was a shift of perspective among welfare-state liberals. The impetus for this often came from large-scale empirical inquiries into social mobility and class formation in advanced societies which enjoyed the assumed benefits of the welfare state. Accordingly this change provides a link between purely ideological shifts (neo-conservatives relied on partisan think-tank research rather than scientific university-based investigations) and careful reanalysis of the social effects of the welfare state – and, by extension, a bridge between continuity and decline-and-fall accounts of its likely evolution. For example, John Goldthorpe argued that social mobility in post-war Britain owed as much to rising living standards as to the development of the welfare state. He warned on the eve of the Thatcher revolution:

> If one anticipates a rather bleak economic future in which competition for higher-level class positions intensifies, and in which the resources necessary for setting social policies against class influences – apart from the political will to do so – will be harder to muster than before, then a decline in openness would seem to have a particularly high probability.[7]

Goldthorpe's conclusion was that there was no half-way house. Egalitarians had to recognize that the potential for social change was bound up in the potential for class conflict. A consensual welfare state was not an easy way out of this dilemma. Christopher Jencks had reached a similar conclusion at the end of his study of inequality in the United States a decade earlier. He believed that, in order to produce greater equality, it was necessary to change the mainstream economic institutions which perpetuated inequality rather than to devise ameliorative social programmes.[8] In the 1970s such conclusions tended to strengthen the case for more radical social interventions, and intensification of the welfare state. In the changed political circumstances of the 1980s and 1990s, certainly in Britain and America, they have contributed towards a culture of pessimism. The impact of neo-conservativism on social thought has been largely mediated through the morale of those who were once the welfare state's core supporters.

But the more critical attitude towards social expenditure can also be explained, perhaps more plausibly, in terms of the inner dynamics of the welfare state as well as of external ideological shifts. Although living standards have continued to rise, the once strong sense of economic well-being, which, rather than economic level, may be a more direct determinant of the growth of welfare states, has been dissipated by a number of factors. These include the crumbling of Keynesianism as a clear conceptual framework which underpinned, and validated, growth; increasing unemployment, which is no longer confined to the marginally skilled but now threatens the 'careers' of the skilled; and the penetration of global competition into every aspect of previously 'national' economies.

Each of these factors has deeply influenced attitudes towards the welfare state – the first towards its legitimacy, because the revival of liberal economics has reopened the arguments about (wealth-generating) private enterprise and (wealth-consuming) public services which Keynesianism appeared to have dismissed; the second towards its affordability, because the universal entitlements of the original welfare state assumed (fairly) full employment, so limiting the burden of social security, and safe jobs as a precondition of stable family patterns; and the third towards its practicality, because (with the possible exception of the European Union) welfare states must operate within the anachronistic framework of nation states. Each strengthens the case for a re-evaluation, although not a rejection, of the intellectual and operating principles of the welfare state.

The two other major determinants identified by Wilensky also strengthen this case. The growing proportion of retired people, the result of shorter working lives and increased longevity, was once a prime cause of the development of welfare states. Now, as the cost of providing pensions and health care for the elderly accelerates, this demographic profile has become a powerful motive for restructuring the welfare state. At the same time, the maturity of established welfare-state bureaucracies has provoked demands for their reform, which have been strengthened by suggestions that they provide secure and well-paid jobs for professional workers rather than being responsive to the needs of their less privileged clients.

In other words, there is no need to invent an ideological revolution to explain the transformation of the welfare state. The imperatives which created it in the first place are the same forces which are now remoulding it. The most powerful motive of governments, left as well as right, is the need to contain a welfare state which has been almost too successful, in expenditure terms although not necessarily in the arenas of emancipation and equality. In the middle of the Thatcher period Dennis Kavanagh wrote that he expected:

> there will be a new 'consensus' on social and economic policy, though it may be more difficult to obtain on the former, and . . . the new policy mix will include most of the social and welfare thinking of the old one and some of the economic thinking of Thatcherism. But rather than 'rolling back the state' the post-Thatcher era will have more to do with holding the line on state provision of welfare.[9]

'Holding the line' makes better sense than 'rolling back the state' as a description of most governments' stance towards the welfare state. A key issue here is the so-called 'sophistication factor', which applies in the social sphere just as much as in the industrial and commercial sectors. It affects the welfare state in two ways. First, even the most basic safety net must be defined in relative rather than absolute terms, because the poverty it is designed to relieve is itself a relative category. The safety net must be raised as material standards and, equally important, non-material expectations rise. Second, Fordist economies of scale, and perhaps also post-Fordist economies of scope, which are used by industry to square the circle by providing more sophisticated products at reduced cost, cannot easily be applied to the welfare state. Health care is the best example. While detailed productivity gains are possible, its overall 'success' is measured in high-technology operations and more sophisticated treatments, both of which lead to longer lifespans.

The case of higher education, although the impact of new technology on unit costs and productivity is more balanced, highlights an additional factor. Rates of return, certainly for the individual, tend to fall in response to increased 'investment' rather than the other way round. This is because higher education, like other welfare-state services, produces more 'positional' goods, the benefits of which are closely linked to their availability, than 'non-positional' goods, which retain much of their value even if they are widely distributed. Universities and colleges provide opportunities and life chances, both of which have a significant positional goods element. As these opportunities and life chances become more widely distributed, which is inherent in the transition from an élite to a mass system, their unit value tends to fall. This is demonstrated by the narrowing differential between graduate and non-graduate earning and employment rates. The general phenomenon of declining rates of return also tends to undermine the case for further investment.

The second issue, which has already begun to be addressed, is whether higher education is special, or whether it can be regarded as just another activity of the welfare state. Although some universities pre-date the welfare-state era, most were established during it. However, as has already been pointed out, their development pattern does not exactly match that of the welfare state, at any rate in Britain. Although the first great wave of expansion took place during the 1960s, when the welfare state was in the ascendant, the second wave in the late 1980s and early 1990s took place at a time when welfare-state values (if not structures) were under attack. One, perhaps trivial, explanation is that there may merely have been a time-lag between this second wave of expansion, the last manifestation of welfare-state higher education, and the imposition of a post-welfare-state policy framework characterized by 'consolidation' of student growth, increased efficiency, greater accountability to 'customers', a more robust management culture and a renewed interest in semi-privatization.

However, a more substantial explanation may lie in the pluralism of welfare states. This pluralism is expressed not only in terms of different national models but also in the diversity of welfare-state initiatives within individual nations. No welfare state was planned as a coherent whole. Even the most systematic tended to be centred around a key reform – in the case of Britain the establishment of a National Health Service – which created a context for other reforms. But many have developed through the accretion of social programmes, designed according to often incommensurable principles. This is the pattern in the United States. This contrast between organic and fissiparous welfare states has an important impact on how the degree of association between the reform of higher education and the development of other welfare-state programmes is interpreted.

In Britain the welfare state's core, moral and administrative, is in the health service, pensions and social security. The development of higher education is peripheral – to such an extent, in fact, that it may not be fair to regard it as a component of the welfare state at all. This distance between higher education and the welfare-state core was underlined by the fact that until recently British universities and colleges made up an élite system organized round notions of social selectivity rather than social mobility. In the United States, with its sprawling aggregation of social programmes without a core focus, the demarcation between higher education and other welfare-state arenas is much less clear. Furthermore, the key role played by a mass system in promoting social mobility represents a strong affinity with these other social programmes.

A second contrast can be drawn between the 'primary' welfare state concerned with social security, health insurance, public housing and unemployment benefit and designed to provide a safety net for the poor, and the 'secondary' welfare state in which political, social and educational institutions (including universities) are mobilized to promote a democratic culture and to encourage social mobility. A similar contrast can be drawn between an essentially reactive welfare state which acts to protect vulnerable individuals and groups, and a more proactive welfare state which seeks to reshape society through legislative, regulatory and redistributive policies. The role of universities in the 'primary' welfare state, as opposed to that of nursery schools, is limited. The links between higher education and the 'secondary' welfare state, although problematical (because universities may be an obstacle to, as well as an agent of, greater social openness), are more significant.

However, it can also be argued that, viewed in another light, the role of universities is still limited. Most state expenditure on education, and especially on higher education, is designed to promote more equal opportunities. It can be distinguished from expenditure on health, social security, housing and other 'primary' welfare-state services which is intended to produce more equal outcomes. The two, therefore, are different in kind even if they are subsumed under the title of the welfare state. A survey of expenditure patterns in the 22 richest countries in the 1970s found a small negative correlation between education and social security spending, although this finding was influenced by the weight of the United States where expenditure on education, especially higher education, is high and expenditure on social security low by international standards.

A third contrast, arising from the pluralism of welfare states, is between the welfare state as a collection of institutions and bureaucratic practices and the welfare state as a set of socio-political and professional values. The two are not necessarily congruent. The normative element in some bureaucratically elaborate welfare states is weakly developed. Conversely, some welfare states with a strongly articulated ideological purpose are institutionally underdeveloped. And normative elements have diverse origins. In the United States the development of social welfare programmes has been stimulated by the politics of race, an orientation which can readily be observed also in the priorities of American universities and colleges. In Europe welfare states have grown out of the politics of class, although religious and charitable traditions were also important motivating forces. The links between class politics and the development of European higher education systems are less direct.

The third issue is the evolution of new forms of the welfare state. The transition from the 'primary' safety-net welfare state to a more elaborate 'secondary' welfare state with a more active and interventionist agenda, which took place in many countries during the 1960s and 1970s, has already been briefly discussed. In the 1990s is the 'secondary' welfare state, in turn, being replaced by a 'tertiary' welfare state, semi-privatized in structure and enterprise- rather than equality-minded? The evidence is suggestive rather than conclusive. The shift from universal to selective benefits, the growing popularity of user payments, the tendency to distinguish between policy-making and service delivery (enabling the latter to be contracted out to non-state providers) – these, and other, significant changes can be observed in most welfare states regardless of their ideological foundations.

However, interpreting these changes is difficult. It has been argued here that they are better explained as 'holding the line' than as 'rolling back the welfare state'. But this does not mean that they are likely to be less radical in their effects. The pressure to control the upward pressure of costs produced by demography, unemployment and other factors is encouraging governments not only to reform delivery mechanisms, for example substituting private for public provision, but also to review fundamental principles such as universal entitlement to free services (at the point of use). The consistency of these responses reflects their structural origins. Ideological interpretations, which emphasize the triumph of an individualistic ethic over collectivism or private enterprise over state planning, are unsatisfactory because they fail to explain that consistency.

The 'tertiary' welfare state which is emerging in many countries, including Britain (although here it is obscured by ideological 'noise'), has two key features. The first is best described as a shift from a fiduciary state to a contractual state. This is clear in the case of higher education, not only in Britain but also in Sweden, the Netherlands and France. Governments are now less likely to see their responsibility for higher education as an absolute duty, the various components of which – social justice, economic efficiency, individual enlightenment and so on – cannot be disaggregated. Instead they have begun to see themselves as the purchasers, on behalf of tax-paying citizens, of a range of teaching, research and consultancy services. An important motive for creating such internal markets, of which the re-formed NHS is the best British example, is to promote efficiency through competition among providers. But it also opens the door to a wider range of paying purchasers – direct users such as students or patients, and indirect users such as their employers as well as the state.

In the contractual state the emphasis shifts from the state as provider to the state as regulator, establishing the conditions under which various internal markets are allowed to operate, and the state as auditor, assessing their outcomes. The first of these latter roles is a historic responsibility of the state. Indeed, it is possible to regard this renewed emphasis on regulation as a regression to a much older conception of the state, as the regulator of voluntary initiatives. Welfare states, of course, developed because this older conception of the state failed to keep pace with the demands of both the industrial and democratic revolutions. The state was obliged first to sponsor, then to fund and finally to organize such initiatives on its own account. In this respect the relationship between the state and the 'old' universities under the UGC regime was archaic. The state's role was largely confined to sponsorship and funding until the late 1960s (or, arguably, the early 1980s).

The second role is more novel, and has important implications for the evolution of the 'tertiary' welfare state. Instead of planning inputs, the state audits outcomes. This is a radical change in the means by which social control is asserted. According to Michael Power,

> audit is not just a series of (rather uninteresting) technical practices. It must also be understood as an *idea* . . . Audit has become central to ways of talking about administrative control. The extension of auditing into different settings, such as hospitals, schools, water companies, laboratories and industrial processes, is more than a natural and self-evidently technical response to problems of governance and accountability. It has much to do with articulating values, with rationalising and reinforcing public images of control.[10]

This is especially true with regard to the welfare state. Although the spread of the audit society is formally justified in terms of better governance and improved accountability, it plays a more influential role in articulating new values, a new political and organizational culture.

Again, compared to the rest of the welfare state, higher education may be untypical. In the 'old' universities little attempt was made to plan inputs, except in terms of broad aggregates such as overall student numbers and capital expenditure. Nor were serious efforts made until recently to audit outcomes, because of a lack of faith in manpower planning and because audit was seen as incompatible with academic freedom. In the 'new' universities most inputs (although not student numbers before the creation of the NAB) were tightly controlled up to 1989 and audit, in the shape of external inspection and validation, was also familiar. In either case, if Michael Power's prescription – 'a broad shift in control philosophy: from long distance, low trust, quantitative, disciplinary and ex-post forms of verification by private experts to local, high trust, qualitative, enabling, real time forms of dialogue with peers'[11] – is adopted, audit is unlikely to articulate new and alien values, or to lead to a significant shift in the inner culture of higher education.

The second feature is the transition from the welfare state to a welfare society, which reflects the broader shift from the corporatist state to civil society. This transition has several dimensions. One is the partial substitution of non-state welfare providers for state welfare bureaucracies, which has already been discussed. Another is the trend away from institutions. In this context the substitution of community care for long-stay hospitals and the increasing significance of distance learning, pioneered by the Open University, in higher education can perhaps be regarded as adjacent phenomena. As a result, the idea of the welfare state as an unambiguously public enterprise is likely to be weakened. Instead a co-mingling of public and private is likely to take place, which will make it increasingly difficult to establish a clear demarcation between them. The long-term importance of privatization may be not to shrink the public sector and expand the private sector but to create a new hybrid arena.

The most important dimension, however, is a shift of priorities. The welfare state was designed to operate in the arenas of health care, formal education, public housing and social security. Its agendas were instrumental, cumulative, progressive and materialistic. The welfare society, in contrast, is more preoccupied with quality-of-life issues, whether rebuilding the idea of community or safeguarding the environment. Its agendas are ethical, cyclical, post-materialistic, utopian even. As Fred Hirsch commented: 'Solutions that work have traditionally dominated solutions that have ethical appeal. The distinction is now blurred: to work it must be ethically defensible.'[12] This issue is discussed further later in this chapter.

The welfare state, albeit in this 'tertiary' form, remains the dominant form of political organization. The underlying social forces which produced it are as strong as or stronger than ever. The ideological counter-revolution has been exaggerated. Opinion poll evidence suggests there has been little change in underlying public attitudes on social policy. Structure, not polemic, is reshaping the welfare state. The pluralism of welfare states, both institutional and normative, is more likely to increase than to diminish, so retrospectively endorsing those who emphasized divergence rather than convergence. Although all advanced societies are influenced by similar socio-economic trends, the keynotes of that post-industrialism are themselves variation, flexibility and customization.

Conceptually, the place of higher education within the welfare state is hard to categorize. Its role in the closed social security model of the welfare state is limited, but it makes a key contribution to the open equal opportunities model. Historically, the articulation between higher education systems and the wider welfare state has followed no consistent pattern. In Britain up to the 1980s it was a weak relationship, because higher education was still an élite system and because the core of the welfare state was elsewhere. In other countries the links between universities and colleges and other social programmes have been closer. Prospectively, as the welfare state evolves into the welfare society and élite systems of higher education are replaced by mass systems, the articulation between polity and academy is likely to become both more complex and more direct.

Control and funding

These changes within the still dominant paradigm of the welfare state have a direct impact on higher education in two areas – the control exercised by governments over universities and colleges; and the funding of these institutions. In the first there has been a trend towards administrative devolution, although in Britain this has been obscured by the imposition of tighter political control and the establishment of formal audit and assessment systems. In the second there has been a trend away from total dependence on state funding; there have also been significant changes in the ways in which state funds are allocated.

The changing relationship between higher education and the state has already been discussed (Chapter 2) in historical and institutional terms in the context of the development of the British system (now systems). However, the evolution of the welfare state, which has just been described, casts new light on this relationship and enables it to be analysed in broader and more conceptual terms.[13] The rise of a new form of welfare state, plural rather than organic and contractual rather than fiduciary, means that state control of universities and colleges, as of all public institutions, has been transformed. This transformation has coincided, in Britain at any rate, with the emergence of a mass system.

The general effect has been to encourage convergence. State universities have tended to acquire greater operational (and entrepreneurial) freedom, as the emphasis has shifted from their absolute ownership by the state to new contractual relationships with governments designed to deliver specified services. Private universities, and those which traditionally have enjoyed a high level of autonomy, like the 'old' universities in Britain, have become increasingly bound to the state by similar contracts. This is an example of the erosion of the once clear demarcation between public and private characteristic of the post-welfare state. It fits the British pattern well. The former polytechnics, which were local state institutions until 1989, and the Scottish central institutions, which were regional state institutions until 1992, have been granted greater autonomy; the 'old' universities have become subject to more detailed controls.

To illustrate the implications of the new welfare state for the public regulation of higher education, it is necessary to identify, and discuss, the five models of university–state relations.

1. *Universities as state institutions.* This category includes nearly all higher education institutions in continental Europe, many state universities and colleges in the United States and, until recently, as has already been stated, the former polytechnics in England and the central institutions in Scotland. Typically university and college staff are state employees and their buildings state property. However, state universities often enjoy considerable autonomy, in terms of governance and academic affairs. In Europe university councils are broadly based, largely made up of elected representatives of teaching and non-teaching staff and students. Rectors are elected from among the professors. Most academic appointments, apart from chairs, are made by the institutions themselves. As has already been pointed out, state universities in several European countries, including the Netherlands and Sweden, have been given greater control over their budgets and buildings.

2. *Chartered and constitutional universities.* In this second category universities have either been chartered by the state or are protected by constitutional safeguards. As a result, they are distanced from the regular state

bureaucracy. Because their regulation is a legal or constitutional, rather than simply administrative, matter, their autonomy is notionally enhanced. In addition, powerful governing bodies, usually termed 'boards of regents' in the United States, often with long terms of office, have been established in order to insulate universities from short-term political pressures. However, these safeguards do not protect chartered universities from budgetary accountability, which may be exercised on a line-by-line basis. Many American state universities fall into this second category, as do many universities in Asia and Africa. Australian universities are also included, since the abolition of the intermediary Tertiary Education Commission in the late 1980s. Although both 'old' and 'new' universities in Britain properly belong in the next category, the former are chartered institutions.

3. *Arm's-length universities.* In the third category universities are public, rather than state, institutions. As well as being, in most cases, chartered institutions or independent corporations, they receive their funds not directly from the state, but indirectly through an intermediary body. That body, rather than a government department, may be responsible for the detailed planning of the higher education system within broad political guidelines. The 'old' universities in Britain (with the exception of the Open University, Cranfield Institute of Technology and the Royal College of Art, which were directly funded by the Department of Education and Science), fell into this category, receiving state grants through the University Grants Committee and later the Universities Funding Council.[14] The 'new' universities became arm's-length institutions in 1989, even before they were formally designated as universities. Arm's-length bodies are rare in the rest of Europe. The Swedish National Board for Universities and Colleges, which was an administrative agency rather than a buffer body, was abolished in 1992. In the USA state-wide bodies are responsible for funding, although generally the aim is to improve co-ordination rather than to enhance autonomy.

4. *Universities in the 'internal market'.* In this fourth category the relationship between universities and the state becomes looser still. Governments, directly or through agencies, establish 'internal markets' designed to encourage universities to be more efficient and responsive. Funding systems are used to generate competition rather than produce planned outcomes. However, two consequences flow from 'internal markets'. First, buffer bodies designed to insulate universities from political and market pressures are transformed into administrative agencies charged with managing 'internal markets'. The evolution of the UGC in its final decade and its replacement by the UFC are examples of this shift.[15] Second, to enable institutions to respond quickly and flexibly to 'internal markets', the burden of state regulations and public service procedures has to be reduced. But this liberalization can raise awkward issues of public accountability. So far, with the exception of the UFC's failed initiative which has already been described, few high-profile attempts have been

made to introduce 'internal markets' into higher education. Most American and continental European systems are funded by politico-bureaucratic allocations. However, market-like mechanisms have been introduced into many of these systems to manage marginal increases and decreases in funding.

5. *Private universities.* The state has no direct financial stake in this last category of universities. However, it may have a residual regulatory role, such as granting charters or authorizing the award of degrees, and it may also have an indirect financial stake, for example granting tax-exempt or tax-favourable status, or making students eligible for public support. In one sense, this is the least significant category. The University of Buckingham is the only example of a private university in Britain. There are very few private higher education institutions in the rest of Europe. The private sector is more prominent in Japan and, especially, in the United States. But, even in the latter, it is overshadowed by the public system and private universities and colleges have become increasingly dependent on public money, in terms of student support and research grants. In another sense, this fifth category is becoming more significant. Public higher education institutions are being discreetly privatized. More of their income now comes from private sources. This is true even of tightly regulated state systems in continental Europe and in the American states.

Two qualifications must be made about this typology of models of university–state relations. First, there is considerable overlap, and blurring, between these five categories. Some state universities, their staff employed and buildings owned by the state, have governance arrangements which nevertheless make it difficult for the state to interfere in their affairs. Politicians find themselves in the unenviable position of having responsibility without being able to exercise power. Some private universities receive almost as much state support as public universities. Arm's-length arrangements have ambiguous effects; protective buffer bodies may also be oppressive administrative agencies.

Second, this typology arguably is both too simple and too complex. These categories represent broad approximations which conceal wide-ranging operational differences. For example, a recent study of university–state relations in Europe and America demonstrated how much detailed controls over state institutions varied.[16] One response to this variation is to devise finer-grain typologies. Another is to simplify it. For example, according to Peter Maassen and Frans van Vught, a simple dichotomy is to be preferred as a conceptual framework, between state-controlled (types 1 and 2) and state-supervised systems (types 3 and 4), the former based on notions of rational planning and the latter more congenial to self-regulation.[17] In their view, state-supervised systems are more likely to encourage innovation and flexibility.[18]

Both qualifications are likely to become more significant as a result of the transformation of the welfare state. State regulation of higher education is likely to become less intense. State universities will be swept up in the wider movement towards contracting-out of public services. Other ministries, apart from education, and other public agencies will develop their links with higher education, on the basis of new-style contracts rather than old-style grants. The multiple missions adopted by mass systems will encourage this growth of plural university–state relations. In contrast, arm's-length universities are likely to find their traditional relationship with the state disrupted, as governments abandon their fiduciary responsibilities in favour of contractual links. Autonomy, as a principle of public policy as well as an operational requirement, may come to be seen as an anachronism. Finally, the blurring of the boundaries between public and private sectors will make the present distinction between state and private institutions, and between public and private income, less significant.

Changes in the funding of higher education, actual and argued-for, similarly reflect changes in the welfare state, in particular the growth of new partnerships between state, voluntary and private sectors. In Britain the opening-up of higher education has been accompanied by the state's effective abandonment of its near-total responsibility for funding the system assumed in the 1960s. As a result there has been a steady increase in the proportion of university and college budgets provided by non-state funds. A similar, although more modest, trend can be observed in the rest of Europe. This pattern is in sharp contrast to the experience of the United States during the two decades after 1945 when American higher education was transformed into a mass system. There, and then, the proportion of private funding fell sharply. The building of mass higher education was largely a public enterprise. The more open the institutions, the more complete their reliance on public funds. Expansion was concentrated in the four-year state colleges and two-year community colleges. The private sector's share of the market dwindled.

This contrast is important because it suggests that those who argue that there is an inevitable link between a move towards mass higher education and a retreat from state funding are wrong. If such a link existed, it would have been most obvious in the United States, with its immature and contested welfare state. Yet, it is in Europe, with its much stronger collectivist ethic, that the link is being made. This suggests that the retreat from state funding is not the result of the move to mass higher education *per se*; the opposite happened in the United States. Nor can it be explained in terms of Europe following the US example; although the US system has many private institutions, they are concentrated in the élite (or, at any rate, pre-mass) sector. Instead the key determinant appears to be the changing character of the welfare state itself. The US system went mass when the welfare state was in its 'secondary' phase; the British is going mass during its 'tertiary' phase.

Two features of the 'tertiary' welfare state are especially significant in connection with the funding of higher education. The first is the shift from a fiduciary to a contractual state. This, in turn, has had two major effects. One is the development of internal markets in which contracts are made between purchasers (the state or its agents) and providers of various teaching, research and consultancy services (universities and colleges). No longer is higher education funded at arm's length, as used to be the case in Britain under the UGC regime, because it is held to be in the highest public interest to maintain the freest possible universities. Nor is it funded as an internal state operation, as is/was the common pattern in the rest of Europe, because universities are themselves part of the state bureaucracy.

This is a crucial reconceptualization of the relationship between higher education and the state, which has already been discussed. In the short term, its practical effects may be limited. Only one serious attempt has been made in Britain to create a genuine internal market among universities and colleges, in which they would bid against each other for funded student places by setting their own prices. This initiative was taken by Lord Chilver, the first chairman of the UFC, in the late 1980s. It was a failure, partly because of its technical shortcomings but mainly because institutions formed an informal cartel and refused to compete against each other. More often existing patterns of funding have simply been rewritten as contracts. Competition has been confined to marginal bids for extra student places or for specially earmarked funds. But, in the long term, the imposition of a new discourse, the language of contracts, may reshape the terms of engagement between higher education and the state.

The other effect is that the public interest has been not privatized, but pluralized. The state is no longer regarded as a monolithic entity with an organic purpose. Instead it is seen as a collection of departments (or ministries) and other agencies, all with their own distinctive agendas. Often the private sector is involved in shaping these agendas. This new pluralism is different from the carefully contrived separation of powers, whether constitutional as in America or conventional as in the case of the UGC and similar buffer bodies, which characterized relationships between the state and higher education in the past. As a result higher education no longer has a single Rousseauesque contract with the state, but individual institutions (and even units within them) have a series of businesslike contracts with its various components.

The effects can be observed on the ground in Britain. Universities and colleges used to have a near-exclusive relationship with the funding councils (and antecedent bodies) which provided core grants, research councils which funded projects, and local education authorities which paid tuition fees on behalf of students, and, through them, with a single parent ministry, the Department of Education and Science. Today, in addition to relating to both the Department for Education and the Office of Science and Technology, they also have important funding links with a wide range of other departments and state agencies. In addition, new relationships have been established with the agencies of the European Union. Most of these new links are contractual in character.

The second key feature of the 'tertiary' welfare state is the fuzzy boundary between public and private sectors produced by the growth in contracting-out, the spread of user payments and similar phenomena. It is this change which has stimulated the search for non-state funding in higher education. Because British universities are public but not state institutions, and other European universities, although state institutions, are autonomous in character, higher education is one of the arenas in which hybrid funding is likely to develop first and most strongly. Yet the nature and purpose of non-state funding have not been properly analysed. The key issue is whether such funding is regarded as supplementary to state funding, or a substitute for it.

In Britain there is considerable support for so-called top-up fees. Under this plan, institutions would be encouraged to charge fees at a higher level than those paid by the state (through local education authorities in England and Wales, or directly in Scotland) on behalf of students. Students would be expected to make up the difference out of their own or family resources or by taking out loans, hence the 'top-up' label. There are no legal obstacles to top-up fees, although there are both equitable objections and uncertainties about their impact on demand. The fundamental logic behind top-up fees is that they are designed to supplement state funding which is perceived to be inadequate. As such the proposal reflects one characteristic of the 'tertiary' welfare state, the crisis of affordability. Seen in that light, the rapid expansion in the number of students can be equated with the growth in the number of elderly people.

However, other characteristics of the 'tertiary' welfare state support a different interpretation of non-state funding of higher education, as representing, at a minimum, a more balanced partnership between public and private income and, eventually, the partial substitution of the former by the latter. The result, it is argued, will be a mixed economy in higher education as in many other social policy arenas. Although at first sight more radical in its likely effects than proposals to supplement insufficient state funding, the emphasis on public–private partnerships and even substitution may more truly reflect the new dynamics of the welfare state. The plan for top-up fees, after all, endorses the hegemony of state funding, if only by drawing attention to its insufficiency. Among the motives of the supporters of top-up fees is the hope the state will be shamed into increasing public expenditure on higher education – or shoved into it by the mobilization of a vocal middle-class constituency very much attached to 'free' welfare-state services.

A broader interpretation which acknowledges, even endorses, substitution and no longer regards public funding of higher education as in any way privileged suggests two different outcomes. The first is that it enables a more pragmatic view to be taken about which classes of student should be expected to contribute directly to the cost of their higher education, and which should continue to receive 'free' higher education, and which courses should be full-cost and which should be low-cost or free. In practice, such choices are already made. Non-EU students in British higher education are charged full-cost fees; universities levy high fees for Master of Business Administration (MBA) and other management courses; and many continuing professional development courses are run on a profit basis. This privatized periphery is likely to grow at the expense of the publicly funded core – but in a piecemeal way.

The second outcome is that a principled debate becomes possible about the changing balance between the public good and the private benefits attributable to higher education. Central to this debate is the identification of the 'users' who should be charged – the state, both as a core provider and a contractor for specified services; other public agencies and private organizations, either as employers of graduates or as research and consultancy customers; and individual students. The last group already contributes to the cost of higher education both prospectively, because students are drawn disproportionately from higher social groups which pay higher taxes, and retrospectively, because graduates have higher lifetime earnings which again are subject to higher rates of personal taxation.

The burden on employers, on the other hand, is reduced because higher education is provided 'free' by the state. As a result, graduate employees do not have to take out loans for tuition, which they would expect to be able to pay back out of higher earnings. However, the suggestion that employers should pay more, perhaps by means of employment insurance surcharges, has generally been discounted. It would be seen as a tax on highly skilled labour, imposing an additional burden on companies already struggling to compete with companies in the NICs with much less elaborate, and expensive, welfare states. It would almost certainly reduce the demand for graduates, so eroding the income differential they enjoyed over non-graduates and making higher education a less attractive option for potential students. As highly skilled workers are the key to the high value-added products and high-technology enterprises of the twenty-first century, the result could be a significant decline in national competitiveness.

Consequently, the presumption is that, if the burden on the state is to be reduced, students themselves must make a direct, and more substantial, contribution to the cost of their higher education. But the case is far from clear-cut. It can be argued that in a mass system vocational-professional higher education becomes comparatively more important and liberal-academic higher education less significant. This tilt to vocationalism apparently endorses the belief that higher education is largely a private good, the value of which is reflected in higher lifetime earnings by individual graduates. On the other hand, as has already been pointed out, the differential between graduate and non-graduate earnings has been eroded. This suggests that graduates of a mass system, and certainly those from mass institutions, should not be expected to make such a large personal contribution to the cost of their higher education as the graduates of an élite system.

Even if it is accepted that user payments should be introduced in mainstream higher education, two distinct strategies are available. The first is to introduce a special graduate tax. The disadvantages are that it might discourage marginally motivated students at whom a mass system is particularly directed, and that hypothecated taxes impose intolerable limits on the state's freedom to determine its public expenditure priorities (and, therefore, never stick for long). The second is to charge students directly for tuition, but to establish a loans scheme. Nicholas Barr and Jane Falkingham have produced a useful analysis of the detailed effects of three different types of potential loan scheme.[19] The best working example is Australia's Higher Education Contribution Scheme (HECS). The disadvantages are that, in the short term, it would probably increase public expenditure because loans are more difficult to cash-limit than grants and because all students, even those who did not need them, would take advantage of low-interest state loans; and that eventual savings might be modest because of the need to address concerns about social equity, because of default difficulties, because low-earning graduates would have to be excused and because many graduates end up working for the state in some capacity.

The changes in control, already far advanced, and in funding, still to be realized, grow out of the larger changes in the character of the welfare state discussed in the first section of this chapter. But, as with the welfare state itself, they represent the continuation, and intensification, of existing trends rather than a clear break with the past. They reflect the inner dynamics of a higher education system caught up in the transition from élite to mass phases, which have been described in the last chapter. But these shifts in control and funding have been more decisively shaped by the outer dynamics of a welfare state in which that system is embedded.

Post-industrialism to post-Fordism

A profound transformation of western, now world, society and of advanced economies is under way which, as has already been argued, coincides intriguingly with the growth of mass higher education in Britain. The class formations produced by the industrial revolution, radically (but recognizably) modified by the rise of a post-war consumer society, have been further eroded by the rise of new, more voluntary and more volatile, identities. 'Work' has been reshaped by new technologies and new organizational patterns in industry and business. Commerce and culture have been globalized. These phenomena have produced far-reaching effects not only in how social life is organized but also in how it is conceived and experienced by individuals. Life chances and lifestyles have been conflated as the former have become more diffuse and the latter have been commodified. The demarcation between the public arena, rational and regulated, and the private world, intimate and affective, has become fuzzy.

A generation ago these trends were bundled together under the label of post-industrialism. The emphasis then was on economic and technological change. The post-industrial revolution of the later twentieth century, if a revolution at all, was analogous to the nineteenth-century industrial revolution. Its progress was likely to be patchy, gradual and incomplete. In the first comprehensive account of post-industrialism, Daniel Bell described the transition in terms of a stately schema emphasizing the shift from manufacturing to services, both private sector (predominantly financial) and public sector (such as health and education); from skilled production workers to scientists and other professional workers; from present-oriented empiricism to future-oriented abstraction; and, most crucially, from energy to information as the key technology.[20] The separate elements within his description were already familiar; the novelty lay in their implied congruence.

Today post-Fordism has replaced post-industrialism as the academic buzzword. In one sense the shift in vocabulary suggests a more limited transition. As a label Fordism describes a particular form of industrial society built round the mass production of consumer durables and its bureaucratic analogues in the business world and in government. It does not cover other forms of industrialism, smaller-scale, service-oriented, artisanal and craft-based, which in terms of employment if not of production were equally important (and on which Fordist mass manufacture and Weberian bureaucracy depended). But in another, and more significant, sense the shift from post-industrialism to post-Fordism suggests a more abrupt transition. Not just an economic system derived from particular technologies but an entire social system, indeed a whole set of ideological norms, is being transformed. The stately progression of social schemas has been replaced by paradigmatic revolution.

One reason for this changed perception is that the emphasis has switched from technological and economic change to wider social and institutional transformations. And the latter are no longer seen as passively growing out of the former but also as actively engineering them. Another is that the socio-economic phenomena so suggestively identified by Bell in the 1970s have both accelerated and coalesced in the 1990s. For example, the shift from manufacturing to services has intensified during the past two decades, nowhere more dramatically than in Britain. Also the erosion of traditional class loyalties – and so, arguably, identities – has entered a new and more radical (and irreversible?) phase, at any rate as expressed in voting behaviour. At the same time, the links between these various phenomena have become clearer. There has been a spate of best-selling books, mostly American, which have attempted to forecast the shape of twenty-first-century society.[21] Finally, post-industrialism apparently took its place in a developmental sequence, in succession to industrial society which, in turn, had replaced pre-industrial society. Post-Fordism implies no such long-haul linearity; only a rupture with the Fordist paradigm.

The development of mass higher education in Britain, therefore, is taking place when post-Fordist interpretations of socio-economic change have become popular, while in the United States the decisive shift towards a mass system took place when post-industrialism had only recently and tentatively been developed as an analytical framework. This is a key difference. Massification in Britain is more likely to be seen as only one, and perhaps

Table 3 Employees in industry (excluding agriculture) and services, 1960–81 (per cent)

	Industry		Services	
	1960	1981	1960	1981
West Germany	49	44	37	50
Sweden	42	31	45	63
USA	37	30	58	66
UK	49	36	47	61

Source: David Harvey (1990) The Condition of Postmodernity. Oxford: Blackwell, p. 157.

a subordinate, phenomenon within a much larger transformation. It cannot reasonably be regarded as an autonomous, distinct or self-referential episode. In contrast, the growth of the American multiversity in the 1960s was interpreted within a more traditional, and arguably anachronistic, framework of liberal values emphasizing democratic opportunity rather than socio-economic responsiveness. In other words, the disaggregated and, from the particular perspective of higher education, 'external' trends of the 1960s have become in the 1990s integrated and 'internal' trends.

The phenomena labelled either post-industrial or post-Fordist can be divided into three groups. The first comprises technological advances and changes in economic structure; these include the shift from manufacturing to services, the emergence of a global economy and the information technology/hyperautomation revolution in industry. The second embraces wider social and cultural shifts; these include the intensification of consumerism, the ambiguous rise of so-called post-materialism and the replacement of class-determined life chances by individualized lifestyles as the primary source of social identity. The third group includes intermediate phenomena, such as changes in the structure of organizations and the pattern of employment, which link 'work', or the economy, and 'life', or society.

The shift from manufacturing to services is generally regarded as the fundamental characteristic of post-industrialism / post-Fordism. However, although accelerating, this shift is a well-established trend. As Table 3 illustrates, industry's share of the labour force in most mature capitalist economies has been declining since mid-century.

These figures point to a number of conclusions. First, the shift appears to be common to all advanced economies regardless of their political cultures: welfare-state Sweden and free-enterprise America are equally affected. Second, the shift away from industry is least pronounced in West Germany and most pronounced in the United Kingdom. These figures cover the period before the deindustrialization of the early 1980s which flowed from the policies of the Thatcher government. The latest statistics suggest that almost three-quarters of employees in Britain are now in the services sector, and only one in five is in manufacturing.[22] Third, in 1960 the occupational structure of the United States was significantly more 'post-industrial' than those of the three European countries, but twenty years later the contrast was less marked. This convergence supports those who argue that a generic shift towards post-industrialism can be identified.

The reasons for this post-industrial shift are less clear-cut. One is the erosion of the manufacturing base in the older industrial countries, as factory jobs have been exported to lower-wage economies. But this is not a novel phenomenon; it is as old as empire. It is not even necessarily radical, if the once hegemonic economies of the West continue to monopolise high-technology, and high value-added, manufacturing. However, it does reflect an intensified globalization of economic activity, which is discussed later. A second reason is a shift in how jobs are categorized, as marketing, legal, advertising and other 'service' functions once provided in-house by large manufacturers have been contracted out to independent services companies. This can be regarded merely as a technical adjustment of job categories, although it reflects significant changes in the organization of industry, which is also discussed later.

A third is that investment in automation has produced far-reaching productivity gains enabling production to be expanded while cutting labour forces. So far, in terms of employment, the impact of robots in the factory, which can be seen as the intensification or culmination of Fordism, appears to have been greater than that of information technology in the office, arguably a purer manifestation of post-Fordism because it has more radical implications for how 'work' is organized and defined. The teleworking revolution looms. A fourth reason is that, because of the increasing velocity/volatility of advanced capitalist systems, the production of material goods, certainly durable goods with comparatively long lives, becomes less important than the production of ephemeral experiences, especially in the mass media, and of short-shelflife goods, for example in the fashion industry.

Nor are the implications of this shift from manufacturing to services for higher education clear-cut. The development of élite university systems was only obliquely and ambiguously related to the emergence of industrial society. The growing demand for university education from the expanding professional and public service classes was not matched by a reciprocal investment in the training of engineers, managers and other highly skilled technical workers. Comparatively few university graduates found jobs in manufacturing industry. Most went into service occupations, disproportionately in the public or quasi-public sectors. The development of the former polytechnics from narrowly focused technical institutions training higher industrial workers into much broader (and fuzzier?) professional institutions developing the generic skills required by service-sector workers owed far more to the dynamics of the jobs market than to so-called 'academic drift'.

Mass higher education systems, therefore, are not faced with a radical reorientation of their mission, in terms of graduate output, as a result of the emergence of post-industrialism. Instead they are likely to be affected in two different ways. First, massification is itself part of the post-industrial shift, because universities and colleges will form an increasingly significant component of the services-dominated economy. They are no longer 'external' to that economy as, arguably, they were to an industry-based economy. Second, mass higher education systems are primary producers of the events and experiences which are displacing consumer durables as the 'outputs' of advanced capitalist economies, as well as of the codified knowledge on which the production of high value-added goods depends and the symbolic knowledge in which social power is denominated. These issues are explored later in this chapter.

The second phenomenon associated with post-industrialism is globalization. This is more than internationalization, or multinationalization. It goes far beyond the development of international markets, which have existed for upwards of two centuries. It also goes beyond the development of international divisions of labour or shifts in competitive advantage between old smokestack unionized economies, national or regional, and new high-technology entrepreneurial economies. The growth of multinational corporations, the national affiliations of which amount to little more than now irrelevant historical accident and are largely determined by tax and other fiscal considerations, is only one aspect of globalization, although their power and prominence now make it difficult for national governments to determine their own economic policies.

It also makes it difficult to label companies and products. According to Robert Reich:

> The new organizational webs of high-value enterprise, which are replacing the old core pyramids of high-volume enterprise, are reaching across the globe. Thus there is coming to be no such organization as an 'American' (or British or French or Japanese or West German) corporation, nor any finished goods called an 'American' (or British, French, Japanese, or West German) product.[23]

But internationalization is only one aspect of this change. Equally significant, in Reich's terms, are the shifts from pyramids to webs (the top of the pyramid, head office, might be clearly American, or British, while webs link together more or less equal units in different countries) and from high volume to high value, much of which is derived not from manufacturing products at central sites but from design, marketing and other service components that are globally distributed.

The key to globalization, however, is the velocity of advanced capitalism which trades not only goods but also symbols (including, of course, that most powerful symbol, money, but also events, lifestyles and experiences), enabled by the new information technologies. According to Paul Kennedy: 'If major corporations have largely broken free from their national roots, this is even more true of the fast-moving, twenty-four-hour-day, border-crossing, profit-hunting system of international finance.'[24] The flows of foreign exchange trading are many hundreds of times larger than the flows of traded goods. In a single day deals are struck, and restruck, which exceed the value of the gross national product of most nations. Nor is foreign exchange trading an exception. It is merely the most striking example of the global market in financial instruments and other symbolic goods. The most powerful post-industrial image is of round-the-clock, round-the-globe stock-market trading, much of it controlled by sophisticated computer programs.

There are many affinities between globalization and the growth of mass higher education systems, not all straightforward. Universities, but not necessarily all higher education institutions, have always been international in their aspirations, even if, as was pointed out in the last chapter, most of them are rooted in national environments. Their internationalization has been accentuated by two new factors. First, international student flows have increased, partly for 'internal' reasons because in Britain, and many other countries, international students provide much needed income for universities, and partly for 'external' reasons because these flows reflect accelerating global mobility. A second, more speculative, factor is that universities are primary producers of symbolic goods, through their research and other knowledge outputs, which have assumed much greater importance in the global post-industrial economy, and also of problem-solving skills, through their graduates, which are needed to produce high-value goods.

However, it can be argued that mass higher education systems are inherently more national, even local, in their orientation than élite university systems.[25] Many more students will be part-time; most graduates will not enter élite occupations; and much research will be guided by more parochial user perspectives. A tension, therefore, may develop between global mission and local accountability which will be difficult to resolve. In Britain the growing popularity of the ungainly term 'glocalization' is evidence of this tension. On the other hand, in mass systems with a much clearer division of institutional labour élite universities may be relieved of their local responsibilities and allowed greater freedom to pursue their international ambitions.

Another, arguably negative, effect of globalization may be to erode the living standards of the traditional middle classes, whose ambitions have been largely responsible for the development of mass higher education systems. Or, at any rate, to erode their sense of security and well-being, the so-called feel-good factor. Globalization is closely linked to what Kevin Phillips has called 'financialization'.[26] He points out that the vastly increased trading flows, through stock-market brokerages and investment banks, which are typical of a global post-industrial economy, have not established a firm base for the creation of middle-class jobs. As a result incomes have failed to keep pace with economic growth. This can be interpreted as a one-off productivity adjustment. But the dynamics of globalization suggests it may become endemic. If this happens, the willingness of the middle classes to invest long-term, whether in housing or higher education, may be eroded. An awkward affinity would then arise between the undermining of middle-class life chances and the massification of higher education.

'internal markets' within the public sector. As was pointed out earlier in this chapter, the National Health Service reforms are the best example. Privatization of state industries and public services has also become popular. Since the fall of communism this policy has been obsessively pursued in eastern and central Europe. Finally, so-called market testing, which requires in-house services to compete with outside contractors, has become common practice in central and local government in Britain. All these policies are likely to have the effect of undermining monolithic bureaucracies, although the ideological intentions that lie behind them are neo-conservative rather than post-industrial. It is also possible to point to smaller firms, often operating at the high-technology frontier, which conform to the post-Fordist model outlined in the preceding paragraph. Even large corporations, and bureaucratic institutions, have experimented with cost-centring (in universities), devolved budgets (in LEAs), and flexible work teams (in manufacturing plants).

However, the post-Fordist shift can easily be exaggerated. Many of these initiatives are designed to modernize, not to abandon, control mechanisms. According to J. K. Galbraith, the large corporation remains the dominant organizational form, even if its authority is now exercised through financial protocols and service standards rather than standardized production processes. It is a key instrument in consolidating the 'culture of contentment' which, in his view, is more typical of the late twentieth-century world than post-Fordist volatility. The 500 biggest US companies still account for more than half of America's economic output.[30] Nor is the alleged hegemony of the post-Fordist organization easy to reconcile with Peter Drucker's schema of industrial change. According to Drucker, the industrial revolution, based on technologies which systematized craft working, was succeeded by the productivity revolution, associated with Fordist mass production and Taylorist scientific management, both of which aimed to disaggregate labour and other inputs. This Fordist paradigm has been succeeded in turn by the management revolution. In this most recent phase management, not production, is the key activity.

The implications of post-Fordist organizations for higher education have already been discussed, in the last section of the previous chapter. Those conclusions will not be repeated, except to re-emphasize that institutions in mass higher education systems, characterized by organizational complexity and multiple missions, cannot be treated as if they were either small-scale, high-technology companies or monolithic bureaucratic or corporate organizations like the NHS or ICI. Instead, they belong in the middle range of organizations that are least susceptible to post-Fordist change. They cannot match the flexibility and volatility of the former, ceaselessly reconfiguring; nor do they possess the (over?)elaborate management structure typical of the latter. The superficial similarity between the post-Fordist firm and the collegial university is treacherously misleading.

There can be less doubt about the second of these mediating phenomena, the changing patterns of employment. Three trends are clear. Unemployment

Table 4 Unemployment, 1976–92 (per cent)

	1976	1984	1992
UK	5.6	11.7	9.9
France	4.4	9.7	10.3
Germany	3.7	7.1	4.6
Netherlands	5.5	11.8	6.8
Australia	4.7	8.9	10.7
Sweden	1.6	3.1	4.8
USA	7.6	7.4	7.3

Source: Central Statistical Office (1993) *Social Trends 1993*. London: HMSO, p. 62.

has risen; self-employment has increased; and the proportion of part-time workers has also grown. Moreover, similar trends can be observed in nearly all advanced countries, as Table 4 demonstrates. Although there are interesting variations, the general pattern is clear. Overall unemployment is significantly higher in the early 1990s than it was in the mid-1970s. And it appears to be a structural rather than cyclical phenomenon.

Self-employment in Britain increased by 16 per cent between 1986 and 1993, from 2.5 to 2.9 million. During the same period the number of employees fell slightly from 20.9 to 20.8 million.[31] Also the number of part-time workers rose by 55 per cent, in the case of men, and 16 per cent, in the case of women, between 1983 and 1993. The number of full-time male workers actually fell during that period.[32] However, there is evidence to suggest that much of this increase in part-time work was involuntary. Barely a third of men and less than half of unmarried women actively preferred to work part-time. Many of the self-employed have been the victims of redundancy. As a result, interpreting these shifts is not easy. Although they generally support the contentions that a more flexible (and entrepreneurial?) post-Fordist workforce is emerging and that the total amount of 'work' is shrinking, other factors are at work.

One certainly is a squeeze on labour costs, made easier by the secular shift from manufacturing, where trade unions have traditionally been strong, to services, where union organization is more limited. Part-time workers are cheaper. According to the latest US census (1991), full-time workers make up 62 per cent of the workforce but receive 82 per cent of the aggregate payroll, while part-time workers, who make up 38 per cent, only receive 18 per cent. According to John Tomaney, restructuring (which he is reluctant to label post-Fordist) is still largely determined by the balance of power between management and workers.[33] Post-Fordism, therefore, may simply be the latest form of labour intensification. Another factor is the impact of the gender revolution on the labour market. Women are getting a fairer share of the full-time secure jobs once monopolized by men. But men are losing more than women are gaining. The overall trend is towards less secure forms of part-time or self-employment.

Mass higher education systems are implicated in these shifts in employment in two senses. First, their own employment structures have followed the same broad pattern. The number of core, full-time and permanent, jobs has declined, while the periphery of short-term contract employees and freelance sub-contractors has expanded. As a result, the character and balance of the academic profession have changed. In this respect higher education teachers have been affected in the same way as many other professional workers, although it is difficult to distinguish between short-term ideological and long-haul structural factors. Harold Perkin emphasized the former, regarding the current check to professional society as an ideological backlash, produced by leftist suspicion of established expertise and rightist enthusiasm for free markets.[34] However, even if there had been no general reaction against professional privilege, massification would still have led to some degree of casualization among university and college teachers. Second, university and college graduates must now be prepared for a world of flexible employment. This is discussed in the next section.

The third group of phenomena associated with post-Fordism embraces social and cultural trends, some contingent on the technological and economic changes which have just been discussed and others which have promoted these changes. The first is the intensification of consumer society. This goes beyond the shift from manufacturing to services, or from durable to symbolic goods. At its root is a shift in social behaviour and individual motivation. Consumers behave in different ways from producers. The former are impulsive and affective, seduced by desirable lifestyles, while the latter must be disciplined and rational, determined to secure improved life chances. In industrial society individuals were producers first and consumers second; in post-industrial these roles are reversed. It is no coincidence that the hedonistic consumer first attracted attention in the 1950s when the balance of mass-production economy switched from industrial to consumer goods.

David Riesman intuitively explored the contrast between the 'inner-directed' personality, disciplined to defer gratification and dutiful towards inherited norms, and the 'outer-directed' personality, searching for present pleasure and prey to peer pressure.[35] This shift contained several elements: a new idea of time as the extended present rather than a flow from past to future; the erosion of vertical, inter-generational, authority and its replacement by horizontal, intra-generational, loyalties; an emphasis on the advanced capitalist system's production of surplus time, the (re?)invention of leisure, rather than its exploitation of surplus value by intensifying the labour process. All these elements have suggestive connections with the larger phenomenon of acceleration which is at the heart of all futurist theories of social change.

But an important element in this shift from 'inner direction' to 'outer direction' was the dynamics of the post-industrial economy. As production switched to more ephemeral goods, it became necessary to accelerate consumption accordingly. Gratification had no longer to be deferred, as in an investment economy, but anticipated. The devices of anticipation were easily available credit, which produced high levels of personal indebtedness, that led in turn to inflationary fiscal policies (because that debt needed to be serviced, hence upward pressure on wages, and its overall burden reduced). At first, the hedonistic consumer was regarded as a threat to the rationalizing and economizing modes characteristic of the technological and industrial arenas. According to Daniel Bell:

> The interplay of modernism as a mode developed by serious artists, the institutionalization of those played-out forms by the 'cultural mass' and the hedonism as a way of life promoted by the marketing system of business, constitutes the cultural contradictions of capitalism.[36]

Today it is the synergy, not the contradictions, which is striking. Modern art, at its highest level a challenge to the banal rhythms of rationality, in its derivative form as lifestyle images which can be produced, and reproduced, at an ever faster rate, has become an accomplice in the regime of capitalist accumulation. The sumptuary affluence of high-consumer society, however much it may offend the rationalizing modes typical of an earlier stage of economic development, is a necessary component of post-industrial production. Indeed, it may not be an exaggeration to argue that hedonism, sumptuary consumption, 'outer direction' and similar essentially cultural phenomena can no longer be regarded simply as the outgrowths of a particular stage of economic development; rather they have become key inputs, prime determinants.

This casts a new light on the growth of mass higher education. In the past higher education was seen as an investment good, even if that investment was in extending democratic opportunities as well as promoting economic efficiency. In élite systems individual rates of return were high. Nevertheless, higher education was acknowledged to be a public responsibility. Everyone would benefit from investment in higher education in the long run, not only those who participated directly. This was the predominant view during the first wave of post-war expansion in Britain, at the time of the Robbins report, and during the development of the American multiversity. However, higher education is now more likely to be regarded as a consumption good (although, paradoxically, individual rates of return have fallen). As a result, the case for regarding it as essentially a public responsibility has been weakened. The second wave, therefore, the development of mass higher education in Britain, is taking place in a changed socio-political climate and in a very different economic context.

It is possible to argue from some characteristics of post-industrialism that investment in higher education should be intensified. Universities and colleges, as key organizations within a wider 'knowledge' industry, are now primary producers of wealth. 'Knowledge' has succeeded energy as the basic resource. But other characteristics point to a different conclusion. If mass higher education is seen as part of a sumptuary and hedonistic society, and is associated with lifestyles rather than life chances, it becomes more difficult to argue that it should be treated differently from other forms of consumption. Of course, higher education is *both* investment in economic efficiency and enhanced life chances *and* consumption of desirable lifestyles and symbolic goods more broadly defined. This ambiguity is reflected in the multiple missions of the mass university discussed in the previous chapter. But, under post-industrial conditions, the balance may be shifting, from investment to consumption. It is at this interesting, but awkward, moment that Britain has developed a mass system.

The second socio-cultural phenomenon associated with post-industrialism is so-called post-materialism, a term first given widespread currency by Roland Inglehart in the 1970s.[37] The idea is simple in outline. As material needs are satisfied, consumers will increasingly seek non-material, or post-material, satisfactions. These satisfactions, it is argued, are likely to take several forms – a preference for social benefits rather than (or, more realistically, in addition to) private goods; a new emphasis on the non-material conditions of work; a heightened sensitivity to environmental issues, and so on. There is suggestive evidence to support this thesis, at any rate among the young and more privileged.

But interpreting the dynamics of post-materialism is difficult. According to one version, it arises because material needs have been largely satisfied. Surplus income and time, therefore, must be spent elsewhere. But, once basic subsistence has been achieved (which itself is difficult to define because increasingly it must be defined in social rather than biological terms), material needs become highly variable and relative. The ingenuity of advanced capitalism in inventing new needs is almost without limit. Indeed, such ingenuity is one of the most important characteristics of a post-industrial economy. According to a second version, post-materialism is a reaction to the *anomie* of high-consumer society, a very different orientation: the New Left of the 1960s transformed into the New-Ageism of the 1990s.

Closely linked to post-materialism is another phenomenon, social scarcity. Again the idea is straightforward. Forty years ago Roy Harrod[38] drew a distinction between 'oligarchic wealth', privileges which could not be widely distributed without being destroyed, and 'democratic wealth', which could be made freely available. This distinction was reiterated, and relabelled, by Fred Hirsch, in terms of individual and social opportunity. Some goods, such as health care, are 'non-positional'; in other words, their individual value is not affected by mass availability. Others, such as cars (and degrees?) are 'positional'; the more there are, the less they are worth. He reached a pessimistic conclusion:

> A major adjustment needs to be made in the legitimate scope for individual economic striving. Individual economic freedom still has to be adjusted to the demands of majority participation. The traditional availabilities, grounded by circumstances in minority status, now represent an overload.[39]

Two interesting questions arise. First, is post-materialism produced by material surfeit, as Inglehart suggested, or by social scarcity, as Hirsch argued?

No single or simple answer is available. The evidence for post-materialism, as an alternative to rather than simply an elaboration of consumerism, is slight, outside the ranks of the New-Ageists. It may be better seen as a particular form of high-status sumptuary behaviour. But neither is there much evidence to suggest that the social limits of growth have been acknowledged by consumers. Rather they have led to intensified competition for 'positional' goods, because the penalties suffered by those who do not possess them have sharply increased. The continuing demand for places in higher education and declining opportunities for non-graduates illustrate this point. Second, has the rise of post-Fordism transcended the terms of the post-materialism debate? In an economy increasingly dominated by services, producing symbolic goods and characterized by flexible employment, it becomes more difficult to distinguish between buying a car and an opera ticket, or being a corporate employee and a community activist.

Nevertheless, post-materialism and social scarcity are troubling concepts for higher education. They imply that mass systems, which have grown up alongside these phenomena, should be regarded either as distinct from the 'real' economy, the icing on the cake of a sumptuary society; or a bastion of alternative, anti-consumerist, values; or as a 'positional' good, which must be rationed if it is to retain its value. None is appealing. The first and second characterizations are not consistent with the synergies between mass higher education and new class formations and employment structures, discussed in the next section. The primary characteristic of the mass university is its reflexivity. The third is more plausible. At first sight, higher education offers a good example of those traditional liberal opportunities which, according to Hirsch, 'offered to the majority, are available only to a minority'.[40] But, although there are some characteristics of higher education – rates of return certainly and academic standards arguably – which are likely to be affected in this way, massification itself is a process deliberately designed to transcend these élite constraints.

The third, and most significant, of the socio-cultural phenomena associated with post-industrialism is the erosion of class as the primary determinant of social identity. Post-industrial change has wider reverberations. According to Stuart Hall:

> Post-Fordism is also associated with broader social and cultural change. For example, greater fragmentation and pluralism, the weakening of older collective solidarities and block identities and the emergence of new identities associated with greater work flexibility, the maximisation of individual choices through personal consumption.[41]

These older solidarities, rooted in the social class identifications produced by the employment patterns of the Fordist age with its large-scale factories and complex corporate bureaucracies, are giving way to new identities, based on race, gender and region and, as Hall suggested, on more individualized lifestyles within, paradoxically, a more integrated consumer culture. Some dispute the decline of class. The Oxford Mobility Project found little evidence for such a thesis in the 1970s and no equivalent large-scale empirical inquiries have been undertaken since. Instead John Goldthorpe and his colleagues identified a different phenomenon, the 'maturation' of the working class, which was smaller but more cohesive and now predominantly second-generation because of declining inward migration from the countryside and reduced downward mobility from an expanding middle class. This interpretation they preferred to the counter-account, of a more porous working class within a more fluid class structure.[42] Also the emergence of a 'service' class, drawn overwhelmingly from the old middle class but containing upwardly mobile members of the working class and so, arguably, above-class, depended far more on economic growth than social mobility.

On the other hand, there is evidence to suggest that class identifications, if they are not being eroded, are becoming more volatile, because they are determined more by patterns of consumption than by employment structures in a post-industrial society. The outcomes have been ambiguous. Convergence can be observed. Writing of the period 1945–70, the high tide of professional society, Harold Perkin argued:

> There came into being a kind of average life-style, home-centred, family-oriented, servantless, with leisure time devoted to home-based activities, television-watching, gardening, do-it-yourself decorating and house improvement with weekend car trips to the country or the seaside, and annual holidays in Britain or abroad, a life-style which encompassed a growing majority of the population.[43]

With minor amendments, Perkin's account could have described British society at any time between the 1920s and the 1990s.

The spread of a homogeneous middle-class-like culture, if a myth, is a powerful one. It is consistent with the accounts of working-class life (Richard Hoggart's *The Uses of Literacy* is the most famous[44]) which emphasized 'bourgeois' respectability rather than 'proletarian' consciousness. And it is supported by evidence of consumption patterns. According to the latest figures, there are only small differences in the percentages of televisions, telephones, washing machines and video recorders possessed by households in the highest (professional) and lowest (unskilled manual) socio-economic groups.[45] It is difficult to reach firm conclusions in the debate about the decline, or the survival, of class because some accounts, such as Goldthorpe's, are empirically based, and concentrate narrowly on job classifications, while others, such as Perkin's, are more intuitive and address broader cultural identifications. The first measure life chances, which arguably have become more unequal; the second measure lifestyles, which are promiscuously available. In industrial society life chances were the dominant category for social analysis; in post-industrial society they may have been replaced by lifestyles.

However, these new social identifications are also more divisive. First, they tend to erode a sense of community. Class identities helped to re-create, in an industrial and urban environment, the familiarities and loyalties characteristic of pre-industrial society. In post-industrial society the growth of flexible employment inhibits the development of work-based social networks, while the individualization of consumer choices and privatization of social life reduce the scope for other forms of interaction and co-operation. The cement of society crumbles. According to Jon Elster, social order depends on both threats, or community sanctions, and promises, or community rewards. 'Scientific, technical, economic and social development tends to erode the ability to make credible threats and promises, by undermining social norms.'[46] Social norms are undermined by mobility and volatility, the process of acceleration characteristic of post-industrial society, because threats and promises become less credible.

Second, social identifications rooted in race and gender are more determinist than those derived from class. The fluidity of class has made it less satisfactory as an identifier in mass society. Arguably individuals have fallen back on older, and more rigid, identifiers. Certainly the importance of the politics of race, notably in America; of the gender revolution, everywhere in the advanced world; and of nationalism, in benign forms in western Europe and more virulent forms elsewhere, cannot be denied. Accounts of post-industrial change find these phenomena intractable, with the possible exception of the gender revolution. They emphasize instead the replacement of given social identities, such as class, by chosen identities, based on individualized lifestyle choices (including participation in post-compulsory education). However, it is important to recognize the significance of the reaction to flexible and volatile patterns of social identification, as well as the power of post-industrial cultural change.

The growth of mass higher education is deeply implicated in these currents, and counter-currents, of social transformation. Access to universities and colleges remains largely determined by social class, despite the expansion of the system and erosion of class identities. Yet, at the same time, massification is among the most powerful instruments of social change, in a double sense. First, mass higher education systems reproduce, and revise, the division of economic labour, no longer only among a small and stable élite but in a more extensive and more volatile arena embracing large parts of society. Second, these systems are themselves manufacturers of new forms of social identity and status which have begun to supersede older categorizations. These issues will be discussed in greater detail in the next section of this chapter.

The final issue to be addressed in this section is whether the eight phenomena which have been discussed justify the grand claims made on behalf of post-industrial society. In particular, can the grander claims of post-Fordism be sustained? Although there can be little doubt about the importance of the various trends which have been described – the cumulative shifts from manufacturing to services; from industrial goods to consumer-durable goods, and then to symbolic goods; from corporate bureaucracy to flexible organization; and so on – and although there can be no doubt either about the acceleration of these trends in the late twentieth century in the key economies of the developed world, their aggregate effect remains contested.

Two broad views have been expressed. The first emphasizes sequential socio-economic revolutions in a grand succession of Kondratieff waves. Each wave has been made possible by quantum gains in productivity, matched by radical innovations. For example, the Fordist economy, produced by the fourth wave, was based on electro-mechanical technologies, the products of mass manufacturing industries, and, as an energy source, oil and petro-chemicals. The fifth wave relies on the same combination of enabling technologies, novel patterns of production (and consumption), and new energy sources. Micro-electronics is the change agent of the late twentieth-century economy, just as oil was half a century ago, and steel in the Victorian age.

According to this view, technological and economic forces predominate; institutional, social and cultural change are subordinate and secondary. Information technology, the key source of productivity and innovation in the fifth wave, requires 'a full-scale reaccommodation of social behaviour and institutions'.[47] Also, the process of change is linear, despite the radical discontinuities which can be observed as one wave succeeds another. This interpretation, although it is consistent with schemas of post-industrialism which focus on technological and economic change, is more difficult to reconcile with the grander claims of socio-cultural transformation and paradigmatic revolution made by post-Fordism.

The second view adopts a dialectical rather than linear perspective. Post-Fordism is much more a rival than the successor of Fordism. The latter is represented by mass production; the former by so-called flexible specialization. In the early and mid-twentieth century mass production came to dominate the economy, relegating craft production to a subordinate (although never negligible) role. Today, changes in production, principally the hyperautomation made possible by new computer-based technologies, and in consumption, the demand for non-standard high-quality goods, have undermined the Fordist paradigm. Craft production, in the guise of flexible specialization, is fighting back. Mass markets are being disaggregated into customized niches. The emphasis on small and medium-sized businesses as the cutting edge of economic development rather than big corporations, the growth of self-employment, even the re-emergence of a sweatshop economy staffed by the under-class are concrete examples of the rise of flexible specialization.

According to this second view, post-Fordism is far more than a shift in the dominant mode of production. It also implies the abandonment of the employment structures, key technologies, consumption habits, social practices, configurations of political power and cultural styles associated with industrial society. Indeed, these abandonments are as much responsible for the shift in production as the other way round. In other words, the transition in the regime of accumulation, from industrial to post-industrial society, reflects a transformation of the mode of social, political and cultural regulation, from Fordism to post-Fordism and from modernity to post-modernity.

There is a third view which interprets post-Fordism in neo-Marxist terms, as the response of advanced capitalism eager to exploit technological changes, the growth of more heterogeneous patterns of 'work', the erosion of class solidarities, the rise of hedonistic consumerism and other phenomena as opportunities in order both to accelerate production and to intensify the labour process.

Choosing between these two broad views is difficult. It may also be unnecessary. Empirically they share much common ground. Their disagreement is conceptual. At this stage it is the empirical phenomena labelled post-industrial which are of interest in developing this account of the growth of mass higher education. In the next section the implications of these phenomena for the inputs (social demand) and outputs (graduate careers) of universities and colleges are examined. The fundamental conceptual question of whether mass systems are better regarded as extensions of élite systems, or as replacements for them, is addressed in the final chapter.

Inputs and outputs

The immediate issues which arise from this discussion of post-industrial society concern its impact on inputs to higher education – in effect, new patterns of student demand which themselves reflect shifts in social stratification (and identification) – and on outputs from the emerging mass system, principally the changing shape of graduate 'careers'. Inputs and outputs are closely linked, because both are aspects of the wider socio-economic articulation of mass higher education, which is distinct from the way in which élite systems related to their external environments.

It was argued in the preceding section that one of the characteristics of post-industrial society is that socio-economic status is coming to depend less on the givens of class and gender and more on attributes, such as educational level and cultural orientation, over which individuals have some control (however strong the historical correlation between such attributes and class origins). It was also argued that socio-economic status could no longer be derived alternatively from occupational level, because of the rise of flexible employment and the adaptable organization; instead it was more likely to be associated with broader socio-cultural attributes labelled lifestyles. If either, or both, of these arguments is true, it suggests that mass higher education systems play a more active role in determining social hierarchies. They no longer simply mediate, as élite university systems arguably did, between entrenched class structures on the one hand and the inflexible division of labour produced by industrial society on the other.

The key quantitative changes in inputs to British higher education were described in the previous chapter. The participation rate among 18–20-year-olds has doubled from 15 per cent in the mid-1980s to 32 per cent in the mid-1990s. Also the participation rate among 20–24-year-olds has risen to 10 per cent, with the result that a third of entrants to universities and colleges are now aged 21 and over. Two social trends have been particularly influential. First, middle-class participation has become universal. A significant proportion of the middle class did not participate in élite higher education, preferring to follow traditional apprenticeship routes into the professions and business. For anyone who enjoys, or aspires to, middle-class status participation in mass higher education has now become compulsory. Second, participation by women has risen sharply, and now approaches parity with men. Between 1987 and 1992, during which period the second wave of post-war expansion was at its peak, the number of full-time female students increased half as fast again as that of men.[48]

Taken together, these trends suggest a modification of the highly competitive culture of élite higher education. For working-class students entry remains competitive, and arguably meritocratic, because it is open to only a minority of their peers. But for middle-class students, who form the majority, a higher education, by itself, offers a reinforcement of their (actual or aspired) social status rather than a significant competitive advantage in the employment market. Increased female participation is also significant. Although the impact of feminism and shifting gender relations have been important factors in increasing participation, the feminization of mass higher education may reduce the competition for occupationally determined and career-driven status – which, in any case, is being undermined by the broader secular trends which can be observed in the post-industrial economy.

The lessening of competitive pressures reflects a shift from opportunity to entitlement (and, then, to contentment?) in mass higher education systems, for those social groups which have been embraced within an expanding 'college culture'. But, paradoxically, the disadvantaged minority may be more categorically excluded. According to Robert Anderson, a tripartite social structure is developing, shaped more like a pear than a pyramid:

> At the top, a large and assured upper middle class, open as always to new money, which has come to take higher education for granted, and uses the school system to secure it; in the middle a broad amalgam of the middle and upper working class, a group . . . which has gained most from state education and the public financing of universities; and the remainder of the unskilled and socially deprived working class, concentrated in inner cities or peripheral housing estates where access to high-quality secondary schools is difficult, and culturally less disposed to seize educational opportunities than the old skilled working class from whom the classic scholarship children were drawn.[49]

As a result, universal middle-class participation in mass higher education (and the rise of female participation which some regard as a parallel phenomenon) can also be interpreted in terms of social exclusion. Phillip Brown and Richard Scase identified two models of the dynamics of modern higher education systems. In the first, which they labelled the technocratic model, a virtuous circle of socio-economic advance is established. Rapid technological change demands more sophisticated skills that lead to the expansion of higher education which produces a shift towards professional society. In the second, which they called the social exclusion model, a vicious circle is created. Increasing competition between social and occupational groups, combined with little change in skill levels (and even deskilling), leads to demands for the expansion of higher education and credential inflation. The outcome is that the middle class tightens its monopoly of superior jobs.[50] Brown and Scase regarded this second scenario as more plausible.

Their conclusion is unduly bleak, although their critique of the linear technocratic model is justified. However, in a mass system, not only has the middle class taken over higher education; higher education has also taken over the middle class. In the process graduate status has become an essential attribute of a middle-class lifestyle, arguably a more important attribute than class origin or occupational category in a post-industrial age. This new affinity between middle-class lifestyles and a 'college culture' on the American pattern, combined with the decay of traditional identifications based on class and gender, is among the most significant characteristics of mass higher education. It reflects two deeply rooted secular trends in modern society, an intensified individualization which is superseding collective solidarities and the growth of a mass global culture which is eroding the particularities of class, gender, religion and nation.

The impact of post-industrial change on the inputs to mass higher education, therefore, is ambiguous. On the one hand, the demand for places in universities and colleges has increased because, in socio-cultural terms, those denied access to the burgeoning 'college culture' (the late twentieth century's equivalent of bourgeois respectability) are disfranchised, and because graduate status is itself becoming a powerful new principle of socio-economic stratification in a volatile post-industrial environment. It is difficult to explain the growing demand for higher education in Britain except in these terms. On the other hand, the graduates of a mass system can no longer be regarded as cadet members of various power élites, because they are too numerous, because élites are no longer formed within the disciplined routines of professional society and because the links between socio-political power and occupational status have become sinuous.

The impact of post-industrial change on the outputs of mass higher education is also far from straightforward. Optimistic (and unreflective?) accounts assert that in the knowledge society, with its vastly accelerated flows and stores of data, symbols and theories, the university will become a truly hegemonic institution. Innovation, and so wealth, will depend crucially on human capital, in the form of expert knowledge and highly skilled graduates. Whatever social prestige the mass university may lose, as a result of wider and more democratic access, will be more than compensated for by its increasing economic power, as the primary producer and authoritative interpreter of the knowledge that will be the key resource in a post-industrial society.

According to Peter Drucker, most advanced nations spend up to a fifth of their gross national product on the production and dissemination of knowledge – as much as 10 per cent on formal education, 5 per cent on training and 5 per cent on research and development.[51] In very few countries has conventional capital formation, in terms of investment in plant and equipment, ever reached the same level. And at the heart of the knowledge society is the educated person. 'In all earlier societies, the educated person was an ornament. He or she embodied *Kultur* . . . But in the knowledge society, the educated person is society's emblem; society's symbol; society's standardbearer. The educated person is the social "archetype".'[52]

But, even within this optimistic scenario, there are doubts about the role of the university. First, the scale, synergy and velocity of knowledge flows have intensified to such an extent that self-developing knowledge systems are being produced. These can no longer be regarded as passive repositories of knowledge but are active and dynamic systems with, in some sense, lives of their own. Within such systems universities may be subordinated components. Second, it is not clear whether universities, as traditionally conceived and organized, will be able to cope with the extra responsibility of leading the 'knowledge industry', or other agencies, whether based in corporate business or formed through informal strategic alliances among creative workers, will take over their leading role.

As has already been argued, the relationship between élite universities and the industrial revolution was oblique and full of contradiction. Perhaps the relationship between mass higher education and post-industrial change will be similarly indirect. Hans van Ginkel concluded that, in the future, universities would concentrate on guiding and combining knowledge flows. Consequently their role as primary producers might be reduced, diminishing their direct stake in cutting-edge research. Their responsibility would be for knowledge management, supervising and integrating research which might have been carried out elsewhere, and for scholarship, preserving, reviewing and transmitting the broader intellectual and scientific cultures within which research was undertaken. He also suggested that, as a result, a new concept of higher education would develop, concerned with general principles and generic skills. And, because a knowledge society must also be a learning society, this new higher education would provide an extended, even lifelong, experience.[53]

But, even if the mass university is not automatically assured of an institutional role at the heart of the knowledge society, nevertheless through their production of graduates higher education systems may still make a key contribution to the post-industrial division of labour. Creative workers, wherever they are located, are increasingly likely to be graduates. But it does not follow that all graduates of a mass system will become front-line workers in the post-industrial economy. According to Robert Reich, a tripartite division is developing. First come routine production services, which he estimated account for a quarter of all American jobs (and a similar proportion in Britain). These include not only production-line jobs but also routine supervisory and managerial occupations. Post-industrialism has affected such jobs in three different ways. Many have been abolished by hyper-automation; but many new jobs have been created in routine information-processing; while globalization of production means these tasks can be undertaken almost anywhere in the world.

Next come in-person services, accounting for perhaps a third of jobs. Because these services must be provided person-to-person, they are less susceptible to automation and globalization. They include jobs in retail sales, customer services, catering, transport and so on. They also embrace many of the so-called caring professions such as nursing and social work. Finally come what Reich called symbolic-analytical services, which he esti-mated make up a fifth of all jobs. These jobs involve identifying, solving and brokering of problems. Their tools are various – legal arguments, math-ematical formulae, scientific principles, psychological techniques, aesthetic symbols. They include lawyers, engineers, designers, writers, managers.[54] Reich excluded the 25 per cent of Americans who worked in the public sector and on the land. But public employees can fairly easily be assimilated into Reich's categories. Most fall into the last two.

If this categorization is accepted, it is no longer possible to establish a broad equivalence between the production of graduates in mass higher education systems and the supply of superior jobs in symbolic-analytical services in the post-industrial economy (as it may have been between the production of élite university graduates and the supply of élite professional jobs). There are simply too many graduates. Many are now employed in the in-person services sector and a growing number in routine production. Furthermore, according to Reich, the new symbolic-analytical services are not necessarily the same as the old professions. Although most symbolic analysts are graduates, they are not necessarily socialized into traditional disciplinary or professional cultures. Indeed, the most successful have gen-erally resisted such socialization.

The impact of post-industrial change on graduate careers, therefore, is twofold. First, the links between graduate and occupational status (and all that this implies in terms of upward social mobility) have become fuzzier. Rates of return on higher education have sharply declined over the past decade as the production of graduates has increased.[55] On the other hand, upskilling is taking place across a wide range of occupations. Graduates are increasingly taking non-graduate jobs, partly because employers are using graduate status as a sieve in a competitive labour market and partly because these jobs have become more technically and conceptually sophisticated (and, generally, because of a combination of these two factors). As a result, the demarcation between graduate and non-graduate status has been eroded in terms of occupations.

The demarcation is being eroded in subtler ways. Not only has the supply of graduates exceeded the demand for élite jobs, but the nature of these jobs has changed in ways hinted at by Reich. They have become more volatile and creative, less hierarchical and disciplined. Moreover, many graduates from a mass system enter non-élite occupations which are also changing. More are working in adaptable organizations – whether public agencies, private companies or their own businesses. Fewer are employed by corporate bureaucracies, whether the Civil Service or ICI. In addition, a growing number of mass university graduates are flexibly employed, unemployed or (early?) retired. As a result, the direct links between higher education and employment may have been weakened. Despite the advance of vocationalism, more graduates are not 'using' the detailed knowledge and expert skills they acquired. Moreover, as occupational hierarchies are undermined by post-industrial change, higher education offers an alternative arena in which personal significance and satisfaction can be achieved.

Second, post-industrial change, which is producing a much more volatile and flexible labour market not only for graduates but for all workers, may also be undermining credentialization, the key dynamic of professional (and industrial?) society. This effect is consistent with the paradigm shift from bureaucratic to adaptable organizations, described in the preceding section. The former depend on formal, depersonalized, rule-bound structures; the latter on flexible, individualized, intuitive, even charismatic modes of operation. This shift is matched by another in the character of higher education and professional training, from disciplined socialization into specialized knowledge cultures to a more open engagement with real-world problems and the skills required to solve them.

There was a close affinity between bureaucratic careers and élite university systems, even in an extended form (which is the best characterization of British higher education between the early 1960s and late 1980s). The credentials gained in higher education were a good predictor of success of these careers. According to Brown and Scase, 'the possession of a graduate qualification provided evidence of the bureaucratic discipline and competence demanded for managerial positions in both private and public sectors'.[56] But the fit between adaptable lives ('careers' is now too narrow a term) and mass higher education systems is more problematical. Formal credentials are a less reliable guide to success in the adaptable organizations of post-industrial society. Often they value habit-breaking more highly than habit-forming. Personal qualities are more important than professional discipline, possession of specific credentials, mastery of specialized knowledge or even of expert skills.

Universities and colleges have responded in two ways to this challenge. The first strategy, strongest in the 'new' universities, has been to develop a more innovative curriculum, based perhaps on the principles enunciated by the Education for Capability movement or the Enterprise in Higher Education initiative. Greater emphasis has been placed on producing adaptable skills, oriented towards practical problem-solving rather than disciplinary or professional socialization. Novel modes of assessment have also been developed which rely on outcomes such as student projects and profiling more heavily than on formal examinations. The second strategy, intuitively popular in the 'old' universities, has been to define post-industrial 'personal qualities' in terms of the common, if tacit, values and instincts possessed by graduates from élite institutions, because they have enjoyed the same élite formation and because they generally come from similarly privileged socio-cultural backgrounds.

Between these two strategies may be poised a new, and more insidious, division of labour. Mass institutions will produce adaptable workers, some engaged in symbolic-analytical services but the majority working in the in-person services sector, to adopt Reich's classification. Élite institutions, meanwhile, will intensify their control over the supply of graduates who fill élite jobs, which demand not only practical problem-solving skills but also the abstract and theoretical capacities for meta-modelling. The develop-ment of mass higher education, therefore, will be accompanied by the decline of distinctively graduate careers. Instead, the bulk of graduate ca-reers will be difficult to distinguish from other jobs, an inevitable outcome of the creation of a wider-access system, while élite jobs, dominated but not monopolized by graduates from élite universities, may become less open.

In conclusion, inputs and outputs coalesce. Élite university systems pro-vided opportunities for upward social mobility. Mobility confirmed existing class structures, because it legitimized their persistence in an open and democratic society and also modernized class structures by conscripting the talented of all classes. But mobility also eroded class hierarchies, because expert knowledge and professional skills, suitably credentialized, offer an alternative basis for social stratification. The link between inputs, the de-mand for and supply of university and college places, and outputs, recog-nizably graduate careers with guaranteed upward social mobility, was direct.

Mass higher education systems, on the other hand, are both less dynamic and more radical in their effects. The emphasis switches from upward social mobility for a meritocratic élite to the development of a 'college culture' for the majority – from life chances to lifestyles, mirroring the larger shift towards post-industrialism. To some extent, and in the short term, class-based hierarchies harden as mobility slows. The decline of graduate careers reflects this change. But, in another sense, class society itself begins to dissolve as the links loosen between socio-cultural status and occupational categories (which themselves are becoming more volatile).

Theorizing modernity

At the end of the last but one section two questions were left hanging. The first was whether it was more accurate to emphasize the continuities, how-ever dynamic, between industrial and post-industrial society, or the more radical discontinuities suggested by the idea of post-Fordism. The second was how the massification of higher education related to these broader socio-economic transformations. The latter has been partly answered al-ready by discussing the detailed consequences for higher education of these new political patterns, social formations and economic structures, in terms of control, funding, demand and outputs. But the central issue – is the growth of mass higher education an active agent of these transformations, or merely contingent upon them? – has not been properly addressed. It is discussed briefly now, although a fuller discussion is postponed until the final chapter. However, the focus of this section is on the first question – continuity or change?

It is possible to identify a number of fundamental shifts transcending the particular phenomena examined in the earlier section. These shifts can be illuminated by using various theoretical perspectives developed by social theorists. The first, and most prominent, is acceleration. The quickening of the rhythms of industrial, social and cultural life is a central feature of the late twentieth century, a global characteristic not confined to the high-technology, hyperconsumption West. But the acceleration of post-industrial society is different from the expansion of industrial society. It is not simply a question of greater velocity. Acceleration has produced a number of effects, not side-effects but primary effects. One is an alarming volatility. According to Jean-François Lyotard: 'The temporary contract is in practice supplanting permanent institutions in the professional, emotional, sexual, cultural and family domains, as well as political affairs.'[57] And, by disordering the time-world, it has sometimes sharpened rather than reduced inequality. Helga Nowotny argued: 'Making an approximate simultaneity possible with the aid of modern electronics has by no means led to a social simultaneity. On the contrary, new inequalities are arising from non-simultaneities.'[58]

The second shift, closely linked to acceleration, is a radically different concept of time. At the start, time became disjointed from space. Universalized, it was no longer defined by local circumstances. As a result, most social theorists have privileged time, which represented change, over space, which represented stasis, becoming over being. According to David Harvey: 'Social theory has always focused on processes of social change, modernisation, and revolution . . . Indeed, progress entails the conquest of space, the tearing down of spatial barriers, and the ultimate "annihilation of space through time".'[59] Modern industrial society required the separation of time from space, and their separate reconstruction as 'empty' categories which could be manipulated for economic, social and personal ends.

Novel concepts of time are now emerging. The future is being reinvented as the extended present. Temporal uncoupling can be observed in a range of technological, economic and social arenas – from food-processing, where tinned and frozen products suspend time and microwave technology accelerates it, to video recorders, which record and play back 'live' performances. As a result, the experience of time is also changing, its traditional sequences transcended yet its use more highly regulated than ever. The need arises for a differently lived time, a Uchronia to substitute for the Utopia that is no longer available, because there are no remote time-places beyond the reach of simultaneity and because the extended present has abolished that idealized future on which utopian hopes could focus.

According to Nowotny, the search for Uchronia takes three forms, all suggestively linked to the idea of post-Fordism. The first is the desire for fuller time, a more intense simultaneity, which can be linked to hyperconsumption and the emergence of a sumptuary society, and also to hyperautomation and the shrinking of 'work'. The second is the reverse, an attempt 'to attain a reduced intensification, to counter the economy of time with its "ecology", to bring work "to life"'. The echoes of post-materialism and social scarcity can be heard in this attempt to reappropriate time. The third is the most radical, an attempt to reverse the rigidities of simultaneity and escape from the extended present by striking a better balance between 'the linearity of mechanised and homogenised time and the unexpected element, the spontaneity of the "vicissitudes of life"'.[60]

The third shift, also a product of acceleration, is the growth of so-called risk society. According to Ulrich Beck, risk society emerges when 'the gain in power from techno-economic "progress" is being increasingly overshadowed by the production of risks'.[61] Modernization has always been accompanied by risks – inequality of wealth, industrial accidents, social divisions, destruction of the environment. But, in the past, these risks could be dismissed as the side-effects, or unintended consequences, of an essentially benign process, and they also tended to be localized, confined to particular social groups and places. In risk society these risks have become global (the proliferation of nuclear weapons, global climate change, the destruction of species diversity and so on). No one can escape. And they can no longer be regarded as unintended consequences, because under conditions of reflexive modernization (a concept which Beck borrowed from Anthony Giddens and which is discussed later) unintended consequences are as powerful as intended consequences in shaping social action.

A fourth shift, to which acceleration, new ideas of time and risk society have all contributed, is the growth of complexity and of non-linearity. The latter is especially important. In industrial society development was linear; in post-industrial society it is multi-dimensional and multi-directional. This shift can be observed in economic theory, where orthodox concepts of 'rational' behaviour in a mechanical, linear world of equilibrium have been rejected in favour of much more fluid and open accounts of economic behaviour. According to Paul Ormerod,

> the strongest manifestations of non-linearity . . . are the two interconnected ideas, first, that there is such a thing as society; and second, that the behaviour of the economy as a whole cannot be deduced from the simple aggregation of its component parts. From the interaction of the myriad decisions taken at the micro-level by individuals and companies, complex patterns of behaviour emerge at the macro-level of the system as a whole. These patterns do not simply relate to the workings of the economy in isolation. They define the social norms, the social and cultural context in which the economy operates.[62]

As basic concepts, complexity and non-linearity were first developed in mathematics and the biological sciences. Closely related is chaos theory, of course, which belies its title. Ormerod's application of these concepts to economics, a social science despite its reliance on mathematics, and to the economy itself, arguably the primary arena for social action in modern society, illustrates how relevant they have become, in a metaphorical but also an exact sense, to wider accounts of modernity. There are suggestive links between complexity/non-linearity and a fifth shift, circularity. All knowledge, especially 'social' knowledge, is circular, according to Giddens, not only because, in principle, it is revisable (an inherent characteristic of progressive science), but also because, in practice, it is revised through interaction with its environment.[63]

Beck reinforced this analysis by distinguishing between 'primary' and 'reflexive scientization'. The former he interpreted as a primary engagement between science on the one hand and nature, people and society, the objects of its research, on the other; the latter as a contest between science and science, by which he means that the objects of inquiry are no longer exclusively 'external' but also include the results, and the methods, of science itself. And reflexivity has a further dimension. 'The "objects" of scientization also becomes subjects of it, in the sense they can and must actively manipulate the heterogeneous supply of scientific interpretations.'[64] This has two effects: first, reflexive science is no longer a monopoly of scientists, which is discussed in the next chapter; and second, in Beck's words, 'science becomes more and more necessary, but less and less sufficient' in risk society.

Circularity is closely related to reflexivity, the sixth shift. Reflexivity takes different forms. It has already been discussed as a scientific, or intellectual, phenomenon. As a social phenomenon, it grows out of one of the primary characteristics of modernity, the decay of 'local' knowledge, rich but limited, and its replacement by a required trust in abstract and expert systems.[65] As a result individuals, and social institutions, are freed from the givens, the fixities, of tradition. Their norms are no longer inherited, organic. Instead they must be constructed, and frequently reconstructed, in the light of the interaction between abstract systems and actual environments. In other words, they become reflexive. Reflexivity can also be explained in terms of the evolution from industrial to post-industrial society. In the nineteenth and early twentieth century modernization had an 'other', traditional society which it was in the process of modernizing. In the late twentieth century modernization has only itself to interrogate. It becomes reflexive.

At a personal level reflexivity leads to individualization, the seventh shift. Beck argued that:

> the individual himself or herself becomes the reproduction unit of the social in the lifeworld. What the social is and does has to be involved with individual decisions. Or put it another way, . . . the individuals becomes the agents of their educational and market-mediated subsistence and the related life planning and organization. Biography itself is acquiring a reflexive project.[66]

Individualization, therefore, is not a passive process, exercising privatized choice within a consumer society; it is also an active process, out of which new social forms are being constructed.

These are the seven shifts which together can be used to shape a general theory of modernity – acceleration; the extended present, or simultaneity; risk society; chaos, complexity and non-linearity; circularity; reflexivity; and individualization. The seamless synergy between them is remarkable. They, and it, suggest that an entirely new kind of society is developing, not simply at the level of grand conceptualizing but in terms of the lived-through experience of individuals and institutions. The sense of change is much more insistent than that of continuity. To explore these changes further it is necessary to inquire into shifts in intellectual culture, and in science and technology, the subjects of the next chapter. The growth of mass higher education, therefore, is taking place at a time not only of urgent socio-economic change, the phenomena discussed in the third section of this chapter, but also when the dynamics of modernity itself are being radically revised. Higher education systems are no longer simply 'knowledge' institutions, reproducing the intellectual and human capital required by industrial society; they are becoming key instruments of the reflexivity which defines the post-industrial (and post-modern) condition.

4

Science and Culture

The university, as an institution and an idea, pre-dates both the scientific tradition first articulated in the seventeenth century and a distinctively modern culture which did not begin to emerge until the end of the eighteenth century. Yet all three – university, science and culture – have reached their respective climaxes in our present century. It is usual, therefore, to discount their separate origins as a historical curiosity without contemporary relevance. The rapid expansion of higher education systems, the explosive growth of knowledge through a progressive science based on the accumulation of expert research and the spread of a culture of rationality rooted in universal values are seen as congruent phenomena. Their mutual dependence, in institutional and political terms, and their creative synergy, in the intellectual sphere, are taken for granted.

As has already been pointed out, the university, for all its assumed antiquity, is a thoroughly modern institution. All but a handful have been founded since 1900; in Britain only 18 universities out of the present total of 93 were established before the death of Queen Victoria. Two-thirds (61) have been founded since 1960. Even those established earlier have been utterly transformed. Indeed these universities, older and therefore generally élite, have often been at the forefront of scientific and cultural change. It is their laboratories which have nurtured Nobel prize-winners; their professors who have produced the most radical reinterpretations of established ideas.

In other words, the connections between university, science and culture are seen as straightforward and unproblematic. The argument in this chapter is that neither is necessarily true. The growth of mass higher education, still a novel phenomenon in Britain, has required universities to evolve in certain directions. The historical, organizational, political and socio-economic dimensions of this evolution have been discussed in earlier chapters. But equally significant changes are taking place in the enveloping intellectual culture. Although always embroiled in, and often generators of, these changes, universities are subject here to a different set of influences. Also, radical shifts are under way in science and technology which are pushing universities in a third direction. There may be affinities between these three axes of change – the creation of a more open higher education system, the replacement of canonical conceptions of intellectual culture by a volatile pluralism and the emergence of new modes of knowledge production. But there is not necessarily any causal correspondence.

Five moments of affinity

In the past there have been examples of intriguing affinity, alignments even, between 'moments' in culture, revolutions in science and technology, and shifts in the socio-economic order. Universities have been implicated in all three evolutionary axes – as transmitters and interpreters of privileged cultural norms; as producers of expert scientific knowledge and technology transferers; and as agents of socio-economic change through their role in professionalization or, alternatively, as aiders and abetters of social hierarchy (although, until this century, their role was often subordinate to those of other institutions). Nevertheless, the development of modern culture, the elaboration of a scientific-technological tradition, the growth of secular-urban-industrial society (and, as a result of democratic reform, of welfare states), and the expansion of higher education systems – all have been contemporaneous, and arguably congruent, phenomena.

It is possible to identify five such moments of affinity. The first occurred in early modern Europe. Renaissance in the cultural and intellectual spheres then scientific revolution were its dominant characteristics. But the impact of the Reformation, in particular the influence of a Calvinistic puritanism, cerebral and severe; the early stirrings of political economy and statecraft; the projection of European power across the confining oceans and creation of the first global markets; the emergence of states which, although not yet national, had ceased to be purely personal and were increasingly bureaucratic in form – these other phenomena reinforced the moment of affinity, or coming together of trends to produce a grand conjuncture.

In Britain this was accompanied by a significant expansion of higher education – the foundation of two of the four ancient Scottish universities, the renewal (and part-laicization) of Oxford and Cambridge and the emergence of the Inns of Court as alternative institutions of higher professional training.[1] Many other universities were established at the same time and against the same cultural background. Leiden in the Netherlands and Harvard in infant Massachusetts are exact examples. Only towards the end of this period did the university decline, to be supplemented – and, in some instances, effectively supplanted – by more explicitly scientific institutions such as the Royal Society or the various European academies.

A second moment of affinity took place in the latter half of the eighteenth century. Enlightenment, the decline and fall of the *ancien régime* and the age of revolution, industrial and political; the conjunctures seem too compelling to be coincidences. The Declaration of Independence and *The Wealth of Nations* published in the same year, 1776; *Don Giovanni* first performed only two years before the storming of the Bastille. The effects of this second moment can be clearly observed in the cultural arena, and not only in the work of philosophers like Hume and later Kant and Hegel, *philosophes* like Rousseau and political economists like Adam Smith. They can also be traced in the world of aesthetics and sensibility. A year after the Europe-wide success of *Werther* in 1775, Goethe wrote the drama *Prometheus*. In his biography of Goethe, Nicholas Boyle wrote of Prometheus' hesitation when faced with Jupiter's offer to make his statues come alive if only he, Prometheus, will end his rebellion against the Gods:

> It is a pause of the deepest significance in the history of modern sen-
> sibility. Is the mortal, transient artist the servant of an independent
> world-order which stretches before and after him, to whose laws he
> acknowledges himself subject and parts of which are imitated in his
> works? If so, a realistic objective living art is possible, of the kind we
> associate with Homer and Shakespeare. But if not, if the artist remains
> an autonomous creator, acknowledging no ordering force except that
> which he finds within himself, can his work ever escape from its de-
> pendence upon him? Must it not remain, as in the start of Goethe's
> drama, stone statues scattered through Prometheus' grove, free but
> motionless – frozen icons of the artist's self?[2]

This tension between, broadly, collectively generated tradition and indi-vidually interpreted genius was first strikingly manifest in the work of Goethe and his contemporaries. It was a tension heroically and metaphorically worked through in Goethe's successive drafts of *Faust*. Freed from the can-ons of classicism and constraints of courts, and yet to be subordinated to the mass market, art no longer had to be mediated through inaccessible conventions and arcane knowledge. It became an independent, and poten-tially critical, force.

But these effects were not confined to the aesthetic plane. Closed systems of thought were replaced by open systems, perhaps the fundamental char-acteristic of modernity. Two Scots were the progenitors of this intellectual revolution, the political economist Adam Smith and the philosopher and historian David Hume. Their personal biographies illustrate the experien-tial shift which accompanied this second moment of affinity.[3] The intellec-tual revolution they represented ran alongside revolutions in political culture, social organization and economic structure – the American and French revolutions and their Europe-wide, world-wide, reverberations; the displace-ment of custom by commerce as society's organizing principle; the growth of urbanism; and, above all, the rise of a technology-driven industrial eco-nomy. In the long haul of human history Goethe's Weimar, that microcosm of refined Enlightenment, and Ironbridge Gorge, among the earliest sites of the new industrialism, were aspects of the same movement, the birth of modernity.

All this was accompanied by significant changes in higher education. It was the apogee of the Scottish universities, the age of northern Enlighten-ment. The University of Berlin was established in 1810, an exemplar for many other university foundations later in the nineteenth century but, more immediately, part of the programme of reconstructing Prussian society after the Napoleonic shock. In other words, its link to the general crisis on the cusp of the eighteenth and nineteenth centuries was direct and explicit. The response in France was different. There the universities were stigmatized as relics of the *ancien régime* and lost their leadership role to other institutions, notably the *grandes écoles*. In the United States the proliferation of colleges laid the intellectual and moral foundations of, a generation or so later, the age of Thoreau and Whitman.

The third moment of affinity, perhaps better seen as an extension, or culmination, of the second, came in the middle of the nineteenth century. By then urbanization and industrialization were recognized as irresistible and irreversible. The eighteenth-century city, Blake's dark-lit 'London' in his *Songs of Experience* or the London of Dickens's memory and imagining, was being succeeded by the nineteenth-century metropolis, all 'improvements' and municipal reform, creating a physical environment familiar today. The growth of an industrial economy which sustained, directly or indirectly, a growing fraction of the population, had produced a dramatic reordering of work, and so of its dependent social structures and the traditional rhythms of time and space.

At the same time, equally radical adventures were under way in the intellectual and cultural arenas. In 1859 Darwin published *The Origins of Species*, the emblematic episode in the retreat of religion before a triumphant science – Matthew Arnold's 'melancholy, long, withdrawing roar' of the Sea of Faith in 'Dover Beach' written eight years later. Also in the mid-nineteenth century, so Roland Barthes has argued, classical writing disintegrated. The whole of literature from Flaubert to the present day became the problematics of language. The refined solidity of Ingres' neo-classical painting gave way to the Impressionists' deconstruction of light and form. The conjunctures could hardly be more impressive. In the case of this period's most famous thinker, Marx, they were explicit. 'Exploitation' in the socio-economic sphere bred 'alienation' in the world of ideas and feelings, and together they were to produce the catharsis of revolution.

The second half of the nineteenth century was the first great age of university building. Indeed, it is hardly an exaggeration to say that, *pace* Humboldt's Berlin, recognizably modern universities did not exist before this date, because the social and intellectual preconditions for their existence had not been established. The most significant of Britain's higher education institutions, the civic universities of the North and Midlands, were founded during this period. Their sponsorship by newly emerging élites – industrial, commercial, professional and civic (often in incestuous combination) – indicated the active role they were expected to play in the reordering of Victorian Britain. At the same time Oxford and Cambridge were partly reformed. Although their new orientation, to produce the higher public service class of the bureaucratic and imperial state and to staff the emerging professions, had a different emphasis, it formed part of the same process of modernization. Similar developments took place elsewhere, notably the establishment of the land-grant universities in the United States as manifest of America's destiny.

The fourth moment of affinity occurred in the early years of the twentieth century but reverberated through later decades. It was the moment when modernity, an evolutionary condition, was transformed into modernism, a movement or ideology. It was when so many of the intellectual contours of our world were first delineated. Einsteinian physics, imaginative and theorizing, displaced the 'mechanical' physics of Newton and his successors. The transformation of political economy, speculatively searching for fundamental principles, into social science, rooted in empirical investigation and fixed by 'theory', which had occupied much of the nineteenth century, reached its climax with the twentieth-century projection of Marxism and in the work of Weber and, later, Keynes.

Marx, at any rate as interpreted by Gramsci and Lukács, Keynes, as much aesthete as economist, and Freud, introduced new notes into intellectual discourse, affective and intuitive, which provided a bridge into the radicalized world of modern art – Picasso and Braque in painting; Schoenberg in music; in literature Proust and Joyce, Virginia Woolf (who famously declared that 'human nature changed in, or about, December 1910') and T. S. Eliot (the radical innovator of *The Waste Land*, not the nostalgic conservative of the *Four Quartets*). The coincidence between these radical shifts in the scientific and intellectual spheres and in the aesthetic arena is too remarkable to be overlooked. Henri Lefebvre, echoing Virginia Woolf, described the shift in these terms:

> Around 1910 a certain space was shattered. It was the space of common sense, of knowledge, of social practice, of political power, a space hitherto enshrined in everyday discourse, just as in abstract thought . . . Euclidean and perspectivist space have disappeared as systems of reference, along with other former 'common places'.[4]

Around the same time Henry Ford was laying the foundations of a mass-production, mass-consumption society and Samuel Taylor was devising the principles of scientific management. This application of 'science' not only to the technological enhancement of industrial products but also to the systematic organization of industry itself was a decisive innovation. Detroit, therefore, has as good a claim as Vienna or Berlin to be regarded as, in George Steiner's phrase, an 'inner capital' of the modern world; the Model T, or the Hoover, as authentic an icon of modernism as the Bauhaus.

Fordism and Taylorism foreshadowed the totalitarian experience, because their techniques of mass organization made it possible (just as modern art's rejection of restraint may have made it morally conceivable). But, in contingent combination with Keynesianism, they were more deeply embroiled in America's successive New Deals and Great Societies and in Europe's more thorough welfare states, which aimed to reconcile the imperatives of the free market with liberal-democratic values. Their efficiencies of scale generated the wealth on which post-war democracy depended. The alliance between a progressive industry, stable and responsible, which had displaced the volatile and reckless capitalism of the past, and a progressive science – or, more accurately, consumer-friendly technology – provided the epistemological security and psychic reassurance so badly needed in a post-Holocaust world. Perhaps it is not an accident that, in the aesthetic arena, modernism became the house style of both the welfare state (public housing schemes by Mies van der Rohe) and of Fordist corporations (works by Jackson Pollock in the boardroom).

It is from this fourth, and most recent, moment of affinity that our present higher education systems date. It was the age of Clark Kerr's multiversity, the second great age of university building. As has already been argued, most of today's universities were founded during this historic conjuncture between modernism, techno-science, Fordism and the welfare state. The higher education 'franchise' was greatly extended, primarily to satisfy rising social expectations and only secondarily to meet the increasing demand for skilled labour (which itself was as much culturally constructed as economically determined). Part of the extension of the franchise took the form of the establishment of new kinds of higher education institutions, distinct from the traditional university. Together these developments, which have been discussed in earlier chapters, redrew the map of higher education.

During this same period, from the 1930s to the 1960s, universities came to be identified not only with upward social mobility and wider opportunities but also with the formation of an intelligentsia, albeit salaried or subsidized, to replace the men of letters (the gendering was no accident). Both developments, of course, were aspects of the open society which is the root characteristic of modernity. Ideas, as well as careers, were now open to the talented. Perhaps for the first time, universities came to be seen as intellectual institutions, in an active and engaged sense, rather than cultural institutions, in a passive and conserving sense. But the most significant change was that, at this fourth moment of affinity, their claim to be the leading scientific institutions (and, according to the contemporary belief in the subordination of technology to science, therefore key instruments of wealth creation) was uncritically accepted.

It is argued that we are in the middle of a fifth moment of affinity. Its elements are the transition from élite to mass forms of higher education; the shift from a conception of innovation, whether technological or social, as predominantly produced by scientists and other experts to a more pluralist interpretation emphasizing the creative role of users and other stakeholders; the contested rise of a playful post-modernism in literature and the arts which denies the claims of universalism and despises an ordered aesthetics; the absorption of such ideas into the mainstream of intellectual culture; the growth of a post-Fordist economy, all flexible organizations and flat hierarchies; and, in the social and political arenas, the apparent enthusiasm for market rather than social solutions.

This fifth moment is the subject of the rest of this chapter. The four earlier moments have only been lightly sketched, to provide an interpretative context. The present moment of affinity, however, must be considered in greater depth because it bears directly on the theme of this book, the meanings of mass higher education. Some effort must also be made to press beyond mere affinity, if not all the way to causality, at any rate to a more precise statement of the intermingling of these varied phenomena. Elements of this affinity, of course, have already been considered in the previous chapter – the so-called crisis of the welfare state, the shift towards a post-Fordist paradigm, and efforts to theorize modernity. Here the focus is more directly on knowledge, its configuration and validation. First, the evolution of intellectual culture is discussed, particularly in the context of the social sciences and humanities. Next, shifts in science, technology and innovation are assessed. Finally, the implications of these changes for both teaching and research in universities are examined.

Intellectual culture

Whatever its historical antecedents, the modern university is rooted in a culture of rationality. Writing in the 1970s, when the hard-won reputation of the university as the leading intellectual institution in modern society was first challenged, Talcott Parsons and Gerard Platt argued that it 'must define values and goals in terms of the primacy of cognitive educational functions'.[5] This primary commitment distinguished the university from other institutions. But the mass higher education system of the future may have to renegotiate its relationship with that culture of rationality, and redefine what is meant by 'the primacy of cognitive educational functions', for two reasons. First, as has been argued in earlier chapters, its relationship with society and the economy is being transformed. Second, that culture of rationality, which was never absolute, is being radically revised. This is the subject of this section.

It is commonplace to argue there has been a decisive shift beyond modernity in intellectual culture over the past generation. The frontier has been crossed between the modern system, organized, for all its restlessness, around universal values and 'unified subjects', and *posthistoire*, the trackless territory of deconstructed meanings, relative values, fleeting truths. Often an analogy is drawn between this shift from modernism to post-modernism and the shift from industrial society with complex corporations, elaborate welfare states and large cultural, educational and scientific bureaucracies, to post-industrial society with its flat-hierarchy organizations, flexible careers and privatization of public choices. The latter shift was explored in the last chapter.

Despite the analogy, the end-of-history claim is a bold one. Post-Enlightenment may be pre-Enlightenment dressed in new clothes. The original spirit of modernism was radically revisionist (on occasion destructive). In music it was associated with atonalism; in art with anti-representationalism;

in literature with stream of consciousness, fragmentation of plot, subversion of narrative and *vers libre*; in architecture with bare, even brutal, functionalism. Critics such as Frank Kermode emphasized modernism's 'decreation', closely linking this quality with its ironical introversion. Perhaps modernism's threat to the comfort of familiar forms provoked *posthistoire*, in its guise as neo-conservatism, and prefigured it, in its guise as post-modernism. The dynamic ambivalences which modernism interpreted as a creative tension, post-modernism is content to redefine as static ambiguities. In the words of George Steiner:

> the equivocations, that word out of the spectral terrors of *Macbeth*, between finite, liberal rationality after 'the death of God' on the one hand, and the questionings of immanence which are radical to myth on the other, have been of peculiar intensity throughout modernism.[6]

The secular, rational, scientific and liberal tradition, associated in its beginnings with the Enlightenment and identified today with modernism, the tradition supposedly on the verge of dissolution, must be carefully defined. It is a much more complex movement than its post-modern and/or neo-conservative critics allege. The simplest shorthand account suggests that this movement, the source of modern consciousness, had its origins in the humanism (and, arguably, the Protestantism) of the sixteenth century; was powerfully reinforced by the scientific revolution of the seventeenth century when man's understanding of the natural world was disciplined by mechanical laws; intensified by the eighteenth-century Enlightenment when it was argued that the social world could be regulated by similar laws; and culminated in the nineteenth century when the power of industrial society and the prestige of modern science seemed to confirm the superiority of this intellectual tradition over all others.

This account identifies secular rationality as a Western, and an élite, tradition, produced in Europe or by the wider 'Europe' beyond the oceans, its direct influence confined to sophisticated élites. As Basil Bernstein has argued, 'historically and now, only a tiny percentage of the population has been socialised into knowledge at the level of the meta-languages of control and innovation'.[7] Equally it is significant that the scientific tradition has been shaped by recession from Christianity; its roots still lie deep in the Judaeo-Christian tradition. But in the late twentieth century this inheritance has been abandoned, this unacknowledged moral capital exhausted. Its prestige now depends on the dissemination of the modern system, based on materialist progress powered by the advance of science and technology. This is what has projected the Enlightenment far beyond its Western heartland.

Because of the élitism and cultural specificity of secular rationality, the link between values and outcomes is now contested. Do modern science and technology still depend ultimately on that bundle of secular, liberal, rationality which has become the dominant intellectual culture in Europe over the past two centuries? Can the process of modernization be divorced from the values of modernity? Or, conversely, does the world-wide success of the way of the 'West' indicate how successfully its specific cultural origins have been transcended? The success of Japan suggests that science and technology can be successfully disembedded from their original intellectual context without sacrificing either their creativity or their dynamism. Far from being exceptional, Japan's and, more generally, the Pacific Rim's selective take-over of Western values may be typical. In a similar way forms of this élite intellectual culture have been diffused throughout Western societies, so that they are no longer the property of social élites. Modernism, modernity, modernization, all imply universalism, a denial of cultural specificity.

However, universalism can take two contrasting forms. Cultural specificity can be either transcended, in the sense that Western values have been universalized, or ignored, in the sense that all values but those of a triumphant techno-science have become redundant. The intellectual culture of the late twentieth century is poised between these two forms. Within the secular tradition out of which it has grown contradictory elements have always been found. That tradition's guiding principle is heterodoxy not orthodoxy. As Ralf Dahrendorf has argued, 'difference and plurality are part and parcel of the moral worlds of discovery and invention'.[8] Its meanings have been shaped at various times and with various degrees of influence by science, politics, industry and culture (élite and popular). Also a powerful current of scepticism flows through the Enlightenment tradition – labelled perhaps 'from Hume to Kuhn'. Much of science is concerned with the limits of knowledge. It is by distinguishing the knowable from the (presently or permanently) unknowable that science makes progress. Most is routine. Despite the heroic examples of a Newton or an Einstein and persistent attempts to construct unified theories, grand holistic explanations are the exception. Difference dominates here, too.

Most important of all, modernity cannot be defined in terms of rationality. Few people, even in the eighteenth century, genuinely believed that the social world could be regulated by reasonable laws. The Age of Reason was also the Age of Sensibility, of *Sturm und Drang*. The sentimental novels of Richardson were as much part of the Enlightenment as Hume's *Treatise of Human Nature* or Diderot's *Encyclopédie*. Indeed, in Rousseau, last and greatest of the *philosophes*, the emotional and the rational were joined. In his study of William Blake, who affirmed 'to Labour in Knowledge is to Build up Jerusalem', E. P. Thompson discussed this tension:

> Blake did not achieve any full synthesis of the antinomian and the rationalist. How could he, since the antinomian premised a non-rational affirmative? There was, rather, an incandescence in his art in which the incompatible traditions met – tried to marry – argued as contraries – were held in a polarised tension. If one may be wrong to look for a coherent intellectual system, there are certainly constellations of related attitudes and images – connected insights – but at the moment we attempt a rational exegesis we are imposing bounds on these insights.[9]

And, in case the contemporary relevance of Blake's 'polarised tension' was overlooked, Thompson continued: 'One might add that these affirmatives cannot be derived from materialist thought today. That is why every realization of these values (such as Blake's) is a plank in the floor on which the future must walk.'[10]

There are other examples, less personal and less visionary than Blake's. According to Wolf Lepenies,

> already by the end of the eighteenth century – and not least as a consequence of a general sobering up engendered by the abuses fostered by the French Revolution – the practice of the social sciences in imitating the natural sciences was coming to seem more and more problematical.[11]

Or, expressed more poetically by Lessing:

> Brooding Reason forces its way into everything,
> And where it does not rule it still demands to be indispensable.
> It imperiously decrees the worth of our senses,
> Makes itself the ear of our ears, the eye of our eye.

From another perspective, Hegel questioned whether triumphant reason might not have suffered the same fate as the barbarians who overwhelmed Rome, holding the upper hand outwardly but 'surrendered to the defeated spiritually.'

By the beginning of the nineteenth century Romanticism had become the central impulse in intellectual culture, although on Biedermeier rather than *Sturm und Drang* terms. There was a strong reaction against the intellectual and moral insufficiency of eighteenth-century rationality – the complacent doctrine of 'benevolence' suggested by naturalistic psychology which so stifled Blake – but also against the machine metaphors of society which were popular in the early stages of the industrial revolution. By the middle of the last century the battle-lines had been drawn between sociology,

> a discipline characterised by cold rationality which seeks to comprehend the structures and laws of modern industrial society by means of measurement and computation and in doing so only serves to alienate man more effectively from himself and from the world around him,

and literature, 'whose intuition can see farther than the analyses of the sociologists.'[12] This tension between Huxley's Science and Arnold's Culture emerged early, and has never been resolved.

This tension, in a more extreme form, has been graphically described by Steiner in his study of Tolstoy and Dostoevsky:

> Tolstoy, 'keeping at all times', in Coleridge's phrase, 'to the high road of life'; Dostoevsky, advancing into the labyrinth of the unnatural, into the cellarage and morass of the soul; Tolstoy, like a colossus bestriding the palpable earth, evoking the realness, the tangibility, the sensible

entirety of concrete experience; Dostoevsky, always on the edge of the hallucinatory, of the spectral, always vulnerable to daemomic intrusions into what might prove, in the end, to have been merely a tissue of dreams.[13]

Towards the end of the nineteenth century machine metaphors and naive positivism fell into disuse, and were replaced by new intellectual formations, 'biological' derived from Darwin and 'sociological' derived from Marx, which came to dominate twentieth-century culture. Their contrasting determinisms have come close to defining the possibilities of modernism. Positivism itself, the linear heir of Enlightenment rationality, narrowed from the grand scheme of Comte to categorize all human roles to the philosophical minimalism of logical positivism in the 1920s and 1930s. In the present century infant modernism absorbed additional strands of thought – the austerely ironic, Wittgenstein's *Tractatus* and Eliot's *The Waste Land*, and, most significantly, the affective, through Freudianism and other interpretations of the psyche. Its intellectual repertoire was almost complete.

The natural sciences, discussed in greater detail in the next section, clung to a mechanistic, cumulative ethos for much longer. But here, too, the verve of Einsteinian physics and quantum mechanics, in the early years of the twentieth century, and analogous creativity in the biological sciences in mid-century, introduced a new element of indeterminacy. Theoretical and experimental science drifted apart. Once-firm conceptual frameworks began to shimmer, while the measurements of 'normal' science became more precise. This tension between empiricism and theorizing, familiar in the social and human sciences, has been intensified by a clearer recognition of the social construction of science. Here the work of Thomas Kuhn has been a powerful influence, even if his account of how science is produced has a greater appeal to social than natural scientists.[14]

His succession of incommensurable paradigms, elaborate intellectual constructions as much cultural as scientific, their rise and fall interspersed between long quiescent periods of cumulative 'normal' science, suggests a different evolutionary pattern than the onward and upward march of progressive science. Instead the door is opened to relativism, although Kuhn himself is reluctant to take responsibility for such an outcome.[15] His emphasis on the part played by communities of scientists in validating successive paradigms seems to cast further doubt on the objectivity of science. From there it is a small step to Edmund Leach's suggestion that 'science and the products of science . . . exist only because they are given names and uses by members of society'.[16]

The modern system, therefore, cannot be reduced to the working-through of Reason into cognitive and social structures, or even to the cultivation of rationality. As Hegel long ago pointed out, 'victorious reason is no longer Reason'. This 'polarised tension', to borrow Thompson's phrase about Blake, between order, or affirmation, and questioning is endemic in Western thought. The Enlightenment, and its successor movements, have offered their own eschatologies to relieve this tension. For God it substituted 'victorious reason', literally so in the contrived rituals of the early years of the French Revolution. Although these excesses were quickly abandoned, modernism has remained an identifiably post-Christian movement.

The metaphysics of the spirit have been reasserted in subtler ways, in an intellectual descent that runs from before Hegel to after Heidegger. The Enlightenment also inspired the two great eschatologies of the modern world, Marxism and Freudianism, which have decisively shaped intellectual culture and modern consciousness, influencing even those who most fiercely rejected them. Both, of course, aspire to be scientific systems and are rooted in inquiry, investigation and analysis. But the sums of both are extra-scientific. They demand faith as much as, if not more than, they require proof.

Such grand theories and meta-discourses have an oblique, even ironic, relationship to the explosion of knowledge. They help to reduce it to some kind of order, but it provides the raw material out of which these over-arching theories are constructed. So grand theories like Marxism and Freudianism both enable and disable; they enable by offering a context of meaningfulness, but they disable by ossifying into orthodoxies. These great meta-discourses of the modern world cease to prescribe ideas, and pro-scribe them instead. But Marxism and Freudianism, even with Keynesianism and a few others thrown in, are not exceptions that prove the rule. They are simply the most prominent examples. The last two centuries are littered with 'isms', and all disciplines possess their own petty discourses which prescribe/proscribe just as fiercely.

The construction of meta-discourses, post-religions, has been one response to the segmentation, even disintegration, of the modern world (which, of course, are the sources of its socio-economic power). The other has been an elaboration of the Arnoldian tactic of defining Culture as an autonomous arena, an aspect of the 'ironic introversion' referred to by Kermode. Terry Eagleton argued that, ever since the Enlightenment, culture has been the 'other' of political society – 'the realm of being as opposed to doing, the kingdom of ends rather than of means, the home of transcendental spirit rather than the dreary prose of daily life'.[17]

If culture split off from society, it was partly because that society, as it fell under the sway of instrumental Reason, had less and less time for the values it nurtured. Cultural values, therefore, had to be cultivated at the margin, in an art stripped of its social functions. But, it was by putting some daylight between itself and the political order (and, still more, mass industrial society) that art could become, for the first time, critique as opposed to celebration, or affirmation. As a result, Eagleton argued, culture was defined as a utopian space, providing images of emancipation only, while 'those precious figures of freedom, sensuousness and happiness became falsely abstract'.[18] In a sense the post-modern turn, and the rise of a post-industrial ideology, have undermined both strategies – the creation of meaningful meta-discourses, and of an autonomous space for Culture.

The key to high modernity, the culmination (but also the contradiction) of the Enlightenment tradition, therefore is what Anthony Giddens called 'the institutionalization of doubt'. Giddens saw utopian realism, whether Marxist, Freudian or of any other kind, as ultimately antithetical to modernity. 'Utopian prescriptions or anticipations set a baseline for future states of affairs which blocks off modernity's endlessly open character.'[19] Eagleton wrote, in similar terms but from a different perspective, about capitalism 'restlessly transgressing boundaries and pitching diverse life-forms together'.[20]

Described in this way, high modernity leads to an intensification of ontological insecurity – which is assuaged by playful post-modernism? It demands to be, in Gidden's words, 'cut loose from its moorings in the reassurance of tradition'.[21] Yet this cutting-loose and institutionalization of doubt are the keys to the transformation of modernity, a secular and liberal scepticism, into modernization, an action plan of global significance. For Giddens, as was explained at the end of the previous chapter, the fundamental characteristic of modernity is 'disembedding', the lifting-out of cognitive and social practices from specific contexts and their restructuring across indeterminate spans of time-space. The mechanisms of disembedding are symbolic tokens that can be passed around without regard to who handles them (his favourite example is money, although information technology offers others even more suggestive), and expert systems, 'systems of technical accomplishment or professional expertise' which also remove these relations from the immediacies of context.

The university plays an important role in both. It is a creator and manipulator of some of the most powerful symbolic tokens, in the form of scientific knowledge. And it is certainly an expert system, providing both technical accomplishment and professional expertise. Yet it is committed to a culture of rationality, a commitment less easy to reconcile with Giddens' analysis. And a more destructive analysis can be offered emphasizing not continuity, however dynamic, but discontinuity. Arnold Gehlen has argued that the premises of the Enlightenment are dead and only its consequences remain. Or, in the words of Jürgen Habermas,

> in view of an evolutionary, autonomous, self-promoting modernization, social-scientific observers can all the more easily take leave of the conceptual horizon of Western rationalism in which modernity arose. But as soon as the internal links between the concept of modernity and the self-understanding of modernity gained within the horizon of Western reason have been dissolved, we can relativize the, as it were, automatically continuing process of modernization from the distantiated standpoint of the postmodern observer.[22]

In short, a rupture takes place between intellectual and technical values, between a culture of rationality and instrumental Reason. The potential for such a rupture has existed throughout the modern period. As Eagleton pointed out: 'If it [capitalism] has need of the "unified subject" in the classroom or law-court, it has little enough time for it in the media or the market-place.'[23] But, until recently, complete rupture was avoided in two ways – by the maintenance of Culture as an autonomous domain, so providing a balance; and by the belief that, far underneath, there was a fundamental affinity, even synergy, between intellectual culture and technical performance. Those who argue that we are witnessing a decisive shift from modernity to *posthistoire* doubt that either condition still applies.

Another tension has also become acute, between the social and intellectual projects of the Enlightenment. The first led ineluctably to the creation of a mass society organized according to democratic principles in the political sphere, and along free-market lines in the economic sphere. As the culmination of many jostling traditions – the universalism of the American and French revolutions, nineteenth-century liberalism and *laissez-faire*, the twentieth-century welfare state and consumer capitalism – modern society is inevitably an egalitarian enterprise. The logic of the marketplace, and less obviously of the legislature, is of pleasure and plurality, in Eagleton's phrase 'of a great decentered network of desires of which individual consumers [he could well have added "voters"] are the passing functions'.[24]

The Enlightenment's intellectual project, in contrast, aimed to establish the rule of Reason. Through philosophical scepticism and empirical inquiry it aimed to come to the truth, regardless of established belief or political convenience. That truth, in turn, would be assailed by new assaults of scepticism. This scientific and professional tradition, as truly an heir of the Enlightenment as democratic politics and mass markets, is rooted in the idea of technical expertise, which could not be guaranteed to produce egalitarian outcomes. The two projects, therefore, are in potential conflict. As Edward Shils has argued,

> the growth of scientific knowledge has not turned out to be compatible with the liberal idea of the equal distribution of knowledge to the adult public . . . The problems created for liberal democracy by the growth of knowledge and its distribution have not been resolved.[25]

This tension, analogous to but differently constructed from those other tensions between a volatile, ephemeral, amoral capitalism and the ideology of political order, and between a techno-science state and an autonomous Culture, is at the root of the neo-conservative backlash, which is the first and more trivial manifestation of *posthistoire*. According to Habermas, 'this neo-conservative leave-taking of modernity is directed . . . not to the unchecked dynamism of societal modernization but to the husk of a cultural self-understanding of modernity which appears to have been overtaken'.[26] The dilemma is real. Clearly science cannot be allowed to be polluted by un-Reason, or subordinated to non-cognitive values. On the other hand, knowledge must be distributed as widely and fairly as possible to allow citizens and consumers to make well-informed democratic and market choices. Mass higher education systems are caught in the middle of this dilemma.

Critics of high modernity tend to emphasize the former, the Enlightenment's intellectual project, at the expense of the latter, its social project.

This preference is reinforced by their distaste for bureaucratization which inevitably accompanied the growth of a mass society organized according to democratic principles. The Tocquevillian ideal of civil society able to resist the pressures of massification through voluntary association is an anachronism at the end of the twentieth century. As has been argued in the last chapter, post-Fordism with its information super-highways and pastiche consumer choice is unlikely to restore its viability.

The cultural significance of the information technology revolution is often misunderstood. Far from leading to a recovery (or 'virtual' representation) of civic intimacy, it is likely instead to promote a far-reaching individualization, or privatization, equally inimical to the voluntarism of civil society and the bureaucracy of the welfare state. As Ithiel de Sola Pool argued more than a decade ago:

> The falling cost of electronic logic supports the trend towards individualization. The growing abundance of bandwidth in transmission and better management of the electromagnetic spectrum creates the technical opportunities for small-group communication. Satellites and fiber optics are making costs more distance-insensitive.[27]

Neo-conservative critics, many of whom started out as élitist liberals, are also concerned to restore the idea of cultural authority, another hopeless ambition. For Shils the key is 'truthful knowledge', recalling Matthew Arnold's strikingly similar phrase in *Culture and Anarchy*,[28] 'the best knowledge'. The connection between knowledge, in the sense of science, and truth, in a moral context, is reasserted. Allan Bloom's preoccupation with Platonic idealism in *The Closing of the American Mind*[29] is typical (earlier Karl Popper had seen Plato in an opposite light, as a proto-authoritarian, in *The Open Society and Its Enemies*).[30] Modernism's apparent refusal to associate the good, the true and the beautiful is one of the principal charges laid against it by neo-conservatives.

They deplore the amorality and ambiguity of modern thought, as two sides of the same coin. Bloom located the roots of modernism in the pre- and post-First World War German world, the world of Vienna and Weimar, an interesting identification in the light of their key role in developing the so-called 'international' style in architecture, which is also the target of post-modern architects. 'The good, the true and the beautiful have been displaced by the amoral, the relative and the banal; Socrates by Heidegger.'[31] The latter Bloom saw, along with Nietzsche, as the 'master lyricists' of modern culture.

A less histrionic target is the relativism embedded in modern thought which arguably is an analogue of the reductionism so powerfully characteristic of modern science. Critics of high modernity are uncomfortable with the ideas of the philosopher Richard Rorty, who sees intellectual progress as the outcome of clashes and negotiation between different vocabularies rather than in terms of the creation of a universal vocabulary capable of expressing all truths.[32] Clifford Geertz, the anthropologist, has offered a similar but more pragmatic account:

The problem of the integration of cultural life becomes one of making it possible for people inhabiting different sorts of worlds to have a genuine, and reciprocal, impact upon one another . . . The first is surely to accept the depth of the differences, the second to understand just what, and the third to construct some sort of vocabulary in which they can be publicly formulated.[33]

Neo-conservative leave-takers worry about such ideas – although Rorty does not deny that progress is possible and Geertz acknowledges the need for people inhabiting different worlds to have 'a genuine, and reciprocal, impact' on each other. They worry about where such ideas lead. Eagleton's description of 'theory' as 'a porous space opened up by an upheaval in the discursive division of labour, in which a whole lot of ways of speaking with almost nothing in common with each other proceed to argue the toss over an object . . . whose definition is part of the problem' would confirm their worst fears.[34]

The rise of theory and the popularity of deconstruction in the humanities are seen as undermining the idea of a canon of excellence validated by intellectual and cultural criteria transcending subjective individual preferences and transient social norms. C. van Woodward, reviewing Dinesh D'Souza's *Illiberal Education: The Politics of Race and Sex on Campus*, wrote:

Recurrent themes [of deconstruction] were the impossibility of objectivity, the futility of the search for truth, and the absence of authority for designating any works whatever as classics or part of a canon. The rhetoric of some deconstructionists is carried to the point of trivializing the idea of the humanities.[35]

The social and now the natural sciences, the supposed stronghold of positivistic truth, have also been invaded by relativism. Here Kuhn is a particular target, although he himself does not see the incommensurability of successful scientific paradigms as an obstacle to the progressive ranking of 'normal science'.

The main difficulty encountered by this neo-conservative critique is that there is an unresolved tension between its commitment to cognitive norms and respect for Culture, a rerun perhaps of the old argument between truth and meaning. If the modern system is defined in terms of scientific progress, or Habermas's societal modernization, the need for an ever finer division of intellectual labour is inescapable. Shils, for one, accepted that such specialization is 'an inevitable and fruitful condition of scientific discovery'. However, if modernity is defined instead in terms of an attempt at, in Habermas's words again, 'cultural self-understanding', then specialization becomes an obstacle. Shils again:

The concern for the whole is a transcendental value. It is not only transcendent of material interests, of the various sectors of society; it is also transcendent with respect to power and the desire for it, and with respect to prestige and pride and the desire for them.[36]

Ultimately the neo-conservative version of *posthistoire*, by insisting on universal, even absolute, values, comes close to denying the dynamism, socially derived as much as intellectually determined, of the very cognitive values it aspires to defend against all-comers, academic relativists, social relevantists, political correctors. This dynamism plainly owes as much to the imperatives of socio-economic change as to the inner life of academic disciplines. Moreover, a key question is ducked – do neo-conservatives actually believe in these absolutes or do they, following Plato, argue that while it is not necessary for the philosophers to believe in the myths it is expedient that the people do so? If it is the latter, they are guilty of a worse *trahison des clercs* than their radical-liberal opponents.

If, less probably, it is the former, they are forced to acknowledge the binding power of these myth-absolutes in the face of the disintegrative forces of empirical science. They must either assert the autonomy of Culture, but on grounds far less confident and sure than Arnold's, or accept an even more radical version of *posthistoire*, which comes close to denying the cognitive dynamism of modernity. For example, around the claims of modern science, at once universalizing and reductionist, Steiner (although not a neo-conservative) drew a still wider circle.

> A positivist cosmology, because it would tie 'strings' (the latest mathematical-imagistic device in the quest for a General Theory) around the universe, is finite. Theories, crucial experiments, algebraic models aim at proof. Proof is, in essence, terminal. Even at infinity – itself a precise, technical concept – there is end-stopping. But the humblest of myths, on the contrary, is open-ended. The inference of trans-rational possibility in all authentic mythical forms – theirs is, indeed, 'the music of what happens' – is not archaic indulgence. Myth offers to our impatient questioning the most vivid perception of the neighbourhood of our everyday experience of the 'otherness' in life and in death.[37]

Steiner, of course, argued that modernism must be seen as an unacknowledged, and therefore unrequited, wager on transcendence, as an attempt to assert 'the ultimately theological re-insurance of the very concept of meaningfulness without offering in return the collateral of an avowed faith'. In other words, the Enlightenment, the scientific tradition, the modern system, all must be read as post-Judaeo-Christian phenomena. 'There is language, there is art, because there is the "the other".'[38]

However, it is *posthistoire* in its other form, as post-modernism, which is the principal challenge to the secular and scientific traditions that make up the modern system. Or, rather, re-echoing Gehlen's phrase about the premises of the Enlightenment being dead and only its consequences remaining, post-modernism has the effect of deconstructing the intellectual and cultural values of modernism, its cognitive practices, while leaving untouched (and uncriticized) the economic and technical relations which these values historically made possible, its social practices. In Habermas's words, a self-sufficient advancing modernization of society has separated itself from the impulses of a cultural modernity that has seemingly become obsolete in the meantime; it only carries out the functional laws of economy and state, technology and science, which are supposed to have amalgamated into a system that cannot be influenced.[39]

Post-modernism's relation to that 'self-sufficient advancing modernization' is one of ironic detachment.

It evades definition – by design. Its intentions are anti-holistic; its theme anti-coherence. One way to characterize post-modernism is to employ a favourite metaphor. Modernism is a grand hotel, related processes organized according to hegemomic themes. Post-modernism, in contrast, is a shopping mall, an infrastructure that services unrelated enterprises devoid of authoritative contexts. The results are not all bad. The rise of post-modernism has, unintentionally, permitted the recovery of social forms of knowledge suppressed by the expert professionalized knowledge characteristic of modernity. If all cognitive structures are 'inventions', the latter's claims are no stronger than the former's. For example, oral tradition and popular memory are just as worthy of the historian's attention as the products of archival research.[40] But the general effect is of incoherence on the grand scale. Jim Collins has described the post-modern perspective in the following terms: 'Culture is no longer a unitary, fixed category, but a decentered, fragmentary assemblage of conflicting voices and institutions.'[41]

Jean-François Lyotard, post-modernism's highest priest, offered a similar account. 'Modern' he designated as

any science that legitimates itself with reference to a metadiscourse . . . making an explicit appeal to some grand narrative, such as the dialectics of spirit, the hermeneutics of meaning, the emancipation of the rational or working subject, or the creation of wealth.[42]

So out go Hegel, Marx, Freud, Adam Smith – and with them much of the intellectual apparatus of the Enlightenment. In contrast, post-modernism, according to Lyotard, 'denies itself the solace of good forms' and 'seeks new presentations, not in order to enjoy them but to impart a stronger sense of the unpresentable'. Jacques Derrida, a powerful precursor of post-modernism, discussed the same paradox, the need to exploit the techniques of modernism in order to explode its intellectual claims. 'It is a question of explicitly and systematically posing the problem of the status of a discourse which borrows from a heritage the resources necessary for the destruction of that heritage itself.'[43]

The origins of an intellectual movement which aims to celebrate the unpresentable are necessarily obscure. But three main currents can be identified. The first provides a bridge back into neo-conservative thought. It is characterized by the title of Daniel Bell's first book, *The End of Ideology*.[44] Although soon after its publication in 1960 the turbulence associated with student revolt in the West and the aftershocks of decolonization in the Third World appeared to contradict his thesis, the title proclaimed the advance of pragmatism, now ironically but suggestively re-echoed in Francis Fukuyama's *The End of History and the Last Man*, a reworking in Hegelian language of a Parsonian text.[45]

Subsequent events – the decline of the New Left during the 1970s (in its socio-political if not its academic manifestation), and the crumbling of communism in eastern Europe two decades later (the trigger for Fukuyama's book) – have tended to confirm the long-term accuracy of Bell's argument that the grand ideologies of the nineteenth and early twentieth centuries had become anachronisms. They led only to bloody and futile revolution, totalitarianism, world war, holocaust. But the modern system cannot easily be absolved from blame, except by unconvincingly privileging its democratic-capitalist variant. Either it has been implicated in the construction of totalizing discourses, as an antiphony to the old religions, or, through the reductionism of its science and technology, created both the moral vacuum these discourses filled and developed the techniques they employed.

Here the two critiques of modernism, the neo-conservative and the postmodern, coalesce. In his memoirs, Karl Popper recalled realizing in the Vienna of the 1920s the hidden arrogance of Marxism: 'It was a terrible thing to arrogate to oneself a kind of knowledge which made it a duty to risk the lives of other people for an uncritically accepted dogma, or for a dream that might turn out to be unrealisable.'[46] *The Open Society and Its Enemies* arose from this simple thought.[47] Writing in the Paris of the 1970s Lyotard associated 'the nostalgia for the whole and the one' with Terror and 'the fantasy to seize reality.'[48]

The movement towards a post-industrial society discussed in the previous chapter also undermined the claims of grand theory. In a post-Fordist economy dominated by service and knowledge industries rather than manufacturing, by consumers rather than producers, by symbols rather than goods, class-based analyses of society seem to make less sense and also the certainties of liberal economics appear to creak. At the same time Freudian categories, generated within the context of high-bourgeois *fin-de-siècle* Vienna, appear less relevant in a late twentieth-century world where outer-directed repression has been replaced by inner-directed hedonism. As a result, two of the main movements on which the modern system historically relied, in both social analysis and psychoanalysis, have lost their bite. Here, too, pragmatism seemed to be vindicated as ideology dwindled.

The shrivelling of the intellectual forms associated with the modern system takes two further forms which can also be interpreted as a (re?)turn to pragmatism. First, the advance of new information technologies, the capacity of next-generation computers to handle immensely complicated data sets and the development of artificial intelligence may enable electronic processes to replace the cognitive structures, based on cultural norms, within which science formerly made progress. Second, as memories of religious categories fade, their ability to suggest what Steiner called 'higher things', contexts of meaningfulness, will become more feeble. He discussed this possibility in suggestive terms that link the technical and the metaphysical:

> It may be that the verticalities of reference to 'higher things', to the impalpable and mythical which are still incised in our grammars, which are still the ontological guarantors of the arcs of metaphor, will drain from speech (consider the 'languages' of the computer and the codes of artificial intelligence). Should these mutations of consciousness and expression come into force, the forms of aesthetic making we have known will no longer be productive. They will be relegated to historicity. Correspondingly, the modes of response, of hermeneutic encounter . . . will become archaeologies.[49]

Post-modernism's second current is more obvious – post-structuralism, which flourished most notably in France in the late 1960s and 1970s. As its name suggests, it succeeded structuralism. Structuralists such as Claude Lévi-Strauss a decade or so earlier, and Ferdinand de Saussure at the end of the nineteenth century, had been preoccupied with the deep structures of language, and consequently with cognitive structures. Post-structuralists, in contrast, were sceptical of such efforts. Instead they saw language as a pattern of *différence* (its internal inconsistencies and volatility) and *différance* (its external deference to the expectations it created). Post-structuralism was treated with suspicion in Britain. The most famous post-structuralist, Derrida, was an ambiguously received figure. But, through his charismatic studies of sexuality and madness, Michel Foucault contributed to the powerful effect of post-structuralism by appearing to deny the possibility of Shils's 'truthful knowledge'.

It is not necessary to follow Derrida, Foucault, Paul de Man and the rest into the thickets of deconstruction. But, by emphasizing the contingency of meaning and the slipperiness of language, post-structuralist thought has become a key component of the post-modern mentality. The same emphasis has encouraged those radicals who aim to deconstruct the very notion of secular rationality. In their view the modern system is flawed, not because modernization has become uncoupled from modernity, but because it embodies the subordination of its cognitive practices to its social practices, Culture to capitalism. Their intention is to pull away 'the veil of reason from the sheer will to power', or to 'shake the iron cage in which the spirit of modernity has been objectified in societal form'.

The third, and most recent, current that has produced post-modernism was a question of style. It all began with buildings, a rejection of the 'international' style, the austere unadorned functional architecture which could be traced back to Adolf Loos, Walter Gropius and the Bauhaus and later Mies van der Rohe, and which came to dominate the skyline of most cities. In this context architecture was much more than style. It was a powerful expression, in values and function, of urbanization. The 'international' style was taken to represent the modern system at its most uncompromising. Moreover, it sprang from modernism's heartland – Vienna before the First

World War, Weimar Germany between the wars and post-war America. And, through this association, it seemed to be related, not simply to urbanism, but also to the wider currents of thought now regarded as typically modern – Keynesian economics, Joycian prose, Freudian psychoanalysis, Parsonian sociology and so on.

Post-modern architects tried to soften, or to subvert, the 'international' style by reattaching ornament, tolerating eclecticism, indulging in eccentricity, denying functionality. Although not necessarily a new approach (there are echoes of the vernacular architecture of the late nineteenth century in many post-modern buildings), it was, cognitively, a representation of anti-coherence and, in terms of social practice, an intriguing reflection of changing patterns of economic organization and new lifestyles. It was the architecture of the out-of-town business park, of the private waterside development.

A prominent post-modern architect, Charles Jencks, described its ideology in the following terms: 'I would define post-modernism as double-coding; the combination of modern techniques with something else (usually traditional building) in order for architecture to communicate with the public and with a concerned minority, usually other architects.'[50] Here is a suggestive affinity with Habermas's generalized account of the divorce between modernization (in this case, modern techniques) and modernity (the styles and values which accompanied the development of these techniques). Double-coding, or multiple-coding, has become a distinctively post-modern device. It not only allows architects – as well as writers, scholars and even scientists – to address several audiences at the same time but also asserts the equal validity of these multiple meanings.

To borrow Eagleton's terminology, transgressive capitalism has invaded the autonomous space of Culture. In the process the notion of a 'unified subject', in art or thought, has been destroyed. Or, alternatively, the social practices engendered by the modern system have overwhelmed its cognitive structures. Or, more simply still, the subordination of popular taste to élite culture, of the people to the philosophers, has been replaced by an anti-hierarchical pluralism. Brian Rotman has described the new aesthetic, and intellectual, environment in these terms:

> where buildings and indeed all cultural texts can, by amalgamating professional and popular codes, simultaneously address different audiences and aesthetic agendas, thus making eclecticism a conscious and deliberate means of stylising and vernacularising the very fragmentation of the contemporary context which appears to the critics of the post-moderns as schizophrenic collapse.[51]

The connections between the popularity of post-modernism, in the aesthetic and intellectual arenas, and the growing preference for free-market rather than welfare-state solutions, in the socio-political arena, are persistent. They are reinforced by the metaphor of the grand hotel of modernism and the shopping mall of post-modernism. The former can be seen as reflecting the reasonable and organized society of the social-democratic age, while the latter is aligned with the more volatile society typical of the present age of enterprise. But the implied identification of modernism with welfare states and post-modernism with free markets is too neat. The state and the market are both components of the modern system.

It is equally plausible to argue that post-modernism is an extension of the post-materialism identified by Roland Inglehart, which has already been discussed in the previous chapter.[52] He argued that, as preoccupation with material needs waned, especially in developed countries and among the professional middle classes (many of whom, suggestively, were employed outside the market economy), there was likely to be increased emphasis on satisfying other needs, which were often expressed in terms of cultural goods. His analysis has much in common with Fred Hirsch's distinction between positional (= material?) and non-positional (= cultural?) goods, which has also been discussed.[53] A not dissimilar analysis was offered by Daniel Bell in his book *The Cultural Contradictions of Capitalism*.[54] Producers must behave in a disciplined, rational (and modernist?) manner, while consumers must react in an impulsive, intuitive (and post-modern?) way. In a society whose centre of gravity is shifting from production to consumption this may have far-reaching cultural consequences. If modernization has become an autonomous techno-phenomenon, no longer reliant on the rationalizing values of modernity, intellectual life can be allowed to become more playful – because its cognitive structures are no longer central to the process of material improvement.

Posthistoire is a fractured phenomenon. In its neo-conservative form it seeks to retreat from the hyperreflexivity characteristic of the modern system; in its post-modern form it aims beyond it. Neo-conservatives are committed to the canon; post-modernists to double-coding. Neo-conservatives to 'truthful knowledge'; post-modernists to *différence* and *différance*. Neo-conservatives aim at a cultural integrity that transcends, but does not contradict, scientific reductionism; post-modernists deny themselves 'the solace of good forms'. It is within these fractures that the mass university has to manoeuvre.

The key questions, however, remain. First, to what extent do the social practices of the modern system – in a word, modernization – depend upon its cognitive (and cultural) structures – modernity? This question is generally posed in terms of the projection of the secular scientific tradition beyond its heartland in the open societies of the West into, for example, the segmented societies of the Pacific Rim. But it can also be posed in the context of the projection of élite culture into a more democratic, or populist, environment at home (whether democratization takes the form of efforts to reduce privilege and expand opportunities to hitherto marginal social groups, or to promote consumer capitalism). The issue is the same. Can, should, the practice of secular rationality be successfully disembedded from the particular cultural milieu within which it first developed?

Second, a more radical question, can it be disembedded from traditional notions of scientific truth and objectivity? The reflexivity characteristic of contemporary intellectual culture can be interpreted in two contradictory ways. Either its open-endedness, its refusal to accept closure of any question, can be interpreted in Popperian terms as an affirmation of two centuries or more of scientific scepticism; no proof, however solid, is for ever. Or, more disturbingly, these qualities can be regarded as licensing the view that, if no final truths can ever be discovered, the very notion of truth becomes problematical. In the modern system reflexivity tended to be interpreted in the first way. In a volatile post-modern environment it is perhaps more likely to be interpreted in the second way.

Universities have been key institutions within the modern system. They are intimately associated with its core values. In élite higher education systems answers to these two questions were straightforward. Modernization and modernity were bound up together. Social practices and cognitive structures could not be separated. Universities were global institutions because their intellectual values were universal, not because globalization was a techno-phenomenon no longer ultimately guided by these universal values. Similarly, the reflexivity institutionalized in universities was an elaboration of a familiar scientific scepticism, not a denial of the possibility of 'truthful knowledge'.

However, the mass university is deeply influenced by these changing rules of intellectual engagement. It cannot give such confident answers. Not only does the entire modern system itself appear less solid, but the purposes of universities have been alarmingly enlarged. The articulation of social practices, which are plural if not always transgressive, is as much their job as the maintenance of coherent cognitive structures, still less fixed cultural values. Moreover, not only have universities become agents of modernization, as a techno-phenomenon to which the values of secular rationality are only lightly attached, but the universalizing claims associated with these values have been largely abandoned. These far-reaching shifts in intellectual culture have radical implications for higher education systems, which are considered in the final section of this chapter. But first the equally fundamental changes taking place in the science and technology system must be examined.

Science and technology

Much of the university's contemporary prestige is derived from its claim to play a leading role in knowledge production. It is commonly regarded as the premier scientific institution. The university is a premium institution, in the sense that it enjoys the highest scientific standing; apparent exceptions such as the Bell Laboratories in the United States simply prove the rule. The university is pre-eminent because it monopolizes definitions of what is, and what is not, science, and so, in effect, validates scientific excellence. The university is also first, in the sense that it seems to be at the beginning of the production line of scientific knowledge; its basic research kick-starts the whole process of innovation. And the university is *primus inter pares*, among rival scientific institutions, because it provides the open environment in which curiosity-driven science, the best and most productive kind in the long run, can flourish.

Two questions are raised by this account of the university's role in the production of scientific knowledge. First, is it an accurate account? Set against the historical record, the university's claim to be the leading scientific institution is not strong. For a long time institutions such as the Royal Society were more effective than the traditional universities which, because of their religious orientation or commitment to liberal (i.e. humanistic) education, often clung for too long to pre-scientific patterns of thought. To the extent that independent scientists required an organizational context for their work, they looked to the learned societies rather than the universities. Scientific advances were reported and discussed in the lecture halls of the Royal Society, the Royal Institution and other learned societies, not Oxford and Cambridge.

Other more modern-minded universities, such as the civic universities established in the second half of the nineteenth century, were initially subordinated to local industry and business – chemicals in Manchester, mining in Newcastle, textiles in Leeds. The technological needs of industry shaped the embryonic research programmes of these universities, which had been founded principally to provide professional training rather than undertake scientific research. Little of their research work was basic in today's terms, or only contingently. The PhD, the foundation of scientific training, arrived in Britain half a century after Germany and the United States.

In the twentieth century the Royal Society, and analogous institutions in other disciplines and other countries, became unable to cope with the logistical sophistication of modern scientific research. Universities, because of their organizational strength, took over as the leading scientific institutions. Thus began the great age of the Cavendish and other university laboratories. But their current dominance is less complete than it seems. Learned societies still represent powerful networks through which prestige and patronage circulate. Renewed emphasis has also been placed on application, utility and relevance, re-echoing the practical orientation of much early university research.

Research councils, first and foremost the heirs of the learned-society tradition as expressed through the practice of peer review, have now come under pressure to represent also the industrial-utility tradition. The councils not only determine scientific priorities but also increasingly define scientific problems, in the context of political agendas and/or on the advice of non-university scientists, and even non-scientists in their role as 'users'.[55] Both traditions, therefore, continue to some extent to compromise the autonomy of university science, and so qualify the university's leading role in knowledge production.

That role, today apparently so dominant, was a late addition to the purposes of the university. It was largely an accident of war. Scientific research which was national (or international) in scope and generally basic, rather than of largely local significance and applied, became embedded in university missions after the shock of the First World War, when coincidentally the PhD was first introduced. But it was only during the Second World War and in the years of post-war reconstruction that universities acquired their present status as the leading institutions of knowledge production. The story is familiar – atomic scientists and code-breakers, social planners and Keynesian economists. The answer to this first question, therefore, is that the standard account probably overstates the leadership exercised by universities in the production of scientific knowledge.

The second question is more important in the context of exploring the meanings of mass higher education. Does this standard account provide an accurate conceptual description of knowledge production, or does it offer an interpretation that is both university-centric and anachronistic, and so doubly misleading? The remainder of this section will be devoted to discussing the issues which arise from this question. The argument can be simply stated. The conditions under which scientific knowledge is produced are being radically revised – partly because of the reordering of the economy, the process labelled either post-industrialism or post-Fordism which was described in the last chapter; and partly for epistemological reasons which reflect the larger shifts in intellectual culture that have just been discussed. The role played by universities under these revised conditions of knowledge production is much less clear.

These changes have been described in terms of a shift from mode 1 knowledge production to mode 2.[56] The former represents the traditional model of how scientific knowledge is produced. Mode 1 had four broad characteristics. First, the production process was seen as linear, causal and cumulative. Science generated within universities or other research establishments was 'applied' to solve practical problems, whether social or commercial. This application normally took the form of science being 'transferred' into or through technology which was the source of innovation. The language of application and transfer was, and is, revealing because it suggested that scientific creativity was seen as the prime mover in the process of knowledge production. Paradoxically, it was also asserted that science was autonomous. Although it might help eventually to solve practical problems, scientific problems were initially defined within and by the scientific community.

Second, under conditions of mode 1 knowledge production, science was thought of as a closed system. Of course, it was not a secret system. It was accepted that scientific findings had to be wide open to scrutiny. It was by being put to the proof or, for Popperians, through the cycle of hypothesis–falsification–thesis that science made progress. It was a closed system in the sense that only scientists counted. Definitions of what science was, and in particular what good science was, had to be left to scientists, acknowledged experts in the various disciplines. Only physicists could comment sensibly on physics. And, because pure science was seen not only as the start of the chain of knowledge production but also as the ultimate source of innovation, this meant that the authority of scientists was not confined to their particular disciplinary territories but extended to the application of their research findings and even to the wider context of innovation.

Third, because scientific authority was vested in communities of scientists and rooted in their disciplinary expertise, mode 1 science was inherently reductionist. A small élite of creative scientists might be able to adopt a synoptic, even holistic, approach without compromising their authority. But for most working scientists their claim to be regarded as experts rested on their command of a limited terrain. Inter-disciplinarity, still more trans-disciplinarity, threatened to dilute that authority and expertise, and so posed an unacceptable professional risk. More sophisticated instrumentation, which was both more expensive and more restricted in its uses, intensified this trend towards reductionism.

But the decisive factors were professional rather than technical in origin, because the same prejudice against inter-disciplinarity and the same tendency to divide into specialities, and sub-specialities, could be observed in scientific fields in which the impact of new instrumentation and experimental techniques was not decisive. Again, the pre-eminence of science in knowledge production enabled these reductionist habits to spread into the wider process of innovation. Techniques which arguably had proved effective in solving scientific problems were instinctively applied to tackling larger problems in society and the marketplace, with less happy results.

Fourth, in mode 1 the funding and organization of science were regarded as public responsibilities – for practical reasons and reasons of principle. Practically, science had to be largely funded from public sources because pure science especially, although the key to consequential innovation, was by definition pre-social and pre-commercial. Its benefits could not be predetermined. Beneficiaries, and so contributors to its cost, could not be accurately identified in advance. In any case, premature identification was considered undesirable for reasons of fundamental principle. The best science, which produced the most successful innovation, was likely to be produced within an open and therefore disinterested environment which encouraged curiosity and creativity. The state was best able to provide such an environment, although as guardian of the public interest not as a direct or proxy customer for research 'services', which could not have been identified at this primary stage in the innovation process. It was also important that the professional autonomy of scientists should be similarly guaranteed, because their collective expertise validated good science (and, by logical extension, successful innovation).

Mode 1 has been summarized in the following terms:

For many, Mode 1 is identical to what is meant by science. Its cognitive and social norms determine what shall count as significant problems, who shall be allowed to practise science and what constitutes good science. Forms of practice which adhere to these rules are by definition scientific while those that violate them are not.[57]

Clearly the university played a key role in knowledge production under such conditions. Its crucial contribution to wealth generation and, more mutedly, social improvement was confirmed as the first link in the chain of innovation. But, at the same time, the autonomy of the university mirrored the autonomy of science. It was the professional home of most working scientists, and so institutionalized their expertise and authority. Reductionism was reflected in its academic structures, through faculties, departments and research institutes. Finally the university was a public institution, able to resist prematurely expressed social and commercial pressures and disinterested because its primary loyalty was to the values of science.

Described in such unqualified terms mode 1 cannot be accepted as an accurate empirical account of how scientific knowledge was (or is) produced. It has already been pointed out that the university's present pre-eminence in knowledge production is both recent in origin, essentially a post-1945 if not a post-1960 phenomenon, and less secure and complete than is commonly supposed. Much university research had severely practical beginnings. Even the Royal Society and similar learned societies were founded with utilitarian purposes in mind. Many 'pure' sciences evolved out of their 'applied' variants, not the other way round. The autonomy of science, and of the university, reflected a congruence of priorities between academic scientists and their paymasters and/or customers rather than a unilateral assertion of independence. But, myth or not, the mode 1 model of knowledge production probably accurately reflects the assumptions still made by many working scientists.

Those assumptions are now being challenged, and undermined, by a new model of how scientific knowledge is produced, mode 2. Its characteristics are very different. First, while mode 1 was linear and cumulative with (pure) science as the ultimate source of innovation, mode 2 is multi-variant, unsystematic and even anti-coherent. The source of innovation is to be found not only, or even especially, in the laboratory. It is just as likely to occur in the dynamics of the marketplace or in larger socio-economic or cultural transformations. Indeed, it is most likely to arise in the often contested borderland between the university and the market/society. As a result technology is not subordinated to, or a derivative of, science. It is an autonomous terrain. For the same reason the language of application and transfer breaks down. So too does the metaphor of a chain of innovation because this suggests causal links for which there is little supporting evidence.

Second, it logically follows that knowledge production is an open system. The 'users' of science and technology are creative agents, not passive beneficiaries. And users extend to all those who are ultimately affected by innovation, not just immediate 'customers'. Their conceptions and needs play a crucial role in determining not only scientific priorities (not too difficult for scientists to accept), but also definitions of scientific problems (harder to accept), and even of scientific solutions (hardest of all to accept). If a privileged status is conferred on particular actors it comes from their experience of innovation as much as their disciplinary expertise. A key group is those who combine this experience and expertise, and are sometimes described as knowledge brokers not only because, in practical terms, they match scientific resources, both intellectual and logistical, to so-called real-world problems but also because, in conceptual terms, they are best able to interpret and integrate the internal and external dynamics of science and technology.

Third, mode 2 knowledge production is synoptic rather than reductionist. The focus shifts from the best way to make progress in just one part of the process of innovation, purish science in university or quasi-university settings, to how best to manage the whole process. Once disciplinary specialization was a powerful tool, although even here scientific breakthroughs often required imaginative leaps, the construction of creative hypotheses, even metaphors, which had little to do with the cumulative accretion of routine research. Now it has become impossible to grasp the totality and the interconnectedness of innovation through a reductionist strategy. To do this it is necessary not just to create multi-disciplinary teams, but to transcend, on occasion even to deconstruct, disciplines because they are organized round internally generated affinities and self-referential norms.

Fourth, under mode 2 conditions knowledge production takes place largely in the market, if the end-products of innovation are tradable goods and services, or in the wider social arena, if they are public goods and services. Unlike mode 1 science, it does not need to take place within a privileged arena, protected by public policy. Such privileges and protection would be counter-productive. Knowledge is not simply a predetermined input into the process of innovation. In advanced economies it is also an output, as has been argued in the preceding chapter. More radically still, knowledge *is* process, in the sense that concepts, techniques and uses are tightly interwoven. Nor under mode 2 conditions is scientific knowledge the near-monopoly of specialized and autonomous institutions which not only provide a home for professional scientists but also an environment in which scientific curiosity can roam at will. Again this would make no sense because mode 2 knowledge is neither pre-social nor pre-commercial.

However, to draw too sharp a contrast between mode 1 and mode 2 can be misleading. This dichotomy serves to highlight trends, not to offer definitive accounts of the process of knowledge production. A number of important qualifications must be made. First, mode 2 is not a new phenomenon. Indeed, it can be argued that it describes the dominant mode of knowledge production until the scientific revolution of the seventeenth century established science as an autonomous domain, or the industrial revolution two centuries later demonstrated the power of a science-derived technology, or even until the professionalization and institutionalization of science and scientists in the twentieth-century university.

The French historian Fernand Braudel, in his great study of civilization and capitalism from the fifteenth to the eighteenth centuries, described the contingency of innovation, on its socio-economic setting, in terms which echo this account of mode 2:

As long as daily life proceeded without too much difficulty in its appointed pathway, within the framework of inherited structures, there was no economic motive for change. Inventors' blueprints (for there were always some) stayed in their drawer. It was only when things went wrong, when society came up against the ceiling of the possible that people turned to technology, and interest was aroused for the thousand potential inventions, out of which one would always be recognized as the best . . . For there are always hundreds of possible innovations lying dormant; sooner or later it becomes a matter of urgency to call one of them to life.[58]

The assumption underlying mode 1, made by many academic scientists, is that the dynamism of modern science has reversed this order, making socio-economic conditions contingent on successful innovation (in which science, of course, plays a leading role). Braudel's anachronistic account, they argue, describes the subordinate role of innovation in a pre-modern world. The theories of post-industrialism, which were reviewed in the previous chapter, tend to support this view. But there are two counter-arguments. First, much routine innovation still occurs in the way Braudel described. It is, in his phrase, 'called to life' by changing socio-economic conditions and by the enlargement of human possibilities in the intellectual and cultural spheres. Second, the success of science has raised expectations of its utility. It now permeates society. It must now operate in arenas in which the cognitive values and experimental techniques typical of mode 1 are no longer sufficient.

A second qualification is that mode 1 and mode 2 may describe different things. The former offers an account of science confined largely to research in a university or quasi-university setting; the latter is applied to knowledge in a wider sense, embracing the whole process of innovation, from initiation to evaluation. Yet there is a tension between the two accounts. Michael Gibbons and his co-authors argued: 'It is our contention that there is sufficient empirical evidence to indicate that a distinct set of cognitive and social practices is beginning to emerge and these practices are different from those that govern mode 1.'[59] In other words, the normative and professional structures of science – and, more controversially, definitions of successful science – are modified by changes in the production of knowledge. The former is ultimately subordinate to the latter.

Another way to describe the tension is as a clash of ideologies, between the individualist ethos of scientific creativity and the corporate ethos of knowledge production. In 1942, just when the university was becoming established as the leading scientific institution, the American sociologist Robert Merton attempted to systematize the ideology, or norms, of academic science. He did so in terms which echo many of the characteristics of mode 1 science. John Ziman described these norms in the following terms:

Communalism: Science is a collective enterprise, and the results of science should be made public at the earliest opportunity;

Universalism: Participation in the scientific enterprise should be open to all competent persons, regardless of race, religion, nationality or other affiliations;

Disinterestedness: Scientists should present their results impartially, as if they had no personal interest in their acceptability;

Originality: Research claims must be novel; copies of previously published work are not acceptable;

Scepticism: All research claims should be subjected to critical scrutiny and testing.[60]

Ziman contrasted these norms, the first letters of which spell out the acronym CUDOS, with another set of characteristics – Proprietary, Local, Authoritarian, Commissioned and Expert (or, as an acronym, PLACE).[61] The fit between CUDOS and mode 1, and PLACE and mode 2, is not exact. But it is suggestive.

A third qualification is that mode 1 and mode 2 are labels attached to bundles of attributes. These attributes are not necessarily internally consistent. For example, Ziman regarded 'expert' as characteristic of corporate research and development rather than of academic science, while others see the professionalization of science, and the expertise in which it is rooted and the reductionism which it engenders, as characteristic of mode 1. Similarly the universalism and disinterestedness celebrated by Ziman are characteristics which it is difficult to reconcile with Kuhn's assertion that 'normal' science is validated by self-referential scientific communities, which again are typical of mode 1.

Nor are these bundles of attributes easily distinguishable. According to Gibbons *et al.*:

Although Mode 1 and Mode 2 are distinct modes of production, they interact with each other. Specialists trained in the disciplinary sciences do enter Mode 2 knowledge production. While some may return to their original disciplinary base others will choose to follow a trail of complexity solving problems that are set by a sequence of application contexts. Conversely, some outputs of trans-disciplinary knowledge production, particularly new instruments, may enter and fertilise any number of disciplinary sciences.

Nevertheless, despite this interaction, what distinguished mode 1 from mode 2, they argued, was that in the former concepts were generated within a disciplinary context and in the latter in a context of application. 'In Mode 2 things are done differently and when enough things are done differently one is entitled to say that a new form has emerged.'[62]

The general characteristics which distinguish mode 1 scientific research from mode 2 knowledge production have already been identified in outline. However mode 2 has a number of fundamental attributes which it is important to consider in more detail – the production of knowledge in the context of application, or socially distributed knowledge; trans-disciplinarity;

heterogeneity and organizational diversity; social accountability and reflexivity; and quality control.

Knowledge in the context of application

In mode 2 the focus of knowledge production is not on disciplines but on applications. This is not the same as applied science, for two main reasons. First, there is often no pre-existing science which can be applied. Admittedly disciplines like computer science were established because existing disciplinary structures were inadequate. But, although their creation was in the context of application, their practice has come to be shaped by more conventional disciplinary norms typical of mode 1. Second, the term 'applied science' suggests that the basic concepts and methodologies are derived from fundamental disciplines which are essentially self-referential and have not been influenced (or contaminated?) by possible applications, and that only subsequently, and separately, are these concepts and methodologies applied to solve practical problems.

A more radical contextualization takes place under mode 2 conditions. Not only are knowledge outputs expected to be useful, knowledge itself is produced as a result of, and in the course of, permanent negotiation between practitioners, whether 'producers', 'brokers' or 'users' (categories which themselves lose much of their descriptive force). Basic science, as well as its applications, is generated within this process of negotiation. Not only commercially profitable or socially beneficial outcomes, not only research methodologies, but also fundamental concepts are negotiated in this way. And this negotiation is not confined to the commercial arena. Instead knowledge production is diffused through society, which is why it becomes plausible to talk of socially distributed knowledge.

The main reason for this new pattern of knowledge production is that, as has already been discussed in Chapter 3, modern economies are increasingly organized around various forms of knowledge – whether expressed in terms of improvement, exploitation or innovation. Two things flow from this. First, the production of knowledge becomes a central economic and social activity. As a result the monopoly of professional scientists is eroded. There is pressure for other actors to exercise greater influence over defining problems and determining priorities in order to increase the all-important productivity of knowledge. Second, the balance of scientific research, to the extent that it is an element within knowledge production, shifts. Its claim to be an autonomous domain is eroded, because knowledge production has become so tightly interwoven with other forms of economic production and social reproduction.

However, it is probably wrong to imply that, because knowledge is now more likely to be produced within a context of application, the creativity of scientists has necessarily been curbed. Fundamental theoretical problems are encountered just as frequently in a socially distributed knowledge system characteristic of mode 2. It is also wrong to exaggerate the novelty of such a system. As has already been argued, many pure disciplines evolved out of their applied analogues – or, rather, first took shape within a context of application. Many continue to display this characteristic. Medicine, technology and business are all negotiated disciplines, even if this negotiation takes place within narrow confines. And the humanities are embroiled in applications in a double sense – because of their links with the media and culture industry; and because creation and contextualization, and so application, are impossible to separate. Truth and meaning, to revisit an old dichotomy, are the same.

Trans-disciplinarity

Mode 2 knowledge production consists of more than simply assembling experts to work in teams on problems in an applications-oriented environment. For mode 2 to be recognized as a valid, and alternative, form of knowledge production, it must also be seen to be able to evolve distinctive cognitive patterns and social practices. To be effective a scientific framework needs to be created which, while inevitably transcending the boundaries and restrictive norms of existing disciplines, nevertheless provides a context in which the assembled experts can make their contributions. That framework is necessarily trans-disciplinary.

Trans-disciplinarity is different from multi-disciplinarity or inter-disciplinarity. The latter not only presuppose the existence of conventional disciplines, shaped by scientific affinities and policed by scientific communities rather than generated within a context of application, but also use components of these disciplines as pre-fabricated elements within larger or more novel scientific structures. Experts agree to co-operate to try to solve common problems while retaining their own distinctive disciplinary perspectives. Scientific coherence and professional continuity are provided by these perspectives which persist even though the problems change.

Trans-disciplinarity has a different starting point. It is volatile and often ephemeral, formed by short-term associations between scientists and others who do not aspire to 'grow' a new discipline such as biotechnology or socio-legal studies. Its theoretical and methodological structures do not pre-exist the applications context from which the trans-disciplinary project has sprung. Both are improvised. Nor is there a striving to integrate these structures into a coherent whole. Trans-disciplinarity persists not because of disciplinary continuities but through the succession of problems generated within a socially distributed knowledge system. It has been described as 'problem solving capability on the move.'[63]

But trans-disciplinarity is not necessarily inferior to discipline-based research. It has the capacity to develop new theoretical insights which are less likely to arise in a disciplinary, or even an inter-disciplinary or multi-disciplinary, setting. These insights cannot readily be redistributed to disciplines. Nevertheless they represent genuine, and often substantial, contributions to knowledge. These contributions are difficult to quantify. There have been significant increases in the number of collaborative papers in many scientific fields, which suggest that trans-disciplinarity is increasing. In electronics the total number of papers published in European journals grew by 48 per cent during the 1980s. But the number of non-collaborative papers was static, while that of collaborative papers increased threefold.[64] However, one of the characteristics of trans-disciplinary knowledge production is that its results are disseminated not so much through journals and conferences but through the scientific and management skills which members of transdisciplinary teams carry from one project to another.

Heterogeneity and organizational diversity

A third attribute of mode 2 knowledge production is that it takes place in a much wider variety of settings. One reason is that the focus has shifted from science, and so scientists, to knowledge, and so to an extended constituency of producers, brokers and users. By definition these participants have always been widely distributed. What has changed, therefore, is not their distribution but the definition of who participates in knowledge production. For example, nuclear energy is no longer seen as solely the business of physicists and nuclear engineers. Other scientists such as economists, risk analysts and environmental scientists are also involved. So too are politicians, planners, the mass media, community groups, activists of all kinds. If all these people are regarded as contributing to knowledge production, it is hardly surprising they are widely distributed.

A second, more substantial, reason is that core scientists, with clear disciplinary affiliations, are in fact more widely distributed. They are no longer concentrated so heavily in universities. They are also to be found working within government and in industry (large multinational corporations and smaller high-technology firms), in think-tanks and independent research institutes, or as consultants. This wider distribution is partly the result of the stagnation of the universities: fewer jobs, reduced prestige and lower salaries have reduced the attractiveness of careers in academic science, while opportunities have increased in other sectors. But it is partly the result of more deeply rooted trends. Government and industry, as the contours of the knowledge society have become clearer, have become more directly involved in knowledge production on their own account. The emphasis on applications, contextualization and trans-disciplinarity has encouraged the growth of more flexible research environments, such as think-tanks and independent research institutes. These trends reflect the transition to mode 2.

Two other aspects of heterogeneity and organizational diversity are important. First, knowledge production is certainly becoming less institutionalized and arguably less professionalized. The growth in the number of sites at which knowledge is produced, brokered or exploited has reversed the trend towards concentrating scientific research in university and quasi-university settings which was so strong between 1945 and 1980 (although the concentration of high-cost, theoretical, discipline-based research has continued). At the same time the structure of scientific 'careers' has been weakened, partly because more scientists are now employed in more flexible institutions and partly because, under the impact of trans-disciplinarity, the process of scientific research has become more volatile.

Second, advances in communications technology have made it possible to reconfigure scientific resources in novel and radical ways. Individual scientists and research sites can now be linked electronically. The need to build up large, cumbersome, resource-hungry infrastructures has been reduced. Access to expensive libraries, large data sets and sophisticated instrumentation has been eased. The 'invisible college' of disciplines and peers has been reinforced, but also modified, by the emergence of the 'virtual university', made up of widely distributed networks of highly diverse knowledge practitioners. Also many of the time-space obstacles to collaborative work have been removed. The mechanisms of publication and dissemination, too, have been transformed. The result is not only an increase in the number of participants in knowledge production but also important changes in the process, and so the nature, of knowledge production. The physical barriers to participation have been lowered at the same time as disciplinary frontiers have been opened.

Social accountability and reflexivity

A fourth attribute of mode 2 knowledge production is its greater emphasis on social accountability and reflexivity. There are two main reasons for this. First, some of the most dynamic scientific fields are in areas of acute controversy. Nuclear energy is perhaps the best example; political opposition has curbed the development of an industry which, with the exception of the disposal of nuclear waste, had largely overcome outstanding scientific and technical problems. But there are many others. Biotechnology and genetic engineering are controversial because they appear radically to upset the balance between the 'natural' and the 'artificial', by creating the capacity to manipulate basic biological processes in plants, animals and, most disturbingly, humans. Information technology and advanced information systems appear to represent threats to privacy and freedom because of their capacity to manipulate very large data sets.

Nor do all the examples of controversies provoked by scientific progress arise in this sombre Huxleyan brave new world. Advances in medicine now mean that doctors are forced to make not life-and-death but cost-benefit decisions. New communication technologies have transformed the organization of the mass media, leading to global concentration at the expense of local variation. However, this association between the cutting edge of science and technology and socio-political controversies is certainly not new; nor probably is it accidental. The links between academic science and military technology have always been close. So have the links of academic science with big business and, in the public sector, big bureaucracy. Science has always been part of the profit/progress nexus and contributed to mechanisms of social control, both controversial associations. And it is almost axiomatic that the most dynamic scientific arenas are also the most controversial, because the most radical advances threaten the greatest disturbance.

The second reason is that the pervasiveness, and permeability, of science have led to an extension of the number of participants in knowledge production. In mode 2 the 'scientification' of society has gone hand-in-hand with the 'socialization' of science. Theoretical science has acquired such importance that it can no longer be left to the scientists, in a narrow disciplinary sense. As a result, research teams are made up not only of core experts. They also include engineers, accountants, lawyers, sociologists, managers, and on occasion philosophers. They even embrace representatives of community, pressure and other interest groups which have a stake in the outcomes of the research. Particularly in areas of acute controversy, which tend also to be at the cutting edge of scientific advance, it is recognized that research cannot be confined to the solution of scientific and technical problems. It must take into account their implementation and broader social consequences. In assessing these the original core experts have no claim to special authority.

Social accountability, therefore, is not an afterthought. It is part of the research design, shaping basic concepts and determining which methodologies are appropriate. Nor is it solely a function of external representation, adding lay members to core experts who make up the research team. In mode 2 social accountability is internalized by scientists, who must be able to conceptualize research issues not simply in terms of their own disciplinary perspectives but in the broader context of the interests and values of other participants. Imagination, empathy and reflexivity are key qualities in mode 2 knowledge production. Far from these characteristics (especially the last) eroding standards of scientific rigour, their absence makes it difficult to engage in high-level science. Without them scientific problems will be inadequately, or mistakenly, conceptualized.

Quality control

The fourth attribute of mode 2 is the emergence of new patterns of quality control and, more fundamentally, of new definitions of scientific excellence. Because the number of participants in knowledge production has increased, and because scientific problems are now generated in a multidimensional context of application rather than the one-dimensional context of individual or allied disciplinary cultures, traditional forms of quality control are no longer sufficient or appropriate. New forms are emerging which have two main characteristics – an extension of the number and definition of 'peers'; and a shift from peer review to other forms of quality control.

Research problems, of course, have never been identified exclusively in terms of their scientific promise. They have always also had to appear timely in order to secure resources, whether from the university or research establishment or, as was nearly always necessary, from external funders such as research councils, government departments and industry. Peer-review judgements, therefore, have always had to embrace criteria which were, in some sense, extra-disciplinary or even non-cognitive. These criteria were often concerned with reinforcing professional hierarchies. But they were also influenced directly by considerations of political expediency or indirectly by assessments of socio-economic relevance.

In recent years these extra-disciplinary criteria have assumed greater importance. Research councils have acquired mission statements and business plans. They have established priorities, often in terms of designated programmes. Ziman described this change as a shift from 'peer review' to 'merit review'.[65] He distinguished between 'internal' criteria which related to the performance of the proposed research and therefore could only be assessed by specialists in the relevant field, and 'external' criteria which related to its anticipated results and consequently could also be assessed by non-specialists. The former he saw as amenable only to peer review, while the latter could be judged through a process of merit review.

However, in mode 2 a further shift takes place. The distinction between 'internal' and 'external' criteria is eroded, because it is no longer possible to separate the performance of research from its anticipated results. Peer-review and merit-review judgements are combined. No longer is research assessed in terms of its scientific promise first, and then, subsequently and separately, in terms of its timeliness. Nor is it simply that new questions – is it cost-effective?, is it socially acceptable?, is it likely to lead to profitable results? – are added to the old questions about theoretical rigour or methodological robustness. They cease to be separate questions. If knowledge is produced within a context of application, theoretical rigour and methodological robustness embrace issues of cost-effectiveness, social acceptability or commercial viability.

The affinities between this interpretation of science and technology, or more broadly knowledge production, and the accounts of post-industrialism offered in Chapter 3 and of shifts in intellectual culture discussed in the preceding section are striking. Both the socio-economic context and epistemological environment exhibit similar characteristics – anti-bureaucratic and anti-canonical, flexible and volatile, adaptable and ephemeral. And these are precisely the qualities which are re-echoed in this account of science and technology. The final section of this chapter considers the impact of these new environments – intellectual/cultural and scientific/technological – on the practice of higher education, in terms of both teaching and research.

Teaching and research

The impact of these new environments on the emerging mass higher education system is both general and specific. Their general impact is on the status of universities as knowledge institutions; their specific impact on detailed practices in teaching and research. The status of universities has been compromised by both changes in intellectual culture and the shift from mode 1 to mode 2 in science and technology. According to the standard account, universities represent the culmination of the educational revolution and are key instruments of the modern system in which cognitive values must always be dominant. Other values – social and political values certainly and cultural ones arguably – need to be subordinated to these cognitive values. To attempt to give equal weight to these secondary values is to undermine both the modern system and the very idea of a university.

Of course, the university has never been seen as simply a cognitive machine. Parsons and Platt argued, at the high tide of the multiversity, that 'cognitive values must somehow be integrated with those of non-cognitive significance'. But they added that

> these other values, for example, in effective attainment of predominantly non-cognitive goals like wealth or economic production, or in effective socialization into the role of educated citizen, should be as fully cognitively grounded as possible, but should not neglect non-cognitive concerns. Non-cognitive concerns are at cultural levels more expressive, more moral-evaluative, or more constitutive and can be combined with the cognitive in complex value structures.[66]

Neil Smelser, too, recognized that the university had to learn to live with conflict: 'to what extent should it be permitted to maximise its own values of cognitive rationality . . . , and to what extent should it be required to "service" the values and needs of other sectors of society?' He acknowledged that 'the institutionalization of cognitive rationality is also closely associated with the potential for conflict *within* educational institutions', because of reductionism between and within disciplines.[67] However, like Parsons and Platt, he was able to regard cognitive values as relatively stable. The trick was to combine these enduring values with ephemeral non-cognitive demands for social justice, wealth creation and so on.

How well this emphasis on the primacy and stability of cognitive values reflected the historical experience of universities, or ever accurately described practice in the humanities and social science, is open to doubt. But, in any case, this account of the status of universities has been undermined by the intellectual and scientific shifts discussed earlier in this chapter. First, it has been argued that cognitive values themselves, far from being privileged, have been radically problematized, which is the thrust of recent changes in intellectual culture whichever label is preferred – high modernity or post-modernism. Second, it has become more difficult to distinguish between purely cognitive values and other values in determining the sources of scientific creativity and innovation, the message of the shift from mode 1 to mode 2. To define the distinctiveness of the university in terms of the primacy of cognitive values, therefore, becomes less convincing.

This does not make the mass university a less significant institution than its élite predecessor. It does mean its significance must be assessed in new ways. Again according to the standard account, the university has pride of place among knowledge institutions which are arranged hierarchically. In the arts and social science its scholarly standards ensure that non-cognitive values, as far as possible, are kept in check; other cultural and intellectual institutions, although important, are more deeply influenced by these values. In science and technology the university is responsible for the purest and freest forms of research which are, by definition, also the primary forms. Both assumptions, on which the traditional hierarchy of knowledge institutions relies, have now been called into question.

One possible conclusion is that the university has become a more powerful institution socially, economically and politically, because of mass expansion, but a less important institution in intellectual and scientific terms. Either its core cognitive functions have been eroded, the intellectual and scientific 'centre' having failed to hold, because such notions have been (rightly or wrongly) deconstructed; or capacities for intellectual creativity and scientific innovation have been more widely distributed across different institutions. Both ways the university loses its monopoly or, at any rate, primacy in the knowledge industry. Potentially this produces more radical effects than the shift from normative to managerial structures discussed in Chapter 2.

It was argued there that the erosion of a common intellectual culture, and its generic cognitive structures and social practices, meant that the integrity of the university was now based on operational rather than cultural principles. But, so long as the primacy of the university in knowledge production was unchallenged (indeed was enhanced by the very reductionism which undermined that common culture), the need to sustain powerful universities remained, albeit as managerial organizations. If, within a much more widely distributed learning society, that primacy is questioned, the need disappears. However, it is also possible to reach the opposite conclusion, that the knowledge capacities of the mass university are greater than those of its élite predecessor, precisely because its heterogeneity reflects the breakdown between cognitive and non-cognitive value structures.

The specific impact of these new intellectual and scientific environments on higher education can be observed in both teaching and research. In the case of teaching, many recent innovations reflect the influence of these environments as well as that of the changing socio-economic context described in the last chapter. Their purpose is not only to act on supply and demand, by widening access to higher education, in the interest of social justice, and increasing the supply of highly skilled graduates, in the interests of economic efficiency. It is also to represent the changing balance of epistemological power, by increasing student choice and offering students a stronger sense of 'ownership' of their courses, through the application of consumerist principles, and by embodying more open interpretations of skills and knowledge.

Some of these innovations are procedural and structural. They include the development of access courses designed to increase the flow of non-traditional students into universities and colleges; a greater willingness to accept non-standard entry qualifications, including the assessment of prior (and experiential) learning;[68] the growth of university/college partnerships which allow students to study the early years of degree courses in local colleges on franchised courses;[69] the increasing popularity of modular degree schemes which enable students to choose more imaginative combinations of units;[70] the introduction of credit accumulation and transfer systems (CATS);[71] the transformation of continuing education, with a new emphasis on continuing professional development; and the provision of higher education in non-academic settings, most prominently in the so-called 'corporate classroom'.

Nearly all these innovations indirectly influence the university curriculum in its widest sense – not only new approaches to teaching and learning but also shifting definitions of desirable outcomes and even, implicitly, interpretations of the validity of different forms of knowledge and skills. There are other innovations which directly address such issues. These include measures to encourage the spread of new teaching technologies which supplement traditional teaching and encourage self-learning;[72] the development of new competence-denominated qualifications; and experiments with new forms of assessment (including self- and group assessment).

There is a powerful dynamic, both organizational and ideological, which binds these apparently eclectic innovations together. Nearly all access and franchised courses are built on the principle of academic credit. So are accreditation of prior learning (APL), accreditation of prior experiential learning (APEL) and other forms of work-based learning. To grant credit for prior learning, whether in a quasi-educational setting or in the workplace, while refusing to apply similar principles of choice and progression to mainstream undergraduate courses is both impractical and illogical. Modular degree schemes, too, are organized around the principles of student choice and academic credit. The accreditation of many continuing education programmes has flowed from the decision to mainstream their funding. The application of new teaching technologies requires a 'systems' approach to course structures, teaching and learning strategies and assessment procedures.

The cumulative effect of these innovations explains their radical impact. Severally modularization, franchising, access courses and credit systems may pose only limited challenges to traditional academic values and institutional cultures. Together they appear to herald the arrival of mass higher education systems, a disturbing phenomenon to many and uncongenial to a significant minority. According to Ronald Barnett, moves are afoot, prompted by social interests, that are also acting to open up the curriculum. Open learning, distance learning, credit accumulation and transfer and transferable personal skills are obliging the academic community to look critically at its educational offerings and to break away from traditional curricula.[73]

Chris Duke put it more bluntly: 'The very idea of CATS implies a paradigm shift in educational provision and curriculum design: from the institution to the individual student.'[74] These accounts do not perhaps go far enough. Both imply the pressure to reform the university curriculum arises from changing socio-economic circumstances, and so is external to the academic system. The argument in this chapter is that this pressure comes as much from inside the academic culture, although it is doubtful whether this demarcation between 'inside' and 'outside' is any longer valid.

Other shifts are at work as part of this transition from the élite to the mass university, the large-scale transformation of higher education systems which is an expression of the socio-economic changes discussed in the previous chapter and reflects the intellectual and cultural shifts described earlier in this chapter. Four broad shifts can be identified.

Courses to credits

The first shift is from courses/qualifications to credits/outcomes. The currency of the élite university has always been denominated in courses/qualifications, whether honours degrees or PhDs. So has the currency of other post-secondary education institutions. The HNC or HND has provided intellectual structures through which appropriate knowledge and relevant skills are validated and organizational contexts within which teaching takes place and students are assessed. Talk of standards, more emotively of a 'gold standard', reflects these fixed hierarchies of merit. The honours degree, in particular, has a normative power transcending any particular curricular context. It embodies academic assumptions about, for example, the need for structured and sequential learning, which demand sustained commitment by students; intellectual assumptions about the organization, and so the nature, of knowledge; and social assumptions about the need to initiate students into particular disciplinary and professional cultures.

These powerful but poorly articulated values are now being challenged by new patterns of academic organization in the mass university. Its currency is denominated in credits/outcomes. Modular degree schemes, CATS and outcomes-based assessments embody different values than those which have been dominant in many higher education systems – or, at any rate, their élite segments. In place of sustained academic commitment a step-by-step, and student-friendly, approach to higher education is offered. Multiple points of entry and exit are opened without regard to the academic symmetry of the whole. In place of grand organic interpretations of knowledge, a pattern of academic progression is provided in which connections, between topics and levels, are pragmatically derived rather than cognitively prescribed. And, in place of socially exclusive accounts of disciplinary and professional cultures, a more diffuse 'college culture' is offered. As a result broader intellectual attributes produced by exposure to higher education itself rather than to particular subjects are inculcated.

This tendency to replace the currency of courses/qualifications with that of credits/outcomes reflects, first, the increasing diversity of student origins and heterogeneity of student destinations and, second, the undermining of canonical knowledge and of expert skills. As such it re-echoes the socio-economic shifts described in the previous chapter and the shifts in intellectual culture and scientific practice discussed in this chapter. The new currency is expressed in new approaches to the inputs of higher education, or access; its outputs, or outcomes and standards; and also the process itself (in both organizational and academic terms). In all three respects it has produced far-reaching transformations.

First, the new currency eases access to higher education, because it enables a much wider range of indicative factors to be taken into account in considering the eligibility of students, rather than simply success in standard end-of-school examinations, and it also provides multiple points rather than a single point of entry. More radically, the general effect of the new currency is to erode authoritative criteria for granting access which have been doubly undermined by the drift towards less selective entry in mass higher education systems and by the problematizing of intellectual hierarchies from which notions of standards, level and so on are derived.

Second, a credit/outcomes currency transforms outcomes. It reduces the risk and stigma of failure by providing multiple exit points which can be certificated. If students pursue diverse trajectories or, increasingly, follow individual learning packages, broad generic norm-referenced assessments will be replaced by detailed criterion-referenced transcripts. This new currency also makes it difficult to label students 'first-class' and so on, because these labels imply broad academic equivalences which can no longer be taken for granted, for both social and intellectual reasons. Again these variable and volatile outcomes reflect the socio-economic and intellectual-scientific shifts already described. The growing difficulty of defining 'quality' – and, in particular, the drift from absolute standards to plural criteria which are relative and self-referential – are further pieces of evidence.[75]

Third, the credits/outcomes currency modifies the transactions which take place within higher education. It enhances student choice by providing greater flexibility. Students are less likely to be trapped in academic programmes for which they have limited aptitude or in which they have lost interest than if they are following conventional courses. It also enables students to 'grow' their own academic interests during their higher education. This flexibility is both characteristic, and a precondition, of a wider-access higher education system which enrols students with less clearly articulated objectives. They are no longer drawn so heavily from the professional middle class with its inherited expectations of and assumptions about higher education, although these expectations and assumptions have already been substantially modified by the shift from, in the terms made famous by David Riesman, inner direction to outer direction among young people and by the erosion of inter-generational traditions.

The new credits/outcomes currency also encourages trans-disciplinarity (or, at any rate, inter-disciplinarity), echoing one of the key characteristics of mode 2 science. Despite the wider focus, depth is not necessarily sacrificed to breadth. Indeed, in the volatile, pluralist, even permissive intellectual environment that now prevails, the old depth–breadth dichotomy has become an anachronism. Depth of understanding is now a function of breadth of reference. Instead students focus on themes which are both academic 'hot spots', produced by the shifts in intellectual culture discussed earlier in this chapter, and topics of urgent social concern, reflecting the shift to mode 2. They encounter, if not problematizing knowledge at the undergraduate level, then problematical connections between different kinds of knowledge. They acquire habits of self-reliance which develop transferable and inter-personal skills. Their development takes place within a context, not of given hierarchies, but of individual enterprise and social application.

Departments to frameworks

The second shift is from discipline-based departments to looser frameworks which set the rules and boundaries within which the new credits/outcomes currency can operate. This is already well under way. The tendency for broadly based faculties to be broken down, effectively if not constitutionally, into reductionist departments has been reversed as more and more universities have developed looser academic structures based on schools, often built round theme categories such as European studies or environmental sciences. More recently, as modular and credit systems have become more popular, some institutions have gone further, establishing still looser frameworks which embrace schools, departments and individual academic programmes.

Faculties and departments have traditionally played a key mediating role within the academic system. They are where the private world of knowledge, whether expressed through teaching or research, and the public world of institutions and systems collide. Departments both embody academic disciplines, by institutionalizing their cognitive codes and value hierarchies, and create the professional structures through which academic careers are realized. Collectively, as has often been pointed out, they form 'invisible colleges', as powerful as the 'visible colleges' of which separately they are constituent parts. Through peer-review networks they establish research agendas and validate curricular innovations, which their parent institutions must follow. Yet departments, or their equivalents, also form the basic units within institutions as well as forming part of institutional structures. Here the values and practices of these different worlds must be harmonized.

Two questions, therefore, are raised by the shift from departments to frameworks. First, can frameworks act as a bridge between higher education's two worlds as effectively as discipline-bound departments? Despite their increasingly managerial role (at the expense of their traditional academic functions?), departments, like honours degrees, are much more than administrative units; they also institutionalize the intellectual values, cognitive structures and social practices of academic disciplines. Second, is the drift towards looser frameworks evidence of a realignment of the frontier between the private and public worlds of higher education – or, more accurately, interpenetration of these once separate worlds which will render the idea of a frontier between them an anachronism?

An affirmative answer to the second question disposes of the first question. If the cognitive and operational domains can no longer be clearly distinguished, for reasons explored earlier in this chapter, the mediating role of the department is transformed. Instead of providing a structured context in which disciplinary expertise is nurtured, it becomes an open environment where knowledge producers/users mingle. Frameworks, within which volatile alliances can be formed, are better designed for such a task than traditional departments. Significantly the latter are already becoming less relevant in the research arena. In many universities they have been effectively superseded by trans-disciplinary research units, institutes with a strong external focus and now separate research schools. Over the next decade similarly flexible organizations are likely to come to dominate the delivery of teaching as well.

Subject-based teaching to student-centred learning

The third shift is from subject-based teaching to student-centred learning. The second part of this shift, from teaching to learning, is a long-established trend which, on the face of it, owes little to the socio-economic and intellectual-scientific transformations which lie at the heart of the development of mass higher education. It can be argued that emphasis on learning by inducing self-criticism, on asking questions rather than providing answers, is the most ancient of all academic methods, the pedagogical principle on which Socrates (according to Plato) relied. It continues to be the principle on which undergraduate tutorials (especially in Oxford and Cambridge), postgraduate seminars and research student supervision are organized. If the development of mass higher education has had any influence on this trend, it has been principally logistical. Student-directed learning, it is argued, is less labour-intensive than teaching and mass systems must exploit all the available economies of scale – and of scope.

The first part of the shift, from subjects to students, is more recent. Arguably it can be attributed to phenomena which grow directly out of the development of mass higher education – the growing presence of new students with less pronounced academic ambitions; and, more significantly, the growing sense of student 'ownership' of their academic programmes, as a result of the introduction of modular schemes, credit systems and user-friendly assessment. Whether such 'ownership' can easily be translated into genuine intellectual independence and whether these new course structures really challenge the hegemony of conventional academic disciplines, however, are open to doubt. Certainly students are expected to be able to negotiate their own customized packages, which itself demands the development of useful learning skills. And, during their progress through higher education they must work out for themselves the academic or vocational coherence of the packages they have chosen, which again puts greater emphasis on learning than teaching.

On the other hand, by chopping up courses into units/modules, orthodoxies whether disciplinary or professional may become more difficult to challenge. Unless great care is taken, knowledge and skills will be reduced to unproblematic sound-bites. Mechanical, even passive, learning may also be encouraged. Students, under appropriate academic guidance, choose prepackaged units. There is a danger these units will be over-structured, both in terms of the teaching and learning strategies they employ and of progression sequences within individual units and also, by prescribing pre-requisites and co-requisites, in terms of their relationship with the broader academic programmes students follow. The paradoxical result may be both greater student choice and an over-determined curriculum.

It can even be argued that the greater social openness of the mass university encourages academic closure. In order to encourage wider access, and to provide for the needs of new kinds of student, a systems approach has to be developed. Those serendipitous connections possible within more traditional, and less systematic, course structures, which stimulate lateral and creative thinking, become more difficult. The complex apparatus of mass access – modular degree schemes, credit systems, accreditation of prior learning, special access programmes, work-based and distance learning – increases the pressure for much tighter control over the structure of academic programmes, within and between units/modules, more explicit descriptions of aims and objectives, and a more prescriptive quality assurance (and assessment) regime. There may also be an intriguing sub-text. Students in a mass system, although formally empowered as customers, are seen as lacking the cultural attributes needed to make genuinely autonomous intellectual decisions. Hence the increasing preoccupation with guidance and counselling, which can empower students but can also be used as a discreet means of academic surveillance.

The links between this shift from subject-based teaching to student-centred learning and the volatility of intellectual culture and the shift from mode 1 to mode 2 in science and technology are not straightforward. But these links can be observed in two further arenas. One is the increased emphasis which both phenomena place on reflexivity. Reflexivity is imported into the university curriculum by two routes. The first is directly through research and scholarship, radically problematized in ways described earlier. The second is through teaching as a context of application. The older idea of learning by doing has been subsumed into the novel idea that all worthwhile knowledge arises, and useful skills develop, within a terrain of (often contested) negotiation rather than as the result of a process of authoritative transmission. The other arena is the effect these intellectual-scientific shifts are likely to have on the authority of teachers in their capacity as experts. Under these new conditions the teacher's role becomes that of a facilitator who provides academic services, of which the once hegemonic function of passing on discipline-based knowledge is only a subordinate part.

Knowledge to competence

The fourth and last shift – from knowledge to competence – embraces and also summarizes the first three. It most directly reflects the shifts in intellectual culture and scientific method discussed in this chapter. Furthermore, it is the most sharply contested. What distinguishes higher education from other levels of education, it is argued, is that the knowledge towards which students aspire, at any rate in their later undergraduate years and as postgraduates, and the skills they acquire, are necessarily provisional, half-formed, indeterminate – and so problematical. As a result, students have to become critical thinkers. Competence, in contrast, implies that the relevant knowledge can be sufficiently complete to be operationalized into identifiable skills, which is difficult to reconcile with permanent problematization.

However, it is difficult to draw a clear demarcation between an élite university curriculum centred on knowledge or high-grade professional skills (generally defined in terms of their constituent knowledge), structured round the honours degree and, in the best cases, embodying a critical and problematizing ethic; and a mass higher education curriculum centred on graded competences derived from uncriticized and unproblematic accounts of knowledge. Historically the higher education curriculum has been permeated by vocationalism, even in élite institutions. As was pointed out in an earlier chapter, the model of the university as a professional institution is as much part of the European university tradition as the scientific university of Humboldtian descent or the 'personality' model associated with Oxford and Cambridge. Moreover, many of the new and non-university institutions which often formed the most dynamic elements within mass higher education systems have inherited an explicit commitment to vocationalism.

Even within the élite university the notion of competence, if not its name, is well understood. Narrowly it is defined as academic competence, mastery of cognitive skills rooted in particular disciplinary traditions, or as technical competence, the job-specific capacities demanded by professional careers. In a wider sense it is interpreted as possession of certain intellectual and cultural attributes, which are often class-influenced. Indeed, according to Patrick Ainley, there is a danger that, as competences defined in terms of

Table 4 Knowledge and culture, by disciplinary grouping

Discipline	Knowledge	Culture
Pure sciences ('hard pure')	Cumulative; atomistic; concerned with universals, quantities, simplification; resulting in discovery/ explanation	Competitive; gregarious; politically well organized; high publication rates; task-oriented
Humanities ('soft pure')	Reiterative; holistic; concerned with particulars, qualities, complication; resulting in understanding/ interpretation	Individualistic; pluralist; loosely structured; low publication rate; person-oriented
Technologies ('hard applied')	Purposive; pragmatic; concerned with mastery of physical environment; resulting in products/techniques	Entrepreneurial; dominated by professional values; patents substitutable for publications; role-oriented
Applied social science ('soft applied')	Functional; utilitarian; concerned with enhancement of practice; resulting in protocols/procedures	Outward-looking; uncertain in status; dominated by intellectual fashions; publication rates reduced by consultancies; power-oriented

Source: Tony Becher (1989) *Academic Tribes and Territories*. Buckingham: Open University Press.

technical expertise are supplemented, or even superseded, by generic skills in a volatile post-industrial culture and in a mass higher education system, the latter, especially so-called personal transferable skills, may tend to be based on these older élite university conceptions of competence.[76]

Too sharp a demarcation between knowledge and competence also suggests that both are homogeneous categories, coherent domains. Neither is. Competences are necessarily plural. Even apparently straightforward categories such as 'core skills' can be defined in many ways, either as the foundations on which more sophisticated skills are built or as generic skills, often at a high level, on which more specialized skills ultimately depend. Ronald Barnett argued for a new, and more humane, conception of competence. His list of its characteristics re-echoes the emphasis on reflexivity typical of post-modern thought. It includes the need for a genuinely open dialogue between teachers and students, respect for the rules of rational discourse (while recognizing that these rules are merely conventions) and a willingness to experiment with new methods of critical inquiry. He concluded:

This list may not seem controversial; yet it runs counter to the positions of either academic or operational competence. In the first case, there is no mention of disciplines, truth, knowledge, objectivity or even auto-

Figure 5   A taxonomy of disciplines

Source: Maurice Kogan and Tony Becher, (1980) *Process and Structure in Higher Education* London, Heinemann, p. 86.

Boundaries

	Closed	Permeable
Cohesive	Single subject, specialized degrees	Inter-disciplinary courses
Discrete	Modular and joint honours	Open learning programmes

Content

nomy, teaching or learning: nor is this an accident. The assumptions of academic competence are deliberately being called into question. In the second case, there is no mention of skills, competence, outcomes, and all the conceptual baggage that goes with the mind-set of operational competence. Both are limiting ideologies.[77]

Barnett's conception of competence, therefore, is very far from either the checklist of reductionist skills definitions favoured by the National Council for Vocational Qualifications or the inward interpretations of merit and excellence generated within disciplinary culture.

Knowledge, too, is a plural category. The cognitive values and social practices of academic disciplines, even as traditionally defined, varied greatly. Tony Becher drew a distinction between different patterns of knowledge, 'areas of contextual imperative' and 'areas of contextual association'.[78] The former offer closely patterned sequences of explanation, with each new finding fitting neatly into place as the whole picture is steadily pieced together; the latter loosely knit clusters of ideas, with no clearly articulated framework of development. His account of the differences between the main disciplinary families is given in Table 4.

However, despite these differences, disciplines as traditionally conceived are largely self-referential, separate worlds embracing their own cognitive structures, professional routines and socio-economic linkages. Becher's account was based on the 'research orientation' of disciplines, which may have emphasized their differences. In the context of teaching they must be expressed through academic programmes, which emphasize linkages and affinities. In another book Becher, together with Maurice Kogan, has suggested the broad-brush taxonomy of course types shown in Figure 5.

This second matrix must be laid upon, and aligned with, the first. The fit is not exact, which underlines once again the pluralism of knowledge and its applications. But, if both knowledge and competence are such broad churches, does it help to argue that the evolution of a mass higher education curriculum is characterized by a shift from one to the other? The answer is still yes. This fourth shift subsumes some significant, and arguably related, trends. These include the increasingly rapid turnover of technical skills, which places a higher premium on generic skills; the opening up (or, better, fraying) of disciplines, linked perhaps with the deprofessionalisation of academic experts; and the erosion of internal epistemological authority, leading to a greater emphasis on skills, competences and other explicit outcomes as substitutes. All these trends reflect the broader shifts in intellectual culture discussed earlier in this chapter.

Concentration or dispersal?

So far, in this final section, the focus has been on teaching rather than research. But the impact of these changes in intellectual culture and, in particular, the shift from mode 1 to mode 2 in science and technology, is likely to be felt most directly and immediately in the context of research. Here the evidence is suggestive rather than conclusive. On the one hand, the emphasis in the recent White Paper on science and technology on interaction rather than origination, on the value of user communities and on the need to generate research problems and solutions within a context of application appears to reflect some characteristics of mode 2 knowledge production.[79] These priorities have been underlined by research council leaders.[80] The growing popularity of research schools can partly be explained by efforts to create organizational structures within which the dynamics of trans-disciplinary research can operate.[81] Even the growth of research assessment may reflect the emergence of new patterns of quality control, in the first place more open and eventually more pluralist.

On the other hand, there are two apparently contradictory trends difficult, at first sight, to reconcile with key characteristics of mode 2 science. The first is concentration, the result of the well-known 'Matthew effect' (unto every one that hath shall be given) powerfully reinforced by three rounds of research assessment in Britain, and of the logistical imperatives produced by the cost and sophistication of instrumentation and by the growth of a higher education system in which not all institutions can have a full research mission. In the United States the research universities' share of federal government research funds and of research and development sponsored by private corporations has tended to grow at the expense of other institutions. In Britain the proposal that all universities and colleges should be categorized as either R (research universities), T (teaching-mainly institutions) or X (institutions with selective research strengths), although dormant, is not dead.[82]

The second trend is towards specialization, the inexorable division, and sub-division, of disciplines to produce an ever-finer division of scientific labour. Together these trends appear to dominate the policy debate. However, neither is necessarily incompatible with the shift from mode 1 to mode 2 described earlier in this chapter. The concentration of (high-cost and/or pure) scientific research on a smaller number of sites is likely to increase the incentive to develop networks, because only through networks will many scientists be able to contribute to such research. It can also be argued that concentration is an attempt (which is likely ultimately to be unsuccessful) to reverse the proliferation of research sites within the wider arena of knowledge production. The number of researchers, conventionally defined, has continued to increase rapidly. Only a small, and probably dwindling, fraction is employed, or active, on the major sites. If all participants in the knowledge industry are taken into account, and if the pre-eminence of university-based science in the innovation process is questioned, the role of the major sites is further reduced.

Specialization, therefore, far from being characteristic of mode 1 science, is perhaps more typical of mode 2 knowledge production. Mode 1 was rooted in well-established disciplines which persisted over time. Expertise and authority were institutionalized primarily through disciplines and only secondarily in universities. The very rapid rate of division into specialisms, and sub-specialisms, is now undermining disciplinary continuities and hierarchies. It is producing instead frequent, and febrile, combinations and recombinations of knowledge production capacity. The cognitive norms and professional structures typical of these volatile specialisms are closer to the pattern of mode 2's temporary research groupings than mode 1's established research teams.

Conclusion

Any direct correspondence between the shifts in intellectual culture and in the character of the scientific system and the changing patterns of teaching and research in higher education is not to be expected. All that can be expected is a broad affinity, like those earlier moments of affinity discussed in the first section of this chapter. Indeed, in one sense, the ambiguities of contemporary intellectual culture and the volatility of modern science and technology mean that any correspondence between these trends and the mass university curriculum and new research agendas is likely to be weaker than at these past moments. Fuzziness, anti-coherence, pluralism shading into relativism, permanent problematizing – these are not characteristics which can easily be translated into operational environments. That is the point.

In another sense, of course, the impact of post-modern thought and a radically contextualized science is likely to be greater, because they represent the breaking down of the frontiers between the private world of ideas and the public world of institutions. Yet it is difficult to understand the detailed changes associated with the shift from élite to mass forms of higher education – the spread of modularization and CATS, the popularity of enterprise and competences in the case of teaching; and the move to research council 'missions' and the preoccupation with end-users in the case of research – without considering the intellectual and scientific environments in which mass higher education systems operate. Above all, it must be recognized that these changes arise from within the academic culture as much as, or more than, they are imposed on higher education by external political and socio-economic imperatives.

5
Understanding Mass Higher Education

Mass, unlike élite, higher education cannot be summed up in a single totalizing idea. Instead, it has plural meanings, being one of a series of multiple modernizations – of society, economy, culture and science as well as the academy. To add to the complexity, these modernizations are linked less by clear causal relationships than by oblique but suggestive affinities. Nor, because of its novel articulation with these other modernizations and because of the acceleration, volatility, simultaneity and non-linearity characteristic of them, can mass higher education be regarded simply as the heir of older élite forms, the next stage in a linear élite–mass–universal sequence or even a one-way paradigm shift. Mass higher education, therefore, is an ambiguous, diverse and volatile phenomenon. Nevertheless, some attempt must be made to conceptualize mass higher education, however difficult or problematical.

This final chapter is divided into two parts. In the first, the arguments put forward in the previous three chapters about the structure of higher education systems and institutions, about the new welfare state and post-industrial change, and about the evolution of intellectual culture and of science and technology, are reviewed as they bear on the development of mass higher education. In the second part, and in the light of that review, two primary characteristics of mass systems are identified. The first, reflexivity, can be observed in the 'public' life of higher education, its political and organizational forms and its interaction with the wider socio-economic arena. The second characteristic, apparent in the 'private' knowledge-based world of higher education, is a shift from closed intellectual systems to open systems. In the former, the academic agenda is determined by the inner dynamics of disciplines and expressed through the professional activities of experts; in the latter, both cognitive values and social practices are shaped by transactions between knowledge producers and knowledge users, a partnership between academy and community.

The higher education system

The two most important features of the structure of mass higher education, discussed in Chapter 2, are fuzziness and permeability. It has become more difficult to distinguish clearly between the four main types of higher education system – dual systems, in which universities stand apart from the rest of post-secondary education; binary systems, where alternative higher education institutions are established to complement or rival the universities; unified systems, in which all higher education institutions are treated (approximately) equally; and stratified systems, characterized by a division of institutional labour (which may take the form of a planned hierarchy or be the result of the differentiating effects of the market). There is a suggestive dynamic, a tendency for dual systems to develop into binary systems, for binary systems to become unified systems, and for unified systems to become stratified, whether formally or informally.

But it is no more than a tendency. The drift from dual to binary, binary to unified, and so on, can also be interpreted as evidence of the erosion of the differences, operational and conceptual, between these types. All systems are responses to complexity. First, upper-secondary education institutions, technical high schools and further education colleges evolve into a distinctively post-secondary sector, initially to satisfy the demand for forms of extended secondary education which are not simply a preparation for traditional university education. Later, as the demand for post-secondary education outstrips the capacity (and mission) of the universities, the role of these institutions is upgraded; they are fully incorporated in a wider higher education system. With the massification of higher education differences between institutions, universities and the rest, are eroded and may finally be abandoned. But, within mass systems with multiple missions, new types of institutional differentiation emerge.

Another way to describe this pattern of evolution, which appears to be more circular than linear, is to say that dual systems tend to re-emerge as stratified systems, while binary systems never disappear; their boundaries merely shift. This pattern is consistent with the second feature of the structure of mass systems, their permeability. Élite higher education systems have clearly demarcated frontiers, even if they are periodically extended to include new types of institution. The frontiers of mass systems are much harder to define. Part of the reason is that successive extensions of higher education have incorporated more and more of post-secondary education; through partnerships with other organizations, these extended systems have come to embrace a wider territory still – corporate training, mass communications, research and development, technology transfer and consultancy. But, part of the reason is not simply that fixed external frontiers have been radically extended, but that permeable internal frontiers have proliferated – within departments and institutions and between institutions as much as between sectors and systems.

Fuzziness and permeability are characteristic of institutions as well as systems. The diversity of British higher education is already greater than is commonly supposed. In Chapter 2, 12 different types of university and three distinct types of college of higher education were identified; in addition, significant higher education is provided by further education colleges. The post-secondary sector is wider still, embracing much of the remaining work of further education colleges, the whole of adult education and the large parts of the 'corporate classroom'. Even if research organizations are excluded, which is difficult to justify in a 'knowledge society', the system is already highly diverse and its institutions differentiated. Both diversity and differentiation are likely to intensify as a mass system develops – the first, because the present division between higher and further education will be further eroded; and the second, because the élite universities will reassert their identity. It is at the base, along the system's open frontier, and at its peak, among these universities, that change will be most vigorous.

In the extended élite system which developed in Britain after 1960, as in many other European countries, reform focused on the development of new institutions – whether new universities or alternative higher education institutions. Because of the system's totalizing instincts, these were sometimes seen as potentially rival hegemonic models. Which would predominate? As a result, differences of ethos and organization were magnified. In a mass system, such as Britain is on the verge of acquiring, dichotomy has been superseded by pluralism. The race for hegemony has been abandoned. It is now recognized that the former polytechnics borrowed much of their spatial, visual and academic language from the new universities of the 1960s, adapting it to the more open tradition they had inherited from further education and to their wider and deeper student constituencies. Equally, the 'old' universities were penetrated by 'polytechnic' practices, especially from the mid-1980s onwards.

The impact of massification on institutions has been twofold. First, they have to develop their own distinctive missions. Because of fuzziness and permeability, real and rhetorical priorities can no longer be derived, normatively, from totalizing ideas such as the liberal university or, operationally, from sector-wide stereotypes such as the standard polytechnic. At present, many institutional mission statements are similar, even identical. But this is likely to change as the burden of past ambitions and expectations is lifted and missions become more individualized. Second, institutions have become much more complex, in size as the system has expanded, and in scope as it has become more heterogeneous. The short-term response has been to tighten up the management of institutions, which explains the grief for the waning of the 'donnish dominion' in the 'old' universities and the antagonism provoked by the advance of 'managerialism', especially in the 'new' universities. But the long-term effect is likely to be the unbinding of the university, as line-management hierarchies crumble to be replaced by networks, webs and other forms of loose association between its constituent units.

The political system

The state is, and is likely to continue to be, the dominant sponsor of mass higher education systems. There is little evidence to support the argument that massification encourages privatization. The 'mass' components of American higher education, four-year state colleges and community colleges, are almost entirely tax-supported; private institutions are crowded into the élite segment. The key shift in the political evolution of mass systems, therefore, is not towards outright privatization but the development of a novel relationship with the late twentieth-century state. Similarly, claims that the welfare state has been 'rolled back' are very much exaggerated. Levels of social expenditure remain high. If there is a crisis of the welfare state, it is the result not of normative collapse, the direly hyped neo-conservative counter-revolution, but of familiar operational strains produced by the difficulty of rationing demand, rising expectations, increasing technological (and sociological) sophistication and higher costs.

Nevertheless, changes in the political system present a powerful challenge to higher education systems, which are themselves caught up in the transition from élite to mass forms. The most significant change is the shift from a fiduciary state, or the state as trustee of the national interest, to the contractual state, or the state as market-maker and over-mighty contractor. A number of secondary effects have been produced by this primary shift. First, the state-as-contractor has taken over from the state-as-provider. Consequently, many public services are now provided indirectly through 'next steps' or arm's-length agencies. Second, there is less emphasis on planning inputs and more on auditing outcomes. Third, the contractual state is eclectic, heterogeneous. Instead of embodying the grand notion of the national interest, it has plural interests which, at the best, are loosely associated under over-arching themes such as 'competitiveness'. Also public, and semi-public, agencies have proliferated, all with their own particular agendas. Fourth, the public–private demarcation has been eroded. Public services are contracted out to the private sector.

On the face of it, this primary shift and secondary effects have produced a congenial environment for higher education, consistent both with the autonomy of élite systems and the heterogeneity of mass systems. The splintering of a single hegemonic national interest into a plurality of more detailed agendas is also consistent with the abandonment of totalizing conceptions of higher education. But the actual impact of these changes is ambiguous. For example, their effect has been to produce convergence among different patterns of university governance. State universities have been given greater operational autonomy, as agencies providing public services on behalf of the state, rather than as previously organic (although privileged) elements within state bureaucracies. On the other hand, institutions, like the 'old' universities in Britain, which were once protected from political interference by buffer bodies have been adversely affected. Through contracts they have been brought into a much closer relationship with the state, which no longer sees itself as a hands-off trustee but as a hands-on customer.

The same has happened with funding. The key changes have not been the slow and unsteady rise in the proportion of private income, but the proliferation of sources of public income, in place of a single income stream, and the replacement of block grants by specific contracts. Again there have been gains and losses. In state systems, and even in arm's-length systems, there has been a retreat from detailed prescriptive planning. Checks now tend to be confined to issues of administrative propriety and financial integrity. To that extent universities and colleges have greater room for manoeuvre. But they must now compete with other institutions to secure contracts, which leads to downward pressure on costs, and also submit to detailed auditing of outcomes, in terms of the quality as well as the quantity of teaching and research.

What is not clear is whether these changes in the political system and the parallel shift towards mass higher education are merely contingent phenomena, or whether they possess a deeper affinity. Certainly there are suggestive similarities – the retreat from totalizing conceptions, the growth of heterogeneity. But welfare states and mass systems are also *sui generis*. The chaotic American welfare state is mainly concerned with promoting equality of opportunity, as a means of realizing democratic entitlements and remedying past racial discrimination. Historically the expansion of higher education has played a central role in that project. In Britain, and the rest of Europe, the welfare state is focused on the reduction of inequalities and the production of social order. The key social policy arenas have been health, housing and employment. Education and, in particular, élite higher education are more closely related to another (arguably secondary) project, the promotion of social mobility. This suggests that it may be difficult to draw any general conclusions about the articulation between mass higher education and the political system.

Socio-economic change

The growth of mass systems is taking place against a background of socio-economic transformations that are both rapid and profound. A generation ago these transformations tended to be described as a shift to post-industrialism, suggesting a linear extrapolation of industrial society. Today more radical accounts are preferred, generally labelled post-Fordism. The emphasis is no longer on continuity but on rupture. New social forms and economic patterns are seen as alternative to, not extensions of, the forms and patterns generated by Fordist mass-manufacturing and the bureaucratic Weberian state. Mass higher education, it has been argued, is also more than the linear successor of élite higher education because sociologically and epistemologically it represents a break with past continuities. It is tempting, therefore, to conclude that massification is one of those broader socio-economic transformations which make up post-Fordism.

They are reshaping both the economy and society in the developed world. A dwindling fraction of the workforce is employed in manufacturing. At the same time, as the 'services' content increases in manufactured goods and the emphasis switches from the production of low-value-added durable goods to high-value-added ephemeral and symbolic goods, the distinction between manufacturing and services is breaking down. The advance of new technologies, hyperautomation in the factory and information technology in the office, has enabled both craft-like customized production to be 'reinvented', and, through just-in-time production and economies of scope, productivity to be intensified and accelerated. It has also produced radical changes in organizations, such as the decline of large vertically integrated corporations and the rise of teleworking. The pattern of employment, too, has been transformed as linear careers have crumbled and short-term contracts expanded.

The social effect of these changes has been to undermine the older solidarities of class relations and gender roles. Old-style producers were clearly stratified by status and occupation; new-style consumers are incoherently generic, distinguished only by the availability of cash and/or credit. The erosion of employment structures has loosened the links between occupation and status, and class and gender. The globalization of culture, fashion and the media has undermined the subtle status distinctions once attached to different consumption patterns. The growth of so-called post-materialism has led to the formation of new attachments no longer grounded in material conditions; the 'green' movement in its widest sense is a good example.

Higher education is embroiled in nearly all these transformations. In terms of inputs, access and demand, expansion has produced near-universal participation by the spreading middle classes. A 'college culture' is being formed within which, for the first time in Britain, anticipations of higher education have been internalized. But, at the same time, mass systems are also more static systems which entrench and legitimate social hierarchies, while élite systems offered upward avenues for able working-class students. Contentment has taken over from entitlement as the *leitmotif* of mass systems, just as entitlement took over from opportunity in extended élite systems.

The balance sheet is difficult to draw up. It is certainly true that higher education has been used by the middle class to preserve not just its cultural hegemony but, more crucially, its privileged access to superior jobs. But it is also true not only that middle-class lifestyles and values have been transformed by participation in higher education but also, crucially, that middle-class identities have also been reshaped by the same process. Individualized lifestyles, admittedly with many echoes of bourgeois culture, may have replaced class or gender-determined life chances as the prime determinants of identity, status and power.

In terms of outputs, both research results and graduate careers, the relationship between mass higher education and the wider 'knowledge society' is also difficult to determine. Optimists argue that the university will become a (possibly the), leading institution; pessimists fear that, in its traditional or even recognizable form, it will be bypassed by other more vigorous elements in the 'knowledge' industry. No single answer is possible. The incestuous interpenetration between élite universities and other cutting-edge research establishments guarantees the former a powerful and privileged role in a society where theoretical models and codified data have become primary resources. To the extent that mass systems are likely to lead to a clearer identification of this élite, and to give it a sharper research-university focus, massification enhances the ability of higher education to play a leading role in post-industrial society.

However, it is less clear where the mass production of graduates fits into the post-industrial picture. The large-scale stable bureaucracies of the industrial age, whether public or private, provided a framework in which traditional graduate careers could flourish; as rational organizations they also valued the rationality reflected in the credentializing of expert skills. The adaptable organizations of the post-industrial age are too volatile to offer the same opportunities for graduate careers; also the skills they value are both generic and charismatic, and so more difficult to credentialize. For many students, of course, mass higher education is an antidote, rather than an avenue, to work. Mass systems shrink the years of structured employment, by delaying entry into the labour market and offering meaningful opportunities to the prematurely retired, and to the growing number of older people. They offer similar opportunities to many employees whose jobs do not provide them with sufficiently stimulating experiences. Under post-industrial conditions mass higher education is as important a form of socio-cultural consumption as investment in high-technology skills.

Academic affinities

Mass higher education does not merely represent a structural shift in the political economy of higher education systems or a novel articulation with emerging socio-economic forces. It is also an intellectual and scientific phenomenon. All three tend to go together. In the past, profound social transformations have generally coincided with periods of intellectual ferment and scientific excitement, which have often (but not always) stimulated reforms in higher education. These conjunctures include the Renaissance and Reformation, the eighteenth-century Enlightenment, the industrial revolution, the rise of modernity in the early years of the twentieth century – and perhaps the 1990s, with the coincidence of massification, post-Fordism and contemporary turbulence in intellectual and scientific cultures.

This is the most difficult meaning of mass higher education to explore, but also the most evocative. The transition from élite to mass forms is taking place at a time of epistemological crisis, in which higher education itself is centrally implicated. This cannot be dismissed as coincidence. The possibility of achieving scientific objectivity even in the most precise experimental arenas, and the claim of long-established normative and conceptual frameworks to provide a context for critical reflection rather than being mere 'stories', the fundamental techniques of the sciences and the arts respectively, both have come under attack. In this contest higher education is both the potential victim, because its core cognitive values are being questioned, but also the aggressor, because these awkward questions are being asked within universities and colleges.

This questioning extends far beyond critical theorists, post-modernists and deconstructionists. Scepticism, constructive and disciplined, is embedded in the university tradition and the scientific method. Socrates, Hume, Popper – all questioned the naiveties of positivistic proof. The role of modern higher education systems has even been described as to institutionalize doubt. Yet the urgings of radical scepticism, to undermine received truths, have been tempered by powerful continuities. Three have been particularly influential. The first is the commitment to a canonical tradition which may be revised, added to, but not utterly rejected. The best example is literature's so-called 'Great Tradition' but there are others, less controversial. The second is the contrast drawn by Kuhn between paradigm shifts in science, violent but brief, and intervening periods of 'normal' science, cumulative and lengthy. The third is the elevation of critical rationality to the status of a universal value immune from its own interrogation.

These continuities are eroded in mass systems. The much wider social constituencies and more diverse cultural backgrounds from which their students are drawn have made it difficult to maintain even the most discreet canonical traditions. Kuhnian ideas have been inappropriately interpreted as an endorsement of permanent intellectual revolution. And critical rationality has been attacked, as a value, because of the oppressive implications of its hegemonic claims and, as a technique, because it fails to provide adequate explanations of key phenomena, especially in the affective and affirmative arenas. As a result, the balance between scepticism and continuity has been upset. Systems of thought are prey to a pluralism hard to distinguish from relativism, which can be traced back to the social construction of mass higher education.

These influences are not confined to the humanities and social sciences. Science and technology are also affected. In Chapter 4 a new mode of science was identified, characterized by the creative combination of discovery and application, by trans-disciplinarity which transcended established subject categories, by organizational diversity and by social accountability. If this characterization is accepted, both the autonomy and linearity of science are called into question. Nor can these intellectual influences be regarded as inherently negative. They arise from the transactions between academy and community which cross, and recross, the permeable boundaries of mass systems. They are an important ingredient in the reflexivity that is a fundamental characteristic of mass higher education.

Reforms in teaching and changes in research reflect these anti-canonical influences. The spread of CATS, modularization, the accreditation of prior learning, self-guided learning packages, new assessment (and self-assessment) methods – these and similar innovations re-echo these larger shifts in intellectual authority. Similarly, the attention paid to the views of 'users' in identifying research priorities and the emphasis on encouraging inter-disciplinary team-work and acquiring research skills can be interpreted as evidence of the shift to mode 2 science. In both cases, difficult issues are encountered. Competences are defined and skills developed in an epistemological vacuum or, at any rate, in a bewilderingly volatile intellectual environment. Students in mass systems, no longer socialized into defined scientific cultures, may be unable to internalize the cognitive values that underpin these competences and skills. It is this process of internalization which enables competences and skills to be creatively applied and critically reviewed. However, these issues arise not because of the extension of the higher education 'franchise' in mass systems but from the inner world of its 'knowledge'.

Reflexivity and open intellectual systems

The two primary characteristics of mass systems are reflexivity, in political and socio-economic contexts, and the shift from closed to open intellectual systems, in the academic arena. Reflexivity is expressed, first, through increased emphasis on accountability, whether in terms of administrative regulation, political priorities or market pressures. Élite university systems asserted a right to enjoy institutional autonomy not simply as a guarantee of academic freedom but as a precondition of their social utility and cultural significance. Universities which were not free were not universities at all. A society without real, i.e. autonomous, universities was not only likely to underperform in scientific and economic terms but also to be intellectually impoverished and socially disempowered.

Mass higher education systems, in contrast, cannot claim the same autonomy, if this means they aspire to be self-referential rather than reflexive. The growing pressure for greater accountability has often been interpreted as illegitimate meddling by politicians, damaging exposure to the market or the price that universities must pay for irresponsibly exercising 'donnish dominion' in the past. All these interpretations may be partly true, but they explain very little. It has also been argued that this pressure is largely a response to increasing operational complexity inside higher education and to external demands for value for money in the competition for scarce (public) resources. This account, too, is plausible. But the over-arching explanation is that reflexivity is an inherent characteristic of mass higher education, which in political terms means accountability rather than autonomy, and, in the context of the market, interaction rather than insulation.

Reflexivity is expressed, second, through a new relationship between higher education and society. Massification is only one of multiple modernizations. It is neither primarily a cause, a precondition, of these other modernizations, as social engineers, human capitalists, Parsonian functionalists and early prophets of post-industrial society claimed; nor primarily an effect, an outcome, as neo-Marxisants are bound to assert. Instead it is poised between cause and effect. It operates not on but inside social change. To claim that mass higher education has the power to reorder social and gender relations, or to provide an alternative or autonomous basis for social stratification, is going too far. But to argue that the extension of the higher education 'franchise' and of graduate careers is merely the product of a social revolution which has taken place elsewhere is not going far enough.

Reflexivity, finally, is expressed in new links between higher education and the economy. On the one hand, élite universities and related research establishments have become primary producers, although their products, not just high technology but 'knowledge' in a broader cultural sense, have transformed older conceptions of primary production. On the other hand, mass institutions have an oblique, even ironic, relationship with wealth creation and the labour market. They educate consumers as much as they train producers; their currency is lifestyles more than life chances; the higher education they provide is an alternative, even an antidote, to rather than a preparation for old-fashioned bureaucratic careers. But, in a post-Fordist environment, conceptions of economic activity have been extended to embrace the ironic, the ephemeral, the alternative. Indeed, it can be argued that these qualities, as economically manifested through the market and politics, are more important than material production (which itself is taking on an increasingly symbolic dimension, in a further illustration of reflexivity).

The shift from closed to open intellectual systems is the second key characteristic of mass higher education systems. The epistemological crisis of the late twentieth century has already been discussed, along with its suggestive affinities to the growth of mass systems. The idea of science as a process of synergy between creative ideas and applications in a trans-disciplinary context rather than a product of linear discovery has also been discussed. Both tend to undermine a fundamental role of élite university systems, to socialize students into distinctive and coherent academic cultures, whether discipline-based or professionally focused. The integrity of these cultures has been questioned and their coherence undermined. Moreover, this socialization relied on tacit knowledge and internalized values, as much as on a structured curriculum or explicitly taught skills. This was, and is, acknowledged by the rhetorical emphasis on learning rather than teaching.

Élite systems draw their tacit knowledge and internalized values from two sources: élite culture and expert knowledge. The first, often in a democratic age coyly disguised as 'the influence of the family' or 'high standards in schools', consisted of the shared references and value structures characteristic of upper-middle class culture. But, well before 1960, the expansion and opening up of higher education meant that a university education could no longer be rooted predominantly in the reproduction of élite intellectual manners, although it would be naive to underestimate their continuing influence. More recently, élite culture has been radically undermined by the gathering of grave doubts about not only its sociological content but also its epistemological validity.

The second source, expert knowledge, was based on the cognitive values and social practices generated within disciplines. Disciplinary traditions, policed by suitably expert scholars and scientists, supplemented, or were substituted for, class cultures. This disciplinary socialization was expressed in terms of being able to 'think sociologically' or labels such as 'physicist'. These traditions, having contributed to the undermining of élite culture by their reductionist techniques, have suffered a similar, often internally induced, epistemological degeneration. But the internalized values of the historian persisted, long after history in its traditional form had been comprehensively deconstructed, just as élite culture has outlasted class hegemony.

Mass higher education systems continue to draw their tacit knowledge and internalized values from élite culture and expert knowledge, but to dwindling effect. One approach is to abandon deep socialization, by concentrating on the development of surface competences and ignoring the epistemological turmoil beneath and absence of firm intellectual foundations. Arguably, this is consistent with the playful nihilism of the post-modern condition. It may also reflect the acceleration, volatility, simultaneity and other characteristics of post-Fordist modernity discussed at the end of Chapter 3. Either there are no deeper values, no connecting themes, to which students can be introduced; or any values and themes are so ephemeral that they cannot and should not be institutionalized through higher education systems.

Another approach is to seek new intellectual resources to supplement and transcend élite culture and expert knowledge. This can only be done by creating open intellectual systems – open to the values of non-élite communities; the practical impulses of life and work; the reflexivity of post-industrial change. For example, mature students on franchised degrees in further education colleges do not possess the same intellectual resources as most (not all) students at Oxford and Cambridge, the tacit knowledge of social élites and the internalized values of expert disciplines. Nor, more practically, can colleges ever expect to possess equivalent resources, in terms of highly qualified teachers or richly stocked libraries. But this does not mean that either mature students or FE colleges are without resources of a different kind. Where Oxbridge students draw on the closed systems of élite culture and expert knowledge, local mature students may draw on the open systems of community involvement or work (or life) experience.

Conclusion

This chapter began with a disclaimer: mass higher education cannot be reduced to either a totalizing idea or a coherent system, so talk of 'ideas' and 'systems' is dangerous. Nevertheless, such terms are probably unavoidable. Therefore, an attempt, partial and provisional, has been made in this book to describe the main outline and key characteristics of mass higher education. It falls far short of offering a 'theory'. Its argument is less grand. Mass systems must be distinguished from élite systems – not in terms of a linear sequence or a paradigm shift because, in crucial respects, they are radically unlike; nor dialectically, although mass systems can be defined by the absence of key features of élite systems; but in terms of their positive attributes.

These attributes have been sought not so much in the inner dynamics of higher education systems and institutions, although this is highly significant (and has been discussed in Chapter 2), as externally in the multiple modernizations of society, the economy, intellectual culture, science and technology, discussed in Chapters 3 and 4. (Part of the argument of this book is that the demarcation between 'internal' and 'external' makes little sense in discussing mass higher education, hence the emphasis on reflexivity and open intellectual systems.) Mass higher education itself is one of these grand modernizations; its influence can be observed in the extension of the higher education 'franchise', the decline of collective solidarities, the ungendering of society, the reworking of graduate careers, the growth of symbolic goods, the acceleration of high technology.

Yet theoretically massification is aligned with modernity, those radically revised but still recognizable normative structures inherited from the past. Through teaching and research universities and colleges play a central role in both the radical revision of these structures and preserving their recognizability. Mass higher education, therefore, may be unique among the transformations of the modern world in that it links modernity and modernization, bridging a fissure between instrumentality and morality which many social analysts see as the decisive dislocation of our global age.

Notes

Chapter 1 Introduction

1. Perry Anderson (1992) Components of the national culture, in *English Questions*. London: Verso.
2. George Steiner (1984) To Civilize Our Gentlemen, in *George Steiner: A Reader*. Harmondsworth: Penguin, pp. 25–36. (Originally published in 1965 in *Language and Silence*.)
3. Martin Trow (1973) *Problems in the Transition from Elite to Mass Higher Education*. Berkeley, CA: Carnegie Commission on Higher Education.
4. J. H. Newman (1976) *The Idea of a University*. Oxford: Oxford University Press. (Originally published 1853.)
5. Clark Kerr (1963) *The Uses of the University*. Cambridge, MA: Harvard University Press.
6. Ronald Barnett (1990) *The Idea of Higher Education*. Buckingham: Open University Press/SRHE.
7. Christopher Duke (1992) *The Learning University*. Buckingham: Open University Press/SRHE.
8. Tony Becher and Maurice Kogan (1980) *Process and Structure in Higher Education*. London: Heinemann.
9. Burton Clark (1983) *The Higher Education System: Academic Organisation in Cross-National Perspective*. Berkeley: University of California Press, p. 274.
10. Philip Larkin (1983) Early Days at Leicester, in *Required Writing: Miscellaneous Pieces 1955–1982*. London: Faber, p. 38.
11. Kingsley Amis (1984) *Lucky Jim*. London: Gollancz (new edn); Malcolm Bradbury (1975) *The History Man*. London: Secker and Warburg.
12. Leslie Wagner (1995) Change and Continuity in Higher Education. Inaugural Lecture, Leeds Metropolitan University, 12 January.
13. Rosa Ehrenreich (1994) *A Garden of Paper Flowers: An American at Oxford*. London: Picador.
14. Claudius Gellert (1993) Structural and Functional Differentiation: Remarks on Changing Paradigms of Tertiary Education in Europe, in Claudius Gellert (ed.), *Higher Education in Europe*. London: Jessica Kingsley, pp. 237–8.
15. Advisory Board for the Research Councils (1987) *A Strategy for the Science Base*. London: HMSO.
16. Sheldon Rothblatt (1993) The Rivals: Historical Observations on an Interesting Competition. Paper given at an international conference on the university in its urban setting at the University of Aberdeen, July.

17. Gaie Davidson (1993) *Credit Accumulation and Transfer in the British Universities 1990–1993*. London: Universities Association for Continuing Education.
18. Office of Public Service and Science: Office of Science and Technology (1994) *Realising Our Potential.* White Paper on Science and Technology. London: HMSO.

Chapter 2   Structure and Institutions

1. Peter Scott (1993) The idea of the university in the 21st century, *British Journal of Education Studies*, XXXXI (1): 4–25.
2. George Davie (1961) *The Democratic Intellect: Scotland and Her Universities in the Nineteenth Century*. Edinburgh: Edinburgh University Press; George Davie (1986) *The Crisis of the Democratic Intellect: The Problem of Generalism and Specialisation in Twentieth-century Scotland*. Edinburgh: Polygon.
3. James Mountford (1966) *British Universities*. Oxford: Oxford University Press, pp. 18–45.
4. Michael Shattock (1994) *The UGC and the Management of British Universities*. Buckingham: Open University Press/SRHE, pp. 99–104.
5. Margaret Archer (1979) *Social Origins of Educational Systems*. London: Sage.
6. Christine Shinn (1986) *Paying the Piper: The Development of the University Grants Committee 1919–1946*. Lewes: Falmer Press.
7. Percy report (1945) *Higher Technological Education*. London: HMSO; Ministry of Education (1956) *Technical Education*. London: HMSO.
8. Shattock, *The UGC*, p. 3.
9. W. A. C. Stewart (1989) *Higher Education in Postwar Britain*. London: Macmillan; Robert Berdahl (1959) *British Universities and the State*. Berkeley: University of California Press.
10. Committee on Higher Education (1963) *Higher Education*, Cmnd. 2154 (Robbins report). London: HMSO.
11. Peter Scott (1988) Blueprint or blue-remembered hills? The relevance of the Robbins report to the present reforms of higher education, *Oxford Review of Education*, 14 (1): 33–48.
12. John Carswell (1985) *Government and the Universities in Britain: Programme and Performance 1960–1980*. Cambridge: Cambridge University Press; Shattock, *The UGC*, p. 13.
13. Department of Education and Science (1978) *Report of the Working Group on the Management of Higher Education in the Maintained Sector* (Oakes report). London: HMSO; House of Commons (1980) *The Funding and Organisation of Courses in Higher Education* (Report of the Select Committee on Education, Science and the Arts). London: HMSO.
14. Maurice Kogan and David Kogan (1983) *The Attack on Higher Education*. London: Kogan Page.
15. Michael Shattock (1994) Financial accountability and the Cardiff affair, in Shattock, *The UGC*, pp. 113–27.
16. Croham report (1987) *Review of the University Grants Committee*. London: HMSO.
17. Department of Education and Science (1987) *Higher Education: Meeting the Challenge*. London: HMSO.
18. Kenneth Baker (1989) *Higher education – 25 years on* (speech at the University of Lancaster). London: Department of Education and Science (press notice).
19. Department of Education and Science (1991) *Higher Education: A New Framework*. London: HMSO, paras 45–53 and 87.

20. Peter Scott (1994) Scottish higher education regained: accident or design?, *Scottish Affairs*, 7: 68–85.
21. Department for Education (1993) *Student Numbers in Higher Education – Great Britain 1980–81 to 1990–91*, Statistical Bulletin 17–93. London: DFE.
22. Peter Scott and David Watson (1994) Setting the scene, in Jean Bocock and David Watson (eds), *Managing the University Curriculum: Making Common Cause*. Buckingham: Open University Press/SRHE, pp. 20–22.
23. Department for Education (1994) *Higher Education Funding 1995–1996 to 1997–1998* (letter from Roger Dawe, Deputy Secretary, to Graeme Davies, Chief Executive of the Higher Education Funding Council for England, dated 29 November). London: Department for Education; Catherine Bargh, Peter Scott and David Smith (1994) *Access and Consolidation: The Impact of Reduced Student Intakes on Opportunities For Non-standard Students*. Leeds: Centre for Policy Studies in Education.
24. Andrew Bain (1993) *Private Sector Funding in Higher Education*. Report to the HEFCE, SHEFC, FCW and DENI. Bristol: HEFCE, p. 15, Table 4.1., and p. 16, Diagram 1.
25. Robbins report, p. 200, Table 54.
26. Ben Jongbloed, Jos Koelman and Hans Vossensteyn (1994) Comparing cost per student and cost per graduate: an analysis of Germany, Great Britain and the Netherlands, in Leo Goedergebuure and Frans van Vught (eds), *Comparative Policy Studies in Higher Education*. Utrecht: Lemma, pp. 65–93.
27. Scott and Watson, 'Setting the scene', p. 28, Table 1.2.
28. Henry Miller (1995) *The Management of Change in Universities: Universities, State and Economy in Australia, Canada and the United Kingdom*. Buckingham: Open University Press/SRHE, pp. 109–18.
29. HEFCE, with SHEFC and FCW (1994) *1996 Research Assessment Exercise*, Circular RAE96 1/94. Bristol: HEFCE.
30. Centre for Higher Education Studies (1994) *Assessment of the Quality of Higher Education*, Report to the Higher Education Funding Councils for England and Wales (Barnett report). London: University of London Institute of Education; HEFCE (1994) *The Quality Assessment Method from April 1995*, Circular 39/94. Bristol: HEFCE.
31. Peter Scott (1993) The transition from élite to mass higher education, in *The Transition from Élite to Mass Higher Education* (Occasional Paper Series). Canberra: Department of Employment, Education and Training (Higher Education Division).
32. Advisory Board for the Research Councils (1987) *A Strategy for the Science Base*. London: HMSO.
33. Burton Clark (1984) Higher Education Systems: Organizational Conditions of Policy Formation and Implementation, in Rune Premfors (ed.), *Higher Education Organization: Conditions for Policy Implementation*. Stockholm: Almqvist & Wiksell International.
34. Peter Scott (1984) *The Crisis of the University*. London: Croom Helm.
35. Organization for Economic Co-operation and Development (1989) *Review of Higher Education in California*. Paris: OECD; Sheldon Rothblatt (ed.) (1992) *The OECD, the Master Plan and the California Dream: A Berkeley Conversation*. Berkeley: Centre for Studies in Higher Education; Clive P. Condren (1988) *Preparing for the Twenty-first Century: A Report on Higher Education in California*. Sacramento: California Postsecondary Education Commission.

36. Susan Davies (1989) *The Martin Committee and the Binary Policy of Higher Education in Australia*, Australian Studies in the Social Sciences. Melbourne: Ashwood House.

37. Peter Scott (1991) *Higher Education in Sweden: A View from the Outside.* Stockholm: National Board for Universities and Colleges.

38. John Brennan, Leo Goedegebuure, Brenda Little, Tarla Shah, Don Westerheijden and Peter Weusthof (1992) *European Higher Education Systems: Germany, The Netherlands, The United Kingdom.* London: Council for National Academic Awards, and Twente: Centre for Higher Education Policy Studies; OECD and the Department for Employment, Education and Training (1993) *Post-Compulsory, Further and Higher Education in the Federal Republic of Germany.* Canberra: Centre for Continuing Education, Australian National University; Ministry of Education and Science, HBO-Raad, VSNU and NUFFIC (1989) *Higher Education in the Netherlands: Characteristics, Structure, Figures, Facts.* Zoetermeer: Ministry of Education and Science.

39. Ulrich Teichler (1995) *Diversity in Higher Education in Germany: The Two-Type Structure.* Kassel: Universität Gesamthochschule, Wissenschaftliches Zentrum für Berufs- und Hochschulforschung.

40. Council for Studies of Higher Education (1994) *Swedish Universities & University Colleges 1992/93*, VHS Report Series 1994: 3 (short version of Annual Report). Stockholm: Council for Studies in Higher Education.

41. Commission of the European Communities (1990) *Structures of the Education and Initial Training Systems of the European Community*, prepared jointly by EURYDICE, the European Information Network in the European Community, and CEDEFOP, the European Centre for the Development of Vocational Training. Brussels: European Commission.

42. Jana Hendrichová (1992) *Recent Developments in Higher Education in Central and Eastern Europe (Czech and Slovak Republics, Hungary, Poland, Romania and the Russian Federation).* Prague: Centre for Higher Education Studies.

43. Guy Neave (1993) Séparation de corps: the training of advanced students and the organisation of research in France, in Burton C. Clark (ed.), *The Research Foundations of Graduate Education.* Berkeley: University of California Press, pp. 159–91.

44. Tony Becher, Mary Henkel and Maurice Kogan (1994) *Graduate Education in Britain.* London: Jessica Kingsley.

45. Bruno de Witte (1993) Higher education and the Constitution of the European Community, in Claudius Gellert (ed.), *Higher Education in Europe.* London: Jessica Kingsley, pp. 186–203; Commission of the European Communities (1991) *Memorandum on Higher Education in the European Community.* Brussels: European Commission; Commission of the European Communities (1993) *Guidelines for Community Action in the Field of Education and Training.* Brussels: European Commission.

46. Ulrich Teichler (1993) Structures of higher education systems in Europe, in Gellert, *Higher Education in Europe*, p. 31.

47. Burton Clark (1993) The problem of complexity in modern higher education, in Sheldon Rothblatt and Björn Wittrock (eds), *The European and American University since 1800: Historical and Sociological Essays.* Cambridge: Cambridge University Press, p. 266.

48. Olaf C. Mc-Danièl and Wiebe Buising (1992) *The Level of Government Influence in Higher Education in the US and Western Europe*, Delphi Research Project. Zoetermeer: Ministry of Education and Science, and Twente: Centre for Higher Education Policy Studies.

49. HEFCE (1995) *Funding the Relationship: Higher Education in Further Education Colleges.* Bristol: HEFCE.
50. Michael Shattock (1991) The pre-history of the university, in Michael Shattock, *Making a University: A Celebration of Warwick's First 25 Years.* Coventry: University of Warwick, p. 9.
51. Gillian Darley (1991) Visions, prospects and compromises, *Higher Education Quarterly,* 45 (4): 354–66.
52. Asa Briggs (1964) Redrawing the map of knowledge, in David Daiches (ed.), *The Idea of a New University.* London: Routledge & Kegan Paul; Asa Briggs (1991) A founding father reflects, *Higher Education Quarterly,* 45 (4): 311–32; Albert Sloman (1964) *A University in the Making.* London: BBC Books.
53. Clark Kerr (1963) *The Uses of the University.* Cambridge, MA: Harvard University Press.
54. Eric Robinson (1968) *The New Polytechnics: A Radical Policy for Higher Education.* London: Cornmarket; William Birch (1988) *The Challenge to Higher Education: Reconciling Responsibilities to Scholarship and to Society.* Milton Keynes: Open University Press/SRHE.
55. Geoffrey Lockwood and John Davies (1985) *Universities: The Management Challenge.* Windsor: National Foundation for Educational Research.
56. National Advisory Body (1987) *Report of the Working Group on Good Management Practice.* London: NAB.
57. Burton Clark (1983) *The Higher Education System: Academic Organization in Cross-National Perspective.* Berkeley: University of California Press, pp. 110–23.
58. A. H. Halsey (1992) *Decline of Donnish Dominion.* Oxford: Oxford University Press.
59. Paul Temple and Celia Whitchurch (1990) *Strategic Choice: Corporate Strategies for Change in Higher Education.* London: Conference of University Administrators.
60. Committee of Vice-Chancellors and Principals (1985) *Report of the Steering Group on University Efficiency* (Jarratt report). London: CVCP.
61. Tony Becher and Maurice Kogan (1980) *Process and Structure in Higher Education.* London: Heinemann, pp. 79–101.
62. Catherine Bargh, Peter Scott and David Smith (1995) *Changing Patterns of Governance in Higher Education.* Leeds: Centre for Policy Studies in Education.
63. Robin Middlehurst (1993) *Leading Academics.* Buckingham: Open University Press/SRHE.
64. Homa Bahrami (1992) The emerging flexible organisation, *California Management Review,* summer 1992, quoted in Charles Handy, *The Empty Raincoat: Making Sense of the Future.* London: Hutchinson.

Chapter 3   State and Society

1. Organization for Economic Co-operation and Development (1981) *The Welfare State in Crisis.* Paris: OECD.
2. Jeffrey Pressman and Aaron Wildavsky (1973) *Implementation.* Berkeley: University of California Press.
3. Harold Wilensky (1975) *The Welfare State and Equality: Structural and Ideological Roots of Public Expenditure.* Berkeley: University of California Press, pp. 1–2.
4. Ibid., p. 48.
5. Ibid., p. 119.
6. Immanuel Wallerstein (1979) *The Capitalist World Economy.* Cambridge: Cambridge University Press, p. 237.

7. John Goldthorpe, in collaboration with Catriona Llewellyn and Clive Payne (1980) *Social Mobility and Class Structure in Modern Britain*. Oxford: Oxford University Press, p. 276.
8. Christopher Jencks (1992) *Inequality: A Reassessment of the Effect of Family and Schooling in America*. New York: Basic Books.
9. Dennis Kavanagh (1987) *Thatcherism and British Politics*. Oxford: Oxford University Press, pp. 308–9.
10. Michael Power (1994) *The Audit Explosion*. London: Demos, p. 5.
11. Ibid., p. 49.
12. Fred Hirsch (1977) *Social Limits to Growth*. London: Routledge & Kegan Paul, p. 190.
13. Peter Scott (1995) Changes in policy affecting public universities: the British experience, in Jim Mauch and Paula Sabloff (eds), *Reform and Change in Higher Education*. New York: Garland.
14. Robert Berdahl (1959) *British Universities and the State*. Berkeley: University of California Press; John Carswell (1985) *Government and the Universities in Britain: Programme and Performance 1960–1980*. Cambridge: Cambridge University Press.
15. Michael Shattock (1994) *The UGC and the Management of British Universities*. Buckingham: Open University Press/SRHE.
16. Olaf Mc-Danièl and Wiebe Buising (1992) *The Level of Government Influence over Higher Education in the United States and Western Europe* (Delphi Research Project). The Hague: Ministry of Education and Science/University of Twente.
17. Peter Maassen and Frans van Vught (1994) Alternative models of governmental steering in higher education, in Leo Goedegebuure and Frans van Vught (eds), *Comparative Policy Studies in Higher Education*. Utrecht: Lemma, pp. 41–43.
18. Ibid., pp. 50–51.
19. Nicholas Barr and Jane Falkingham (1993) *Paying for Learning*. London: London School of Economics (Department of Economics and Welfare State Programme).
20. Daniel Bell (1973) *The Coming of Post-Industrial Society*. London: Heinemann, p. 117.
21. Examples include Alvin Toffler (1990) *Powershift: Knowledge, Wealth and Violence at the Edge of the 21st Century*. New York: Bantam Books; Charles Handy (1994) *The Empty Raincoat: Making Sense of the Future*. London: Hutchinson; and Paul Kennedy (1993) *Preparing for the Twenty-First Century*. New York: Random House.
22. Central Statistical Office (1993) *Social Trends 1993*. London: HMSO, p. 58.
23. Robert Reich (1992) *The Work of Nations*. New York: Vintage Books, p. 110.
24. Kennedy, *Preparing for the Twenty-First Century*, p. 55.
25. Peter Scott (1994) Wider or deeper? International dimensions of mass higher education, *Journal of Tertiary Education Administration*, 16 (2): 179–94.
26. Kevin Phillips (1994) *Arrogant Capital: Washington, Wall Street and the Frustration of American Politics*. New York: Little, Brown.
27. David Harvey (1990) *The Condition of Postmodernity*. Oxford: Blackwell, p. 156.
28. Handy, *The Empty Raincoat*, pp. 65–79.
29. Peter Drucker (1993) *Post-Capitalist Society*. New York: HarperBusiness, p. 92.
30. J. K. Galbraith (1992) *The Culture of Contentment*. London: Penguin, pp. 68–9.
31. Central Statistical Office, *Social Trends 1993*, p. 58.
32. Ibid., p. 59.
33. John Tomaney (1994) New work organization and technology, in Ash Amin (ed.), *Post-Fordism*. Oxford: Blackwell, p. 183.
34. Harold Perkin (1989) *The Rise of Professional Society: England since 1880*. London: Routledge, pp. 472–519.

35. David Riesman, with Nathan Glazer and Reuel Denney (1950, revised edn 1969) *The Lonely Crowd: A Study of the Changing American Character.* New Haven, CT: Yale University Press.
36. Daniel Bell (1976) *The Cultural Contradictions of Capitalism.* London: Heinemann, p. 84.
37. Roland Inglehart (1977) *The Silent Revolution.* Princeton, NJ: Princeton University Press.
38. Roy Harrod (1958) The possibility of economic satiety – use of economic growth for improving the quality of education and leisure. *Problems of United States Economic Development,* 1: 207–13.
39. Hirsch, *Social Limits,* p. 188.
40. Ibid., p. 11.
41. Stuart Hall (1988) Brave New World, *Marxism Today,* October, p. 24.
42. Goldthorpe, *Social Mobility,* pp. 257–71.
43. Perkin, *The Rise of Professional Society,* p. 421.
44. Richard Hoggart (1957) *The Uses of Literacy.* London: Chatto and Windus.
45. Central Statistical Office, *Social Trends 1993,* Table 6.7, p. 85.
46. Jon Elster (1989) *The Cement of Society: A Study of Social Order.* Cambridge: Cambridge University Press, p. 284.
47. Christopher Freeman and Carlota Perez (1988) Structural crises of adjustment, business cycles and investment behaviour, in G. Dosi, C. Freeman, R. Nelson, G. Silverberg and L. Soete (eds), *Technical Change and Economic Theory.* London: Pinter, p. 59.
48. Leslie Wagner (1995) *Change and Continuity in Higher Education.* Leeds: Leeds Metropolitan University, p. 4.
49. R. D. Anderson (1992) *Universities and Elites in Britain since 1800.* London: Macmillan, p. 67.
50. Phillip Brown and Richard Scase (1994) *Higher Education and Corporate Realities: Class, Culture and the Decline of Graduate Careers.* London: UCL Press, pp. 16–17.
51. Drucker, *Post-Capitalist Society,* p. 190.
52. Ibid., p. 210.
53. Hans van Ginkel (1994) University 2050: the organisation of creativity and innovation, in *Universities in the Twenty-First Century: A Lecture Series.* London: National Commission on Education/Council for Industry and Higher Education, p. 76.
54. Reich, *The Work of Nations,* pp. 174–9.
55. Institute of Manpower Studies (1994) *The US Labour Market for New Graduates,* Report 267. Brighton: IMS.
56. Brown and Scase, *Higher Education,* p. 25.
57. Jean-François Lyotard (1984) *The Postmodern Condition.* Manchester: Manchester University Press, p. 66.
58. Helga Nowotny (1994) *Time: The Modern and Postmodern Experience.* Cambridge: Polity Press, p. 10.
59. Harvey, *The Condition of Postmodernity,* p. 205.
60. Nowotny, *Time,* p. 137.
61. Ulrich Beck (1992) *Risk Society: Towards a New Modernity.* London: Sage, p. 10.
62. Paul Ormerod (1994) *The Death of Economics.* London: Faber, p. 179.
63. Anthony Giddens (1990) *The Consequences of Modernity.* Cambridge: Polity Press, pp. 153–4.
64. Beck, *Risk Society,* pp. 156–7.

65. Giddens, *The Consequences of Modernity*, pp. 36–45.
66. Beck, *Risk Society*, p. 90.

Chapter 4   Science and Culture

1. Lawrence Stone (1983) Social control and intellectual excellence: Oxbridge and Edinburgh 1560–1983, in Nicholas Phillipson (ed.), *Universities, Society and the Future*. Edinburgh: Edinburgh University Press, pp. 3–30.
2. Nicholas Boyle (1991) *Goethe: The Poet and the Age. Vol. 1, The Poetry of Desire*. Oxford: Oxford University Press, pp. 165–6.
3. Charles Camic (1983) *Experience and Enlightenment: Socialization for Cultural Change in Eighteenth-Century Scotland*. Edinburgh: Edinburgh University Press.
4. Henri Lefebvre (1991) *The Production of Space*. Oxford: Blackwell, quoted in David Harvey (1990) *The Condition of Postmodernity*. Oxford: Blackwell, p. 47.
5. Talcott Parsons and Gerard Platt (1973) *The American University*. Cambridge, MA: Harvard University Press, p. 387.
6. George Steiner (1989) *Real Presences*. London: Faber, p. 21.
7. Basil Bernstein (1971) *Class, Codes and Control*. London: Routledge & Kegan Paul, p. 239.
8. Ralf Dahrendorf (1979) *Life Chances: Approaches to Social and Political Theory*. London: Weidenfeld and Nicolson.
9. E. P. Thompson (1993) *Witness Against the Beat: William Blake and the Moral Law*. Cambridge: Cambridge University Press, p. 227.
10. Ibid., p. 228.
11. Wolf Lepenies (1988) *Between Literature and Science: The Rise of Sociology*. Cambridge: Cambridge University Press, p. 8.
12. Ibid., p. 13.
13. George Steiner (1960) *Tolstoy or Dostoevsky*. London: Faber, p. 347.
14. Thomas Kuhn (1962, revised edition 1970) *The Structure of Scientific Revolution*. Chicago: Chicago University Press.
15. Peter Scott (1990) Thomas Kuhn, in *Knowledge and Nation*. Edinburgh: Edinburgh University Press, pp. 90–95.
16. Edmund Leach (1965) Culture and social cohesion, *Daedalus*, 94 (Winter): 24–38.
17. Terry Eagleton (1994) Discourse and discos, *Times Literary Supplement*, 15 July, p. 3.
18. Ibid., p. 3.
19. Anthony Giddens (1990) *The Consequences of Modernity*. Cambridge: Polity Press, p. 176.
20. Eagleton, 'Discourse and discos', p. 4.
21. Giddens, *The Consequences of Modernity*, p. 178.
22. Jürgen Habermas (1987) *The Philosophical Discourses of Modernity*. Cambridge: Polity Press, p. 3.
23. Eagleton, 'Discourse and discos', p. 4.
24. Ibid., p. 4.
25. Edward Shils (1989) The modern university and liberal democracy, *Minerva*, (Winter).
26. Habermas, *The Philosophical Discourses of Modernity*, pp. 3–4.
27. Ithiel de Sola Pool (1990) *Technologies of Freedom*. Cambridge MA: Belknap Press of Harvard University Press, p. 52.

28. Matthew Arnold (1932, first published 1869) *Culture and Anarchy*. Edited by J. Dover Wilson. Cambridge: Cambridge University Press, p. 70.
29. Allan Bloom (1988) *The Closing of the American Mind*. New York: Simon and Schuster.
30. Karl Popper (1945) *The Open Society and its Enemies* (Vols 1–2). London: Routledge & Kegan Paul.
31. Allan Bloom (1988) *The Closing of the American Mind*, p. 178.
32. Richard Rorty (1991) *Objectivity, Relativism and Truth*. Cambridge: Cambridge University Press.
33. Clifford Geertz (1983) *Local Knowledge*. New York: Basic Books, quoted in Tony Becher (1989) *Academic Tribes and Territories*. Buckingham: Open University Press/SRHE, p. 171.
34. Eagleton, 'Discourse and discos', p. 3.
35. C. Van Woodward (1991) Freedom and the universities, *New York Review of Books*, 18 July, pp. 32–7.
36. Shils, 'The modern university and liberal democracy'.
37. Steiner, *Real Presences*, p. 219.
38. Ibid., p. 21.
39. Habermas, *The Philosophical Discourses of Modernity*, p. 3.
40. Raphael Samuel (1994) *Theatres of Memory*. London: Verso, pp. 3–8.
41. Jim Collins (1990) *Uncommon Cultures: Popular Culture and Post-Modernism*. London: Routledge.
42. Jean-François Lyotard (1984) *The Postmodern Condition: A Report on Knowledge*. Manchester: Manchester University Press.
43. Jacques Derrida (1967) *L'Écriture et la Différance*. Paris: Éditions du Seuil, p. 289.
44. Daniel Bell (1960) *The End of Ideology: On the Exhaustion of Political Ideas of the 1950s*. Glencoe, IL: Free Press.
45. Francis Fukuyama (1993) *The End of History and the Last Man*. Harmondsworth: Penguin.
46. Karl Popper (1976) *Unended Quest*. London: Pan Books, p. 34.
47. Karl Popper (1945) *The Open Society and its Enemies*.
48. Jean-François Lyotard (1984) *The Postmodern Condition: A Report on Knowledge*, p. xxiv.
49. Steiner, *Real Presences*, pp. 230–31.
50. Charles Jencks (1991) *The Language of Post-Modern Architecture*. London: Academy Editions.
51. Brian Rotman (1990) The grand hotel and the shopping mall, *Times Literary Supplement*, 6–12 April.
52. Roland Ingelhart (1977) *The Silent Revolution*. Princeton, NJ: Princeton University Press.
53. Fred Hirsch (1977) *Social Limits to Growth*. London: Routledge & Kegan Paul.
54. Daniel Bell (1976) *The Cultural Contradictions of Capitalism*. London: Heinemann.
55. Office of Public Service and Science: Office of Science and Technology (1994) *Realising Our Potential*, White Paper on Science and Technology. London: HMSO.
56. Michael Gibbons, Camille Limoges, Helga Nowtny, Simon Schwartzman, Peter Scott and Martin Trow (1994) *The New Production of Knowledge: The Dynamics of Science and Research in Contemporary Societies*. London: Sage.
57. Ibid., pp. 2–3.
58. Fernand Braudel (1981) *Civilization and Capitalism: Fifteenth-Eighteenth Century. Vol. 1: The Structures of Everyday Life*. London: Fontana, p. 435.
59. Gibbons *et al.*, *The New Production of Knowledge*, p. 3.

60. John Ziman (1994) *Prometheus Bound: Science in a Dynamic Steady State*. Cambridge: Cambridge University Press, p. 177.
61. Ibid., p. 178.
62. Gibbons *et al., The New Production of Knowledge*, p. 10.
63. Ibid., p. 11.
64. D. Hicks, P. Isard and B. Martin (1995) An analytical comparison of research in European and Japanese laboratories, Research Policy, (forthcoming) quoted in Gibbons *et al., The New Production of Knowledge*, p. 116.
65. Ziman, *Prometheus Bound*, pp. 100–2.
66. Parsons and Platt, *The American University*, p. 88.
67. Neil Smelser (1973) Epilogue, in Parsons and Platt, *The American University*, p. 401.
68. Norman Evans (1992) *Experiential Learning: Its Assessment and Accreditation*. London: Routledge.
69. Jean Bocock and Peter Scott (1994) *Re-drawing the Boundaries: Further/Higher Education Partnerships* (interim report). University of Leeds: Centre for Policy Studies in Education.
70. Gaie Davidson (1993) *Credit Accumulation and Transfer in British Universities 1990– 93*. London: Universities Association for Continuing Education (UACE).
71. David Robertson (1994) *Choosing to Change*, report of the National CATS Development Project. London: Higher Education Quality Council.
72. Committee of Scottish University Principals (1992) *Teaching and Learning in an Expanding Higher Education System* (MacFarlane report). Edinburgh: CSUP (SCFC, P.O. Box 142, Holyrood Road, Edinburgh EH8 8AH).
73. Ronald Barnett (1992) *The Idea of Higher Education*. Buckingham: Open University Press/SRHE, p. 199.
74. Christopher Duke (1993) *The Learning University*. Buckingham: Open University Press/SRHE, p. 52.
75. Lee Harvey, Alison Burrows and Diana Green (1992) *Criteria of Quality*. Birmingham: Quality in Higher Education Project (University of Central England at Birmingham); Diana Green (1994) What is quality in higher education? Concepts, policy and practice, in Diana Green (ed.), *What is Quality in Higher Education?* Buckingham: Open University Press/SRHE, pp. 3–20.
76. Patrick Ainley (1994) *Degrees of Difference: Higher Education in the 1990s*. London: Lawrence and Wishart.
77. Ronald Barnett (1994) *Limits of Competence*. Buckingham: Open University Press/ SRHE, p. 186.
78. Tony Becher (1984) The cultural view, in Burton Clark (ed.), *Perspectives on Higher Education*. Berkeley: University of California Press, p. 190.
79. Office of Public Service and Science, *Realising Our Potential.*
80. David Clark (1994) A view from the research councils, in *Graduate and Research Schools* (conference report). University of Leeds: Centre for Policy Studies in Education; Howard Newby (1993) The devil will be in the detail, *Times Higher Education Supplement*, 27 July.
81. Tony Becher, Mary Henkel and Maurice Kogan (1994) *Graduate Education in Britain*. London: Jessica Kingsley; UK Council on Graduate Education (1995) *Graduate Schools*. Coventry: UK Council on Graduate Education (University of Warwick).
82. Advisory Board for the Research Councils (1987) *A Strategy for the Science Base*. London: HMSO.

Index

The Society for Research into Higher Education

The Society for Research into Higher Education exists to stimulate and co-ordinate research into all aspects of higher education. It aims to improve the quality of higher education through the encouragement of debate and publication on issues of policy, on the organization and management of higher education institutions, and on the curriculum and teaching methods.

The Society's income is derived from subscriptions, sales of its books and journals, conference fees and grants. It receives no subsidies, and is wholly independent. Its individual members include teachers, researchers, managers and students. Its corporate members are institutions of higher education, research institutes, professional, industrial and governmental bodies. Members are not only from the UK, but from elsewhere in Europe, from America, Canada and Australasia, and it regards its international work as amongst its most important activities.

Under the imprint *SRHE & Open University Press*, the Society is a specialist publisher of research, having some 45 titles in print. The Editorial Board of the Society's Imprint seeks authoritative research or study in the above fields. It offers competitive royalties, a highly recognizable format in both hardback and paperback and the world-wide reputation of the Open University Press.

The Society also publishes *Studies in Higher Education* (three times a year), which is mainly concerned with academic issues, *Higher Education Quarterly* (formerly *Universities Quarterly*), mainly concerned with policy issues, *Research into Higher Education Abstracts* (three times a year), and *SRHE News* (four times a year).

The Society holds a major annual conference in December, jointly with an institution of higher education. In 1992, the topic was 'Learning to Effect', with Nottingham Trent University. In 1993, it was 'Governments and the Higher Education Curriculum: Evolving Partnerships' at the University of Sussex in Brighton, and in 1994, 'The Student Experience' at the University of York. Future conferences include in 1995, 'The Changing University' at Heriot-Watt University in Edinburgh.

The Society's committees, study groups and branches are run by the members. The groups at present include:
Teacher Education Study Group
Continuing Education Group
Staff Development Group
Excellence in Teaching and Learning

Benefits to members

Individual

Individual members receive:

- *SRHE News*, the Society's publications list, conference details and other material included in mailings.
- Greatly reduced rates for *Studies in Higher Education* and *Higher Education Quarterly*.
- A 35% discount on all Open University Press & SRHE publications.
- Free copies of the Proceedings – commissioned papers on the theme of the Annual Conference.
- Free copies of *Research into Higher Education Abstracts*.
- Reduced rates for conferences.
- Extensive contacts and scope for facilitating initiatives.
- Reduced reciprocal memberships.

Corporate

Corporate members receive:

- All benefits of individual members, plus
- Free copies of *Studies in Higher Education*.
- Unlimited copies of the Society's publications at reduced rates.
- Special rates for its members e.g. to the Annual Conference.

Membership details: SRHE, 3 Devonshire Street, London WIN 2BA. Tel: 0171 637 2766
Catalogue: SRHE & Open University Press, Celtic Court, 22 Ballmoor, Buckingham MK18 1XW. Tel: (01280) 823388